THE CAROLINA COLLECTION

The Junior League of Fayetteville, Inc.
Fayetteville, North Carolina
1978

Cover Design and Illustrations by E. Janet Parks

Direct all inquires to:
THE JUNIOR LEAGUE OF FAYETTEVILLE, INC.
THE CAROLINA COLLECTION
P.O. Box 53232
Fayetteville, North Carolina 28305

COOKBOOK COMMITTEE

Executive Committee:

Mrs. Gary B. Copeland (Joanne), Chairman

Mrs. Samuel W. Bowyer (Frances)
Mrs. Richard M. Lewis, Jr. (Linda)
Mrs. Robert W. McCreary (Susan)
Mrs. Hubert D. Reaves, Jr. (Ann)
Mrs. Theodore Rhodes, Jr. (Susan)
Mrs. John W. Taylor (Sarah)

Staff:

Mrs. Janet W. McLeod, Typist
Mrs. John M. Harry, Jr. (Lulie), Historical Consultant
Mrs. Alston G. Cain (Mary Grace), Art Consultant

Mrs. Robert E. Bryan, Jr. (Jerry)
Mrs. John W. Butler (Susan)
Mrs. James S. Hall, Jr. (Mary)
Mrs. Marland C. Reid (Nancy)

Proceeds from the sale of this book go into the League's Community Trust Account and are returned to the community through Junior League projects in education, health, welfare and the arts.

International Standard Book Number — 0-918544-16-5

First Printing	August, 1978	10,000 copies
Second Printing	June, 1981	10,000 copies
Third Printing	September, 1982	10,000 copies

Printed in the United States of America

P.O. BOX 15428 • 1012 LOCUST • KANSAS CITY, MO 64106
816/842-3188

CONTENTS

Over 1500 recipes were submitted and tested by the members of the Junior League of Fayetteville. The 700 recipes contained in this book were selected, retested for quality and edited for clarity by the Cookbook Committee. We hope that your enjoyment of our book will be as great as ours was in compiling the contents.

COLLECTION OF FACTS ON FAYETTEVILLE, CUMBERLAND COUNTY, NORTH CAROLINA

Settled on the banks of Cape Fear River at the mouth of Cross Creek in 1736 by Scots who named the area Campbellton.

Named Fayetteville in 1783 after the French General Marquis de LaFayette, thus becoming the first American town to be named in his honor.

Most famous landmark is the Market House, built in 1789 and once called the State House when it served as temporary capitol of North Carolina in the late 1700's. There the Federal Constitution was adopted in 1789, and the charter was granted for the University of North Carolina, America's oldest state university.

Fayetteville Independent Light Infantry, second oldest military organization in America, was organized in 1793.

Location of Ft. Bragg, one of America's largest and most important military installations, in Cumberland County in 1918 was the beginning of a change for Fayetteville. It is also the home of the 82nd Airborne Division and Pope Air Force Base.

Agricultural activities have been of prime importance over the years, including tobacco, cotton, soybean and livestock markets. Within the last 15 years, industry, rather than the military has become a prime ingredient of development. Over 100 industrial payrolls are now in the county. In commerce, Fayetteville now stands as the shopping center of southeastern N.C. Retail sales during 1975 were in excess of $600,000,000.

The City Itself:

a. Educational: Fayetteville State University — 1867; first teachers' college for Blacks in U.S.
   Fayetteville Technical Institute — largest in state.
   Methodist College — 4-year liberal arts institution.

b. Churches: Over 200 representing all major denominations.

c. Physical Assets: Cumberland County Memorial Auditorium and Arena Convention Center in Bordeaux Section.

d. Government: Fayetteville is the county seat of Cumberland County. The county is governed by a Board of Commissioners. The city has the Council-Manager form of government.

e. Area and Population: City is 29 square miles. 1978 population estimates 241,400 for Cumberland County.

appetizers

THE CAROLINA COLLECTOR'S CONCOCTIONS

. . . Sauté bite size pieces of scallops in butter, garlic & a dash of vermouth.

. . . Knead 4 c whole-wheat flour, 1 t salt, ½ c oil, 3 T brown sugar & 1 c milk; roll into sticks. Bake 15 min. at 375°.

. . . Marinate artichokes & mushrooms in Italian dressing & lemon juice.

. . . Marinate avocado slices in lemon juice & sprinkle with curry powder.

. . . Sauté cherry tomatoes in butter seasoned with garlic salt or Parmesan cheese & serve.

. . . Slice fresh coconut in thin strips; toss with melted butter, lightly salt & serve warm.

. . . Serve crab claws with a spicy chili sauce & horseradish dip.

. . . A good seafood fondue is made with 2 cans cream of shrimp soup, 1 c milk & 1 lb. grated cheese.

. . . For Mexican fondue, heat 1 package processed American cheese & 1 cup chili without beans. Serve with taco chips.

. . . For a good vegetable, fruit & cold meat dip, blend 1½ c cottage cheese, 1 c applesauce, 1 envelope onion soup mix & 2 t curry powder.

. . . Stuff small hollowed out cucumber cups with tuna or deviled ham.

. . . Marinate olives in French dressing to which a minced clove of garlic has been added.

. . . Shrimp cooked & marinated in vinegar & spices keep 3 weeks in refrigerator.

. . . Add ginger or curry powder to cocktail sauce.

. . . Blend 1 envelope instant tomato soup, 1 t paprika, 1½ t oregano, 1½ t onion salt & 1 t chili powder. Toss with buttered popcorn.

CURRY CHEESE BALL

1 tablespoon chutney, finely chopped
1 tablespoon butter
1 teaspoon curry powder
8 ounces cream cheese, softened
coconut

Mix first 4 ingredients together. Form into a ball; roll in coconut. Serve with wheat thin crackers.

HOLLY DAY CHEESE BALL

"Absolutely the best ever cheese ball!"

16 ounces cream cheese, softened
8 ounces sharp cheese, grated
8 ounces Roquefort cheese
6 ounce bacon cheese roll
6 ounce garlic cheese roll
8 ounces pimento cheese
2 teaspoons onion, grated
dash Worcestershire sauce, or to taste
dash hot sauce, or to taste
dash salt, or to taste
dash red pepper, or to taste

Mix all ingredients together thoroughly; form into a ball.
Hint: May be made into 4 balls for Christmas gifts. Roll in chopped nuts, chopped parsley, or ground paprika.

CHEESE BISCUITS

"For those lovers of cheese biscuits who like a sharp flavor, these are really good."

10 ounces extra sharp Cheddar cheese, grated
1 cup butter, softened (use only butter)
2 cups plain flour, sifted
1 teaspoon salt
1 teaspoon Worcestershire sauce
1 teaspoon hot sauce
¼ teaspoon paprika
dash or 2 of cayenne pepper
pecans for garnish (optional)
confectioners' sugar (optional)

Preheat oven to 325°. Thoroughly blend first 8 ingredients together and roll into logs on waxed paper. Freeze and slice when needed. If not freezing, be sure to chill before baking. Bake 15 minutes. Yields: Approximately 10 dozen.
Note: Top with pecan slice before baking. Dust with confectioners' sugar, if desired.

SESAME CHEESE STICKS

2¼ cups plain flour
1 teaspoon salt
1 cup margarine
1 cup Cheddar cheese, grated
⅓ cup honey
1 egg, separated
1½ teaspoons cream of tartar
¾ teaspoon baking soda
1 cup sesame seeds, divided and toasted

Preheat oven to 350°. In medium bowl stir together flour and salt. Cut in margarine with pastry blender or 2 knives until mixture is well mixed and coarse crumbs form. Stir in cheese, honey, egg yolk, cream of tartar, baking soda and ¾ cup of sesame seeds; mix with fork just until blended. Chill dough 15 minutes. On lightly floured surface, roll dough into ¼x3 inch sticks. Place on greased cookie sheet ¼ inch apart, brush with beaten egg white, sprinkle with remaining sesame seeds. Bake 10 minutes or until golden brown. Yields: 5 dozen.

4 ozs. grated cheese yields 1 c.

Marinate leftover cheese in a little wine for good flavor.

ROQUEFORT PUFFS

Cream Puffs:
¼ cup shortening
½ cup water, boiling
½ cup plain flour
dash salt
2 eggs

Preheat oven to 450°. Melt shortening in water and bring to a boil. Remove from heat; add flour and salt, beating until mixture leaves the side of the pan. Add eggs, 1 at a time. Drop by ⅔ tablespoonfuls on cookie sheet. Bake 10 minutes. Reduce heat to 400° and bake 20 minutes more. Cool.

Filling:
6 ounces cottage cheese
4 ounces Roquefort cheese, crumbled
1 tablespoon sour cream
dash A-1 sauce

Thoroughly blend all of above. To fill puffs, slice off top, remove soft centers and fill with filling. Replace tops. Yields: 25 puffs.

TOASTED CHEESE ROUNDS

⅓ cup Parmesan cheese, grated
¾ cup mayonnaise
½ cup onion, chopped
dash Worcestershire sauce
salt
pepper
1 loaf Pepperidge Farm party rye

Mix ingredients well. Spread over entire slice of bread. Broil on cookie sheet until bubbly. Serve warm. Yields: 40.

BEAUMONDE DIP

"None will be left!"

⅔ cup sour cream
⅔ cup mayonnaise
1 teaspoon Beaumonde seasoning
1 teaspoon dill weed
1 teaspoon parsley flakes
1 tablespoon onion, minced
½ teaspoon salt
dash Accent
raw vegetables

Mix together thoroughly and use as a dip for raw vegetables.

CHEDDAR BROCCOLI DIP

"Serves a large group. A nice main course luncheon dish."

20 ounces frozen chopped broccoli
8 ounces sharp Cheddar cheese, cubed
16 ounces Cheddar cheese soup
3 ounces canned mushrooms, sliced and drained
4 ounces pimento, finely cut
⅓ cup sherry
toast points (if used as main course)
crackers (if used as a dip)

Cook broccoli according to package directions. Drain. Mix all ingredients (except toast points or crackers) in top of double boiler until cheese is melted.

"Serve on toast points as a main dish or on crackers as an hors d'oeuvre."

CHIVE-CHEESE DIP

"This may be used as a cold dip, a hot spread or a hot supper dish."

16 ounces cream cheese
6-8 tablespoons salad dressing
6 scallions, green part only (or chives), chopped
12 drops Tabasco sauce
1¼ cups Parmesan cheese, grated
assorted crackers (only if used as an hors d'oeuvre)
¼-½ pound ground round, or sausage (only if used as supper dish)
English muffins (only if used as supper dish)

To use as cold dip:
Soften cream cheese to room temperature. Mix next 4 ingredients in a crock. Add softened cream cheese. Chill overnight. Let it sit out several hours before serving with assorted crackers. Yields: 50 servings.
To use as hot hors d'oeuvre:
Spread mixture on melba toast rounds and run under broiler until bubbly. Yields: 50 servings.
To use as a supper dish:
Brown ground round or sausage and add to cheese mixture. Spread on English muffins and broil until done. Yields: 30 servings.
"This is equally good hot or cold. When hot, it resembles a pizza in taste and smell."

To pulverize a garlic clove, place it between two pieces of waxed paper and hit with a hammer.

HERB AND CURRY DIP

1 cup mayonnaise
½ cup sour cream
⅓ teaspoon dill weed
⅓ teaspoon thyme
⅓ teaspoon marjoram
¼ teaspoon salt
⅛-¼ teaspoon curry powder
½ teaspoon dried parsley
½ teaspoon dehydrated onion
1½ teaspoon lemon juice
½ teaspoon Worcestershire sauce
2 teaspoons capers, minced (optional)
raw vegetables

Mix all ingredients, except raw vegetables, at least 24 hours before serving. Cover tightly and refrigerate.
Variation: Add ¼ cup chili sauce for a different taste.
"This must be made ahead."

HOT CHEESE DIP FOR APPLES

6 slices bacon
8 ounces cream cheese
8 ounces Cheddar cheese, shredded
6 tablespoons half and half
1 teaspoon Worcestershire sauce
¼ teaspoon dry mustard
¼ teaspoon onion salt
2-3 drops Tabasco
6 apples, unpared
1 cup lemon juice

Cut up bacon; sauté until crisp, and drain. Combine remaining ingredients, except apples and lemon juice, in double boiler or heat over low heat, stirring occasionally until cheese melts and mixture is hot. Add bacon pieces. Cut apples in wedges and dip in lemon juice to keep from discoloring. Use as dippers. Yields: 40.

SHRIMP DIP

7 ounces frozen pre-cooked shrimp, thawed, drained and chopped
8 ounces cream cheese, softened
¼ cup salad dressing
¼ cup mayonnaise
1 small onion, finely chopped
2 teaspoons prepared mustard
dash Tabasco sauce
crackers

Cream softened cream cheese. Add salad dressing and mayonnaise. Mix well. Add onion, mustard, Tabasco and shrimp. Mix well. Serve with crackers. Yields: 6 servings.
"May be made a day ahead and refrigerated."

SPINACH DIP

10 ounces frozen chopped spinach
½ cup salad dressing (or sour cream *or* a mixture of both)
4-5 green onions, green part only, chopped (or chives *or* minced onion)
8 drops Tabasco sauce
1 tablespoon Worcestershire sauce
salt to taste
pepper to taste
¼ cup Parmesan cheese, grated (optional)

Thaw spinach and drain very well. Add other ingredients to taste. Place in a crock. Refrigerate overnight. Yields: 20 servings.
"Serve with assorted crackers or melba toast."

HOT ARTICHOKE SPREAD

"A real favorite with everyone."

9 ounces frozen artichoke hearts
1 cup boiling water
½ teaspoon salt
¾ cup mayonnaise
1 cup Parmesan cheese, grated
⅛ teaspoon garlic salt
melba rounds

Preheat oven to 350°. Place frozen artichoke hearts in boiling salted water. Bring to boiling point again, cover, reduce heat and cook until tender, about 8-10 minutes. Drain well and chop. Set aside. Combine mayonnaise, Parmesan cheese and garlic salt; mix well. Add chopped artichokes to mayonnaise mixture. Blend well. Spoon into 8 inch pie plate and bake 20-30 minutes until top is golden. Serve hot on melba rounds or bland crackers. Yields: 3 cups.

"This recipe may be prepared in advance and refrigerated uncooked. Just before guests arrive, pop into hot oven."

HAM ASPARAGUS ROLLS

8 ounces cream cheese
4 tablespoons mayonnaise, or enough to thin mixture
1 teaspoon prepared horseradish
2 teaspoons lemon juice
4 dashes Tabasco
salt to taste
white pepper to taste
18 thin slices boiled ham, approximately 1 ounce each
20 ounces asparagus spears, drained

Blend well first 7 ingredients. Spread each ham slice with 2 teaspoons of cheese mixture. Place 1 large or 2 small asparagus spears along the edge of each ham slice and roll up jellyroll fashion. Chill overnight. Cut rolls in fifths to serve. Yields: 90 rolls.

OLIVE TEA SANDWICHES

8 ounces stuffed olives, drained
1 medium onion, chopped
2 hard cooked eggs, sliced
1 cup pecans
1 cup mayonnaise
40 slices bread

Mix first 4 ingredients. Put ¼ mixture at a time in blender. Blend only until coarsely ground. Mix with mayonnaise and chill. Cut crust from bread and spread with olive mixture. Cut into finger sandwiches or halves. Yields: 20 large sandwiches.

"Tea sandwiches can be made the day before by spreading a damp tea towel over the tray of sandwiches and refrigerating them."

MUSHROOM TURNOVERS

Turnovers:

9 ounces cream cheese, at room temperature
½ cup butter, at room temperature
1½ cups plain flour

Thoroughly mix cream cheese and butter. Add flour and work until smooth. Chill well, at least 30 minutes. Preheat oven to 450°. Roll dough ⅛ inch thick on lightly floured surface; cut into 3 inch rounds. Place approximately 1 teaspoonful of filling on each and fold dough over the filling. Press edges of dough together with water moistened fork. Prick top to allow steam to escape. Place on ungreased baking sheet; bake until lightly browned, about 15 minutes.

Filling:

3 tablespoons butter
1 large onion, finely chopped
½ pound fresh mushrooms, finely chopped
¼ teaspoon thyme
½ teaspoon salt
pepper, freshly ground
2 tablespoons plain flour
¼ cup half and half

In a skillet, heat butter and sauté onion until golden. Add mushrooms and cook, stirring often, about 3 minutes. Add seasonings and sprinkle mixture with flour. Stir in cream and cook, stirring gently, until thick. Yields: 20-24 turnovers.

OYSTER STUFFED TOMATOES

"These will quickly disappear."

1 quart cherry tomatoes
8 ounces cream cheese, softened
3 tablespoons dry sherry
½ cup Parmesan cheese, grated
¼ teaspoon paprika
1 teaspoon onion, grated
½ teaspoon dill weed
7½ ounces canned smoked oysters, drained and chopped
½ cup whipping cream, whipped

Wash tomatoes, cut small slice off top and take out pulp. Turn upside down, to drain, on paper towels. While tomatoes are draining, prepare oyster spread. Beat cream cheese with sherry until smooth. Blend in Parmesan cheese, paprika, onion and dill. Chop oysters and fold into cheese mixture. Whip cream until stiff and add. Refrigerate a few hours before stuffing tomatoes for flavor to improve. Yields: 3 cups (for about 50 tomatoes).

Variation: This is excellent used as a spread for crackers. Salt is really not necessary as oysters provide enough.

OYSTER STUFFED CELERY

2½ ounces canned smoked oysters, drained
1 cup cottage cheese
2 tablespoons whipping cream
1 teaspoon soy sauce
1 bunch celery
dash paprika

Chop oysters and mix with cheese, cream and soy sauce. Cut celery into pieces 2 inches long and fill with mixture. Sprinkle with paprika. Chill. Yields: approximately 50.

TANGY MARINATED MUSHROOMS

2 pounds fresh mushrooms
1½ cups tarragon vinegar
1½ cups salad oil
1 medium clove garlic
1 tablespoon sugar
1½ teaspoons salt
dash pepper
½ cup water, scant
dash Tabasco sauce
1 medium onion, sliced

Wash mushrooms and remove stems. Mix remaining ingredients and pour over the mushrooms. Refrigerate overnight. Drain before serving. Yields: 24.

BRAUNSCHWEIGER PATÉ

"People who don't like liver even enjoy this."

1 pound Braunschweiger liver
2 packages green onion dip mix
1 teaspoon sugar
2 teaspoons water
1 tablespoon garlic butter spread
6 ounces cream cheese, softened
1 tablespoon milk
⅛ teaspoon bottled hot pepper sauce
parsley, snipped
radishes, sliced
crackers

Mash liver; combine dip mix, sugar and water. Add to liver and blend thoroughly. Form mixture into igloo shape; place on serving plate. Chill. Melt garlic spread; whip cream cheese with milk and hot pepper sauce. Blend in melted garlic spread. Spread cream cheese mixture over liver. Chill. Before serving, garnish with parsley and radish slices. Serve with crackers. Yields: 30-40 servings.

MARINATED OLIVES

2 teaspoons red pepper, crushed
2 teaspoons pickling spices
2 garlic cloves
¼ cup red wine vinegar
¼ cup olive oil
16 ounces pitted black olives, drained

Tie red pepper and pickling spices in cheese cloth. Combine all ingredients. Marinate at least 24 hours. Yields: 20 servings.

SPINACH BALLS

20 ounces frozen chopped spinach
2 cups Pepperidge Farm seasoned dressing
1 large onion, chopped
6 eggs, beaten
¾ cup butter, melted
½ cup Parmesan cheese, grated
1 teaspoon garlic salt
1 teaspoon pepper
1 teaspoon Accent

Preheat oven to 350°. Cook spinach according to package directions; drain well. Mix all ingredients with spinach. Shape into balls and bake 20 minutes. Yields: 120 balls.

Note: Balls can be frozen, before cooking. Thaw for 1 hour; bake 20 minutes. To use as a casserole, place ingredients in casserole and increase baking time to 30 minutes.

CHAFING DISH CRAB MEAT

"Easy and tasty – beer gives it a zing."

10 ounces sharp Cheddar cheese spread
16 ounces cream cheese
13 ounces canned crab meat, drained and flaked
¼ cup half and half
1 teaspoon Worcestershire sauce
¼ cup beer
1 loaf French bread (cut in cubes)

Over boiling water, combine Cheddar spread and cream cheese, stirring constantly until smooth. Stir in crab meat, half and half, Worcestershire sauce and beer until thoroughly blended. Transfer to fondue pot or chafing dish. Serve piping hot with cubes of French bread for dunking. Yields: 20 servings.

CRAB SUISSE

8 ounces cream cheese
7½ ounces canned crab meat, drained
¼ cup Swiss cheese, grated
1 tablespoon lemon juice
½ teaspoon salt
dash pepper
dash Worcestershire sauce
8 ounces canned water chestnuts, thinly sliced
8 ounces refrigerated crescent rolls

Preheat oven to 400°. Mix cream cheese, crab meat, Swiss cheese, lemon juice, salt, pepper and Worcestershire sauce. Pinch perforated edges of rolls together to form rectangles. Spread crab mixture over rectangle. Roll jelly roll fashion; chill. Slice each chilled roll into 10 slices. Top each slice with a water chestnut. Bake 10 minutes. Yields: 40 rolls.

CRAB MEAT SPREAD

12 ounces cream cheese with chives, softened
7½ ounces canned crab meat, reserve ½ of the juice
1 teaspoon lemon juice
few drops hot sauce
8 ounces cocktail sauce

Mix cheese, crab, lemon juice and hot sauce. Spread onto serving plate as if forming a pie shell. Pour cocktail sauce in center indentation. Yields: 12-20 servings.

"Serve with melba toast or crackers; have spreaders handy."

Note: This can be fashioned into any shape such as a heart for Valentines. Sprigs of parsley are nice at Christmas around base. Looks beautiful on a silver tray.

BAKED BOLOGNA

1 midget kosher bologna
midget rye bread
prepared mustard

Preheat oven to 450°. Score bologna as you would a ham. Place in shallow pan and bake 45 minutes. Bologna will expand during cooking. Serve whole on a platter for cocktails with midget rye bread and mustard. Bake just before serving. Yields: 4-6 servings.

"Let guests carve their own slices."

SWEET AND SOUR MEATBALLS

3 pounds ground beef
1½ cups cracker crumbs
12 ounces evaporated milk
1 cup onion, chopped
2 teaspoons seasoned salt
1 cup oil
1 cup chicken bouillon
3 green peppers, diced
8-10 slices pineapple, in chunks
4 tablespoons cornstarch
4 tablespoons soy sauce
2 teaspoons Accent
1½ cups vinegar
1½ cups pineapple juice
1 cup sugar
1 teaspoon salt
pepper

Mix first 5 ingredients and shape into tiny balls. Cook in oil until brown; remove. Drain oil from skillet, reserving about 2 tablespoons. Add bouillon, green peppers and pineapple. Cover and cook over medium heat for 10 minutes. Meanwhile, mix cornstarch, soy sauce, Accent, vinegar, pineapple juice, sugar, salt and pepper. Add to mixture in skillet. Simmer, stirring constantly, until mixture thickens. Return meatballs to sauce. Serve in chafing dish with cocktail picks. Yields: 20-30 servings.

Variation: This recipe can be halved. Make larger meat balls and serve on rice or chow mein noodles. It makes a colorful, tasty main dish. It can be made ahead and refrigerated or frozen. Have meatballs in 1 container and sauce in another. Mix together at last minute.

Try pickled or spiced fruits with cocktails.

CHAFING DISH MEATBALLS

2 pounds ground chuck
2½ cups Rice Krispies cereal
½ cup milk
0.6 ounces Good Seasons blue cheese salad dressing mix
10¾ ounces canned cream of mushroom soup
10¾ ounces canned tomato soup
½ cup water

Thoroughly mix ground chuck, cereal, milk and dressing mix. Form into balls, using approximately 2 teaspoons per ball. Brown in a little oil in electric skillet. Drain on paper towels. Add soups and water to skillet, return meat balls and simmer 20-30 minutes. Transfer to chafing dish and serve with cocktail picks. Yields: 25 servings.

TERIYAKI TIDBITS

1 pound round or sirloin steak, cut into thin strips
¼ cup soy sauce
4 tablespoons water
2 tablespoons brown sugar
¼ teaspoon pepper
¼ teaspoon ginger
⅛ teaspoon garlic, minced

Tidbits:

mushroom caps
water chestnuts
cocktail onions
pineapple chunks
cherry tomatoes

Cut steak into thin strips. It is more easily sliced if the meat is partially frozen. Mix next 6 ingredients. Add meat strips and marinate 6-12 hours. Stir occasionally. Wrap marinated steak around any of the suggested tidbits and secure with a toothpick. Broil until meat reaches desired doneness, 3-5 minutes; serve immediately. Yields: 36 appetizers.
"For special flair, these could be cooked by the guests on a hibachi or in a fondue pot with hot oil."

MINIATURE QUICHE LORRAINE

"These will make you the envy of all – easy to prepare and very gourmet."

Shells:
3 ounces cream cheese, softened
½ cup butter, softened
1 cup plain flour

Preheat oven to 375°. Cream butter and cheese; add flour and mix by hand. Press into miniature shells.

Filling:
6 slices bacon
1 cup onion, chopped
2 eggs, slightly beaten
¾ cup sour cream
½ teaspoon salt
dash pepper
12 ounces Swiss cheese, grated

Fry bacon crisp, drain and crumble. Reserve 2 tablespoons drippings, add onion and cook until tender. Combine all ingredients and spoon into shells. Bake 20-30 minutes. Yields: approximately 40.
"Freezes beautifully after baking."

HOT DRIED BEEF SPREAD

"Everyone loves this spread!"

1 cup pecans, chopped
2 teaspoons butter
16 ounces cream cheese, softened
4 tablespoons milk
5 ounces dried beef, minced or shredded in blender
1 teaspoon garlic salt
1 cup sour cream
4 tablespoons onion, minced
4 tablespoons green pepper, minced
2 dashes Worcestershire sauce
crackers

Toast pecans in butter. Reserve. Mix all remaining ingredients, except crackers, thoroughly. Place in pie plate; top with pecans. Chill until serving time. Preheat oven to 350°. Bake for 20 minutes. Serve hot with crackers. Yields: 25 servings.
Hint: For best flavor, mix and refrigerate a day before serving.

VEGETABLE SANDWICH SPREAD

8 ounces cream cheese, softened
¼ cup celery, grated
¼ cup green pepper, grated
¼ cup cucumber, grated
¾ cup carrots, grated
2 tablespoons onion, minced
3-4 tablespoons mayonnaise
1 tablespoon lemon juice
salt

Combine all ingredients, using enough mayonnaise to thin to spreading consistency. Yields: 10 large sandwiches.
"This is best when made the day before and refrigerated overnight."

SAUSAGE KABOBS

8 ounces sausage links
13¼ ounces canned pineapple chunks
⅓ cup soy sauce
¼ cup brown sugar, firmly packed
1 tablespoon oil
1 clove garlic, minced
8 ounces canned water chestnuts, drained and halved
2 medium green peppers, cut in ¾ inch squares

Cut sausage in thirds crosswise. Drain pineapple, reserving ½ cup syrup. Combine reserved syrup, soy sauce, brown sugar, oil and garlic; stir until sugar dissolves. Add sausage and water chestnuts; let stand 2 hours at room temperature or 6 hours in refrigerator. Drain. Thread 1 piece each of sausage, pineapple, water chestnuts and green pepper on short skewers. Broil 3 minutes on each side. Yields: 30 appetizers.

MARINATED SHRIMP IN FRESH DILL

boiling water
salt
1 teaspoon dill seed
1 lemon, sliced
2½ pounds shrimp, in shell

Bring salted water, dill seed and lemon to a boil. Add shrimp and simmer until pink, 5-6 minutes. Immediately drain and chill shrimp. Prepare Marinade of Fresh Dill.

Marinade of Fresh Dill:
½ cup oil
½ cup dry white wine
4 teaspoons fresh dill, chopped (or 2 teaspoons dried dill weed)
1 teaspoon fresh pepper, cracked
dash garlic powder
2 drops Tabasco sauce
½ cup lemon juice
1 tablespoon chives
salt to taste

Mix all ingredients well. After shrimp have chilled, peel and devein them. Place in crock or bowl. Pour marinade over. Cover; store in refrigerator 24 hours. Serves: 8-10.

PICKLED SHRIMP

5 pounds shrimp, cleaned and cooked
3 large onions

Dressing:
2 teaspoons dry mustard
2 teaspoons curry powder
3 teaspoons celery seed
1 teaspoon salt
3 cups oil
3 cups white vinegar
1½ cups catsup
1 tablespoon soy sauce
2 tablespoons Worcestershire sauce
1 tablespoon capers and juice
3 whole cloves
4 bay leaves
dash Tabasco sauce
lettuce

In large container, layer shrimp and onions. Mix all dressing ingredients and cover shrimp with dressing. Cover container; refrigerate for 3 days. Stir well each day. When ready to serve, drain and serve on bed of lettuce with cocktail picks. Yields: 20-25 servings.
Note: Make 3 days before serving.

NITA'S SEAFOOD MOUSSE

⅓ cup catsup
2 teaspoons unflavored gelatin
10¾ ounces canned cream of mushroom soup
9 ounces cream cheese, softened
1 cup celery, diced
1 cup mayonnaise
2 envelopes unflavored gelatin dissolved in ¾ cup cold water
6½ ounces canned lobster
6½ ounces canned shrimp
6½ ounces canned crab meat
½ cup onion, finely chopped
white pepper to taste

Heat catsup; stir in 2 teaspoons gelatin until dissolved. Pour into bottom of decorative seafood mold and refrigerate until firm. Heat soup; add cream cheese. Stir until smooth. Add gelatin and other ingredients, blending well. Pour into mold. Refrigerate until firm. Unmold and serve. Yields: 14-16 servings.

Note: Serve with crackers.

Frozen seafood may be substituted for canned. The kinds and amounts can be varied according to individual taste.

Every successful cocktail party should include a seafood, meat, vegetable, cheese & 1 dip.

ASHEVILLE SEAFOOD MOLD

1 envelope unflavored gelatin
¾ cup cold milk
10¾ ounces canned tomato soup
8 ounces cream cheese
½ cup green onion, chopped
½ cup celery, chopped
½ cup mayonnaise
1½-2 cups seafood (shrimp, crab meat or lobster), cut up
¼ cup green pepper, chopped
1 tablespoon Durkee's dressing
1 teaspoon Worcestershire sauce
¼ teaspoon salt

Dissolve gelatin in cold milk; set aside. In top of double boiler, heat until smooth and hot but not boiling, the tomato soup and cream cheese. Add gelatin mixture. Fold onions, celery and mayonnaise into tomato mixture. Fold in seafood, pepper, Durkee's dressing, Worcestershire sauce and salt. Grease a 4 cup mold with mayonnaise and pour in above mixture. Chill well. Yields: 8-12 servings.

"*Serve with crackers.*"

COLLECTION OF NORTH CAROLINA SYMBOLS

State Toast — Here's to the land of the longleaf pine,
The summer land where the sun doth shine.
Where the weak grow strong and the strong grow great,
Here's to "Down Home", the old North State!

State Song — *Old North State* by Judge William Gaston

State Flag — May 20, 1775
Mecklenburg Declaration of Independence
April 12, 1776 — Halifax Resolves

State Seal —

State Motto — Esse Quam Videri — "To be rather than to seem"

State Insect — Honey Bee

State Bird — Red Cardinal

State Tree — Longleaf Pine

State Flower — Dogwood

State Shell — Scotch Bonnet

State Mammal — Grey Squirrel

State Mineral — Emerald

State Fish — Channel Bass

State Nickname — "Tar Heel State" — It was during one of the fiercest battles of the Civil War, so the story goes, that the column supporting the N.C. troops was driven from the field. After the battle, the North Carolinians who had successfully fought it out alone were greeted from the passing derelict regiment with the question, "any more tar down in the Old North State, boys?". Quick as a flash came the answer, "no, not a bit. Ole' Jeff Davis bought it all up." "Is that so, what is he going to do with it?" was asked. "He is going to put it on you-uns heels to make you stick better in the next fight." General Robert E. Lee, on hearing of the incident, said: "God bless the tar heel boys," and from that they took the name.

beverages

THE CAROLINA COLLECTOR'S CONCOCTIONS

. . . To cranberry juice add cinnamon, allspice &/or cloves. Serve hot or cold.

. . . Blend until frothy, 1 c dry milk, 2 c orange juice, 2 c ice water, ¼ c honey & 2 ice cubes for a refreshing shake.

. . . Spice 9 large cans apple juice with 2 t each cinnamon, cloves, nutmeg & allspice. Serve hot to 100 people.

. . . Add lemon juice & whiskey to sugared iced tea & chill for 1 day.

. . . Crumble 1 T whole cloves, 1 c loose tea leaves, ½ c dried mint & 2 T dried orange peel. Use 1 t in hot water for mint tea.

. . . Mix 2 cans chilled beef broth with ¾ c dry sherry. Pour over ice & add a twist of lemon peel.

. . . Mix 1 c freeze dried coffee, 4 t lemon peel, 4 t cinnamon, 1 t ground cloves. Use 1 t in hot water for spiced coffee.

. . . Make apricot liquor with 1½ c dried apricots, ⅔ c sugar & 1 pt. vodka. Let sit 1 week turning jar twice daily. Strain & refrigerate.

. . . Pour ½ red or white wine & ½ tonic water over ice & serve with a lemon slice.

. . . Combine 3 T concentrated orange juice & ½ pt. yogurt for a delicious health drink.

. . . Whip 1 c frozen evaporated milk to a froth; add ½ t vanilla, 3 t confectioners' sugar, 1 t cinnamon. Fill cup ¼ full, pour in coffee & add a pinch of nutmeg. Serves 12.

. . . To make a Hot Toddy add ¼ c dark rum & lemon slice studded with cloves to a cup of hot tea.

. . . Partially freeze tomato juice with a bit of onion juice — serve in champagne glass with a dollop of curry mayonnaise on top.

. . . For the most delicious coffee ever, freeze extra strong coffee in ice cube trays. Put frozen cubes in tall glasses & pour warm milk over them. Top with 1 T whipped cream.

AMARETTO ALEXANDER

12 ounces Amaretto liqueur
1 pint half and half
6 ounces white crème de cacao
1½ quarts vanilla ice cream

Combine Amaretto, crème de cacao, and half and half in blender. Place scoop of ice cream in each sherbet glass and place the remainder in blender. Blend well. Pour in glass and serve. Yields: 10 servings.

BLOODY MARY

"Perfect seasonings – very, very good."

juice of ½ lemon
juice of ½ lime
5-6 drops Tabasco sauce
6-10 drops Worcestershire sauce
2 ounces clam juice
6 ounces V-8 juice
vodka, according to taste

Shake together over ice and strain into glasses. Yields: 3 drinks.
"Perfect for a brunch. If you want that extra special touch, coat rims of glasses with salt, by dipping each glass into a saucer of slightly beaten egg whites and then into a saucer of salt. Garnish with celery sticks."

Rule for cocktail parties — 3 drinks per person; 1 fifth serves 5 guests or yields 15 drinks.

EGGNOG

"Serve in glasses with a teaspoon for reaching the last drop."

8 eggs, separated
1 cup sugar, divided
1¼ cups bourbon
1 cup whipping cream
2 cups half and half
2 quarts milk
nutmeg, freshly grated or ground

Beat egg yolks with ½ cup sugar and bourbon. Set aside. Beat egg whites until stiff, adding ¼ cups sugar gradually. Set aside. Whip cream until stiff with remaining sugar. In punch bowl, combine half and half with milk. Add yolk-whiskey mixture. Gently fold in egg whites and whipped cream. Serve cold with a sprinkle of nutmeg. Yields: 12 servings.

FROZEN BANANA DAIQUIRI

2 ripe bananas
1½ cups cold water
1 cup light rum
½ cup lime juice
⅓ cup orange liqueur
2-3 tablespoons sugar
fresh strawberries, optional
mint sprig, optional

In blender, combine bananas, water, rum, lime juice, orange liqueur and sugar. Blend 30 seconds. Pour into ice cube trays and freeze. At serving time, transfer frozen mixture to blender and blend until ice dissolves. Serve in chilled cocktail glasses. If desired, garnish each glass with a fresh strawberry and a sprig of mint. Yields: 6 servings.

PEACH FUZZ

1 fresh peach, pitted and sliced but *not* peeled
6 ounces frozen lemonade concentrate
6 ounces vodka or gin
sugar to taste
2 cups crushed ice
4 sprigs fresh mint

Combine first 5 ingredients in blender container. Blend at high speed for 1 minute. Serve in chilled daiquiri glasses with a sprig of mint. Yields: 4 servings.

1 medium orange yields ⅓ c juice & 2 T grated rind.

1 lemon yields ¼ c juice & 1 T grated rind.

PIÑA COLADA

"A summertime favorite which we love all year long."

4 ounces Coco Lopez
8 ounces pineapple juice
6 ounces light rum
20 ice cubes
6 chunks pineapple, fresh or canned
6 maraschino cherries

Combine first 4 ingredients in blender. Store in freezer (will not freeze hard). Serve in champagne glasses and garnish with a chunk of pineapple and maraschino cherry. The drink should be the consistency of a frozen daiquiri. Yields: 6 servings.

Note: Coco Lopez is found with cocktail mixes in grocery store.

MOCHA FRAPPÉ

2-3 cups marble fudge ice cream
½ cup brandy
½ cup vodka
⅓ cup coffee liqueur
⅓ cup crème de cacao

Combine all ingredients in blender container and blend until smooth. Serve in wine or champagne glasses. Yields: 6 servings.
"This should take the place of dessert and liqueur."

HOT BUTTERED CIDER

2 quarts apple cider
2 oranges, juiced
2 lemons, juiced
15 whole cloves
6 sticks cinnamon
1 tablespoon honey
1 tablespoon ground allspice
1 tablespoon ground cinnamon
½ teaspoon ground nutmeg
2½ cups dark rum
3 tablespoons butter
6 additional sticks cinnamon

Combine first 9 ingredients. Simmer, covered, for 2 hours. Strain. Add rum and pour into mugs. Float about ½ tablespoon of butter on surface and use additional cinnamon sticks for stirring. Yields: 6 servings.

LARRY'S STUMP JUICE

"Serve as an after dinner drink."

30 ounces frozen red raspberries (or 1 quart of any fresh fruit)
½ cup sugar (or 1 cup if using fresh fruit)
1 fifth of bourbon whiskey

Combine all ingredients in gallon jug with tight fitting cap. Allow to stand, unrefrigerated, 10 days, being sure to shake the mixture each day. Strain through cheese cloth after 10 days. Chill. Yields: 1 gallon.

HOT SPICED WINE PUNCH

½ cup sugar
½ cup water
24 whole cloves
2 sticks cinnamon
½ lemon, sliced
2 cups unsweetened pineapple juice
2 cups orange juice
1½ quarts red wine

Boil sugar, water, cloves, cinnamon and lemon slices for 20 minutes. Strain. Heat fruit juices and add to first mixture. Add wine. Stir and serve hot or cold with a lemon slice. Yields: 3 quarts.

CHAMPAGNE PUNCH

6 ounces frozen lemonade concentrate
6 cups unsweetened pineapple juice
2 bottles Brut or extra dry champagne
1 bottle sauterne or Rhine Castle

Chill wine and champagne thoroughly. Combine lemonade concentrate, pineapple juice and chilled wine. Chill this mixture. At serving time, combine chilled wine mixture and champagne. Yields: 50 servings.

ALMOND FRUIT PUNCH

4 cups sugar
3 cups water
6 ounces gelatin (flavor determined by color chart below)
1 gallon water
8 ounces lemon juice
46 ounces unsweetened pineapple juice
2 tablespoons almond extract

Boil water and sugar until sugar dissolves. Add gelatin and cool. Combine with remaining ingredients and freeze. To serve, thaw until mushy. Yields: 30-40 servings. (This may be stretched by adding chilled ginger ale or Sprite.)

Color Chart:
Yellow: lemon gelatin
Green: lime gelatin and a few drops of green food coloring
Pink: strawberry gelatin
Red: cherry gelatin
Orange: orange gelatin
Purple: grape gelatin and red food coloring

COFFEE PUNCH

"Rich and creamy, absolutely delicious!"

1 gallon strong coffee, chilled
¾ cup sugar
1 tablespoon vanilla extract
1 gallon vanilla ice cream, softened
1 pint whipping cream, whipped and sweetened to taste
nutmeg, grated

Combine coffee, sugar and vanilla. Stir to dissolve sugar. Refrigerate. At serving time, scoop ice cream into punch bowl. Add chilled coffee mixture and gently fold in whipped cream. Sprinkle top with grated nutmeg. Yields: 45 punch cup servings.

Variation: For a mocha punch, use chocolate ice cream.

CAROLINA-IN-THE-MORNING PUNCH

80 ounces cola beverage
½ gallon coffee ice cream

Chill cola. Soften ice cream. Combine gently in punch bowl. Yields: 25-30 servings.

HOT CRANBERRY-APPLE PUNCH

2 quarts cranberry juice
3 quarts apple juice
4 sticks cinnamon
12 whole cloves
½ lemon, sliced
½ cup brown sugar

Combine ingredients and simmer 1 hour. Serve hot. Yields: 5 quarts.

CINNAMON PUNCH

"This quick and easy punch is a real pleaser at a Christmas Open House."

46 ounces pineapple-grapefruit drink
¼ cup red hot cinnamon candies
½ cup sugar
1 quart ginger ale, chilled

Heat juice, candies and sugar until dissolved. Chill. Add ginger ale and crushed ice to serve, or freeze juice and mix with ginger ale to a slushy consistency. Yields: 20 servings.

JULIA'S PUNCH

"An inexpensive, but delicious fruit punch to have on hand during the hot summer months."

0.6 ounces Cherri-Aid imitation lemonade mix, with water called for on package
46 ounces pineapple juice
46 ounces unsweetened orange juice
3 cups sugar, dissolved in a little water

Combine all ingredients and freeze. To serve, allow to partially thaw and mash with a potato masher. Serve mushy. Yields: 2 gallons.

MOCK PINK CHAMPAGNE PUNCH

½ cup sugar
1½ cups boiling water
2 cups cranberry juice
1 cup pineapple juice
½ cup orange juice
14 ounces lemon-lime carbonated beverage, chilled

Dissolve sugar in boiling water; cool. Stir in fruit juices. Chill. Just before serving, add lemon-lime carbonated beverage. Yields: 14 servings.

WATERMELON PUNCH

2½ cups water, divided
½ cup lemon juice, divided
1 cup sugar
3 cups watermelon juice
2 cups orange juice
lemon, lime, and orange slices

Combine 1¼ cups water, ¼ cup lemon juice and sugar in a saucepan. Boil for 3 minutes. Cool. Mix 1¼ cups water, ¼ cup lemon juice, watermelon juice and orange juice. Add cooled sugar syrup and chill thoroughly. Pour over ice in punch bowl. Yields: 2 quarts.

To make watermelon juice:
Place 5½ cups diced and seeded watermelon in blender container and blend at high speed until liquified. Strain through a fine sieve or cheesecloth.
"This may be served in a scooped out watermelon shell which has been scalloped around the edges."

SOUTHERN MINT TEA PUNCH

"A refreshing summertime punch perfect for morning parties."

1 quart boiling water
7 regular size tea bags
2 cups sugar
2 cups fresh mint
6 ounces frozen orange juice concentrate
7½ ounces lemon juice
water

Pour boiling water over tea bags, sugar and fresh mint. Steep 20 minutes. Strain. Add orange juice concentrate, lemon juice and enough water to make 1 gallon of punch. Chill. To serve, pour over crushed ice or ice block in punch bowl. Decorate with additional fresh mint. Yields: 1 gallon.

PINK VELVET PUNCH

72 ounces cranberry juice cocktail
¾ cup lemon juice
1½ cups orange juice
1 cup sugar (or 3 cups juice from canned fruit)
½ gallon vanilla ice cream, softened
1 quart ginger ale

Mix all ingredients except ice cream and ginger ale. Let stand in refrigerator overnight. At serving time, scoop ice cream into punch bowl and add fruit juices and ginger ale. Yields: 30 servings.
"For a plain red punch, omit the vanilla ice cream."

SUMMER FRUIT SLUSH

"Delightful on a hot summer day."

6 lemons, juiced and divided
6 oranges, juiced and divided
2 cups sugar, divided
2 quarts water, divided
3 ripe bananas, mashed

Combine juice of 3 lemons, 3 oranges, 1 cup sugar and 1 quart water. Stir to dissolve sugar. Pour into ice trays and freeze. Combine juice of 3 lemons, 3 oranges, 1 cup sugar and 1 quart water. Chill. At serving time, fill glasses with frozen juice cubes. Spoon mashed bananas over cubes and fill with chilled juice. Yields: 6-8 servings.
Variation: For a Banana Punch, combine frozen juice, chilled juice, 2 cups pineapple juice, mashed bananas and 42 ounces chilled ginger ale.

RUSSIAN TEA

"Well worth your time to make on a cold day."

2 family size tea bags
6 cups boiling water
1¼ cups sugar
5 cups water
12 whole cloves
1 stick cinnamon
4 oranges, juiced and rind of 1 orange
1 lemon, juiced

Pour boiling water over tea bags. Cover and steep 5 minutes. Make a syrup of remaining ingredients, except fruit juices, by boiling them together 5 minutes. Strain. Add syrup and fruit juices to tea. Keep hot, but do not boil. Yields: 16 servings.

HOT CRANBERRY TEA

2 quarts tea, sweetened to taste
1 quart cranberry juice cocktail
6 ounces frozen pink lemonade concentrate
6 ounces frozen orange juice concentrate
1½ cups water
3 drops oil of cinnamon (found in pharmacy)

Combine all ingredients in a large pot and simmer 15 minutes. Serve hot. Yields: 1 gallon.

FROZEN STRAWBERRY DRINK or DAIQUIRI

6 ounces frozen lemonade concentrate
10 ounces frozen strawberries, thawed
3 tablespoons confectioners' sugar
ice cubes

Place ingredients in blender container and fill almost to the top with ice cubes. Blend on high speed until smooth. Yields: 4-5 servings.
Variation: Add 6 ounces of rum for a strawberry daiquiri.

HOT TOMATO PUNCH

"Excellent flavor. Should be served in demitasse cups."

2 10¾ ounce cans tomato soup
2 10½ ounce cans consommé
1 soup can water
good dash of Worcestershire sauce
1 teaspoon celery salt
½ teaspoon lemon pepper or black pepper
2 beef bouillon cubes

Combine and heat almost to boiling point. Serve with cheese sticks or biscuits. Yields: 10-12 servings.

TASTY TOMATO COCKTAIL

"Serve this delicious appetizer with a stick of fresh celery for munching."

46 ounces tomato juice
1 lemon, juiced and grated rind
2 tablespoons white vinegar
2 tablespoons Worcestershire sauce
2-3 tablespoons sugar
2-3 tablespoons catsup

Mix all ingredients in large container. Chill. Yields: 8 servings.

SPICED ICED TEA

5 tea bags
1 quart boiling water
2 sticks cinnamon
1½ cups sugar
1½ cups pineapple juice
1 cup juice from spiced pickled peaches
juice of 3 lemons
juice of 3 oranges
2 quarts cold water
orange or lemon slices
fresh mint sprigs
whole cloves

Pour boiling water over tea bags and cinnamon. Steep 15-20 minutes. Strain into a gallon container. Add sugar and shake to dissolve thoroughly. Add fruit juices and water. Refrigerate until serving. Yields: 3-4 quarts.

INSTANT HOT CHOCOLATE MIX

1 pound Coffeemate
1 pound Nestle's Quick
29.6 ounces non-fat dry milk
1 pound confectioners' sugar
cinnamon

Blend all ingredients except cinnamon. Store in airtight container. To serve, use ⅓ to ½ cup of mix per cup of boiling water. Add a dash of cinnamon to each cup. Yields: 4 quarts.
"For a delicious Mocha Chocolate Mix, add ½ cup instant coffee granules to basic mix."

Place fresh or dried mint in bottom of hot chocolate cups.

POTPOURRI PUNCH

"This recipe is not for consumption but will fill your home with a marvelous Chrismastime odor."

1 quart pineapple juice
1 quart water
1 quart apple cider
4 pieces ginger
3 three inch cinnamon sticks
16 whole cloves
1 teaspoon whole allspice
1-2 teaspoons pickling spice

Combine all ingredients. Bring to a boil and boil for several minutes. Reduce heat and allow to simmer. Yields: 3 quarts.
"This may be stored in the refrigerator."

COLLECTION OF NORTH CAROLINA FIRSTS

First English Colony in North America — Roanoke Island: 1585

First child of English parents born in North America — Virginia Dare: August 18, 1587

First flight by machine heavier than air: Wright Brothers flight at Kitty Hawk: December 17, 1903

First wireless telegraph experiment by R.A. Fessender: 1906 (became the basis for the development of radio broadcasting)

First gold discovered in America: 1799 — Reed Mine, Cabarrus County (28 lb. gold nugget found)

First state university — UNC-Chapel Hill: 1789 chartered in Fayetteville; 1795 opened to students

First state supported symphony — 1946

First state museum of art — Raleigh, 1956

First state school of arts — Winston-Salem, 1963

First forestry school in America — Biltmore, 1898

First state supported teachers college for blacks — Fayetteville State; Fayetteville, 1877

First woman state supreme court justice — Susie M. Sharp

First town in U.S. to be named for LaFayette — Fayetteville, 1783

First state to seek independence — April 12, 1776, Halifax Resolves: "First in Freedom"

First homerun hit by Babe Ruth — Fayetteville, 1914

First national seashore park in U.S. — Cape Hatteras

First in world in tobacco, textiles, furniture and brick industries

First national sea historic preservatory in U.S. — Civil War iron clad Monitor — off coast of Cape Hatteras

First American poet and playwriter — Thomas Godfrey; born Philadelphia, 1736; died Wilmington, August 3, 1763; buried in St. James Church yard

First X-Ray photograph made by Drittany Smith at Davidson, 1896

Longest plank road in world — 129 miles long — Fayetteville to Bethania

First radio SOS in history sent when the liner Arapahoe radioed for help off Cape Hatteras — 1909

First Division to break Hindenburg Line during World War I — Old Hickory Division (13th of N.C.) — 1918

First meeting in U.S. by women for political reason — Edenton Tea Party: 1774

breads

THE CAROLINA COLLECTOR'S CONCOCTIONS

. . . A basic cracker mix: mix 3 c flour, ½ t salt & 1 c each butter & cottage cheese. Roll out ⅛″ thick & cut into crackers. Bake 12-15 min. at 400°. Add herbs or seeds for a variation.

. . . Orange French toast is made by dipping raisin bread into mixture of orange juice & eggs. Dredge bread in graham cracker crumbs & fry.

. . . A basic biscuit mix is 8 c self-rising flour, 1⅓ c dry milk & 1 c shortening. Store in air tight container in cool place. For angel biscuits, add 1 package yeast, 1 c warm milk & 2 T sugar to 4 c mix. Knead & shape into biscuits. Let rise once.

. . . For quick crepes, blend 2 eggs, ⅔ c milk, 2 T vegetable oil & ⅔ c pancake mix in blender until smooth.

. . . One T brandy added to basic crepe batter makes a delicious variation.

. . . A good spread for French bread is a mixture of ½ c butter, ½ c Roquefort cheese & 2 T minced chives.

. . . Spread bread with mixture of grated cheese, caraway seed, onion salt & mayonnaise.

. . . A good bread spread is made of ½ c sour cream, dash pepper, ¼ t salt, horseradish, ¼ t garlic salt & ½ t poppy seed.

. . . Make honey butter for waffles by beating ¼ c honey, 2 T butter & 2 T whipping cream.

. . . For quick croutons, fry bite size cereals in butter & garlic salt.

. . . Put canned biscuits in muffin tins, indent with thumb & put butter & preserves in indentation. Bake 12-15 min. at 450°.

. . . Dip flaky biscuit quarters in mixture of melted butter, lemon juice, lemon rind & sugar. Bake 12-15 min. at 450°.

. . . Add drained, crushed pineapple to your favorite waffle or pancake mix. Syrup is made with pineapple juice diluted with water & boiled 5-7 min. Butter may be added.

. . . Sprinkle corn bread batter lightly with sesame seeds before baking.

. . . Brush bread sticks with poppy seed butter.

. . . Over French toast sprinkle mixture of 4 t lemon peel & ½ c sugar.

. . . For quick beer biscuits, mix 4 c Bisquick, 12 oz. beer & 3-5 T sugar. Bake in greased muffin tins 8-10 min. at 425°. Yields 18-20.

SNOWFLAKE BISCUITS

2 packages active dry yeast
5 tablespoons lukewarm water
1 cup buttermilk
5 cups plain flour
2 tablespoons sugar
1 tablespoon baking powder
1 teaspoon baking soda
1¼ teaspoons salt
1 cup shortening

Stir yeast into warm water to dissolve. Mix with buttermilk. Combine all dry ingredients in mixing bowl; cut in shortening. Add buttermilk-yeast mixture. Stir to form a soft dough. Roll ½-1 inch thick on lightly floured surface. Cut; place on two greased 10x15 cookie sheets so they do not touch. Cover; let rise in warm place 1-1½ hours. Preheat oven to 400°. Bake 15 minutes. Yields: 60 biscuits.

Note: These biscuits may be baked 8 minutes at 350°; frozen and used as needed. To serve, thaw and bake at 400° 10 minutes.

Kneading biscuit dough for ½ minute after mixing improves the texture of baking powder biscuits.

Use the divider from an ice tray to cut biscuits in a hurry. After baking, biscuits will separate at the dividing lines.

BEST BUTTERMILK BISCUITS

2 cups plain flour, sifted
1 tablespoon baking powder
¾ teaspoon salt
¼ teaspoon baking soda
6 tablespoons butter, cut into bits
¾ cup buttermilk
2 tablespoons butter, melted

Preheat oven to 450°. Mix flour, baking powder, salt and soda. Cut in butter until mixture resembles corn meal. Add buttermilk, stirring until a soft dough is formed. Turn dough onto a floured surface; knead 30 seconds. Pat or roll to ½" thickness. Cut as desired. Place on greased baking sheet. Brush with melted butter. Bake 12-15 minutes. Yields: 8-2½ inch biscuits or 12-15 smaller size biscuits.

Variation: For a cheese biscuit, add ½ cup sharp Cheddar cheese, grated, to the dough.

OVEN-BUTTERED CORNSTICKS

"A quick and easy bread that will please your guests with its buttery flavor."

4 tablespoons margarine
2 cups Bisquick
8¾ ounces cream style corn

Preheat oven to 450°. Melt butter or margarine in 10½x15½x1 jelly roll pan. In mixing bowl, combine Bisquick and corn. Stir to form a soft dough. Knead dough 15 strokes. On a lightly floured surface, roll dough into a 6x10 rectangle. Cut into 1x3 inch strips. Roll strips in melted butter or margarine; lay in a single row in pan. Bake 10-12 minutes. Yields: 20 strips.
"These may be prepared up to baking point, refrigerated and baked at serving time. Cover them with a damp paper towel while in refrigerator."

CAPE FEAR CORN BREAD

"This is a very moist corn bread."

12 ounces Flako Corn Bread Mix
1 cup sour cream
3 eggs, well beaten
½ cup corn oil or butter, melted
1 teaspoon salt
16 ounces cream style corn

Preheat oven to 375°. Mix all ingredients well. Bake 35 minutes in a greased 9x12 pan. Cut in squares to serve. Yields: 12-15 servings.
Variation: Add 4 ounces grated Swiss or sharp Cheddar cheese to top of bread during last 10 minutes of baking time. For Onion Corn Bread, add the cheese, 1½ cups chopped onion and 2 drops red pepper sauce.

CALABASH HUSHPUPPIES

1 cup yellow corn meal
1 cup plain flour
1 teaspoon baking powder
1 teaspoon salt
1 teaspoon baking soda
½ teaspoon onion salt
½ teaspoon granulated garlic powder (optional)
1 egg, well beaten
¾-1 cup buttermilk
½ cup green onion, finely chopped
oil for deep fat frying

Preheat oil in deep fat fryer or electric fry pan to 350°-375°. Stir all dry ingredients together. Make a well in dry ingredients; add egg and ¾ cup buttermilk. Stir thoroughly; add ¼ cup buttermilk if needed. Add green onions; mix well. Drop by teaspoons into hot oil. Brown and turn to brown on other side. Drain on paper towels. Yields: 10-12 servings.

BUTTER MUFFINS

5½ cups plain flour
4 tablespoons baking powder
½ cup sugar
1½ teaspoon salt
½ cup butter, softened

Combine dry ingredients. Cut in softened butter until mixture resembles corn meal. Store, tightly covered, in refrigerator until ready to use. Yields: 6 cups.

To Bake:
2 cups muffin mix
1 tablespoon sugar
1 egg, slightly beaten
¾ cup milk

Preheat oven to 425°. Combine all ingredients just until moistened. Well grease muffin tins. Fill ⅔ full. Bake 20-25 minutes. Yields: 12 muffins.
Variation: For Blueberry Muffins add 1 cup of blueberries to above batter.

French bread, rolls & muffins can be restored to original freshness if placed in brown paper bag with ½ t water added & heated in oven.

BANANA BRAN MUFFINS

1 cup bran cereal
1 cup buttermilk
1 large ripe banana, mashed
1 egg, beaten
1¼ cups whole wheat flour
1 tablespoon baking powder
4 tablespoons brown sugar
½ teaspoon salt
1 cup raisins, optional

Preheat oven to 400°. Combine cereal and buttermilk in mixing bowl; allow to soften 15 minutes. Add mashed banana and beaten egg. Mix well. Combine in small bowl flour, baking powder, sugar, salt and raisins. Gently fold dry ingredients into moist batter. Fill greased muffin tins ⅔ full. Bake 30-35 minutes. Yields: 12 muffins.
"Serve hot or cool completely on wire racks and wrap securely in foil and freezer wrap to freeze. These will keep in the freezer 2-3 months. To serve, thaw and heat 5 minutes at 400°."

POTATO ICE BOX ROLLS

1½ cups milk, scalded and cooled to lukewarm (or ½ cup powdered milk mixed with 1½ cups water, do not scald)
½ cup potatoes, mashed
½ cup water from cooked potatoes
½ cup sugar
½ cup butter
1 package active dry yeast
½ teaspoon baking powder
½ teaspoon salt
6-7 cups plain flour, divided

Combine first 8 ingredients in large bowl of electric mixer. Add 3 cups flour; beat well and allow to rest 15 minutes. Add remaining 3-4 cups flour gradually to make a stiff but sticky dough. Attach dough hook to mixer and process adding a little flour, if necessary, 5 minutes. If not using a dough hook, turn dough onto lightly floured surface and knead 10 minutes. Transfer to a greased bowl; cover, refrigerate. Punch dough down every hour for 3-4 hours or until dough is completely cool. Use immediately or refrigerate up to 5 days. For dinner rolls: Roll dough to ½ inch thickness on lightly floured surface; cut in desired shape. Place on greased cookie sheet; cover loosely. Let rise in warm place 1-1½ hours. Preheat oven to 400°. Bake 20 minutes. Yields: 5-6 dozen dinner rolls.

Variations:

Sticky Buns:

potato ice box roll dough
butter, softened
cinnamon
sugar
whipping cream or evaporated milk
brown sugar
pecans, chopped

Using desired amount of dough, roll out on lightly floured surface into a rectangle ¼ inch thick. Spread generously with butter, sprinkle with cinnamon and sugar. Roll as for jelly roll. Cut into 1 inch pieces. In a baking pan with sides, cover bottom of pan with a thin layer of brown sugar. Pour in cream or milk to ¼ inch depth. Sprinkle heavily with chopped pecans. Place rolls, cut side up, in pan. Cover; let rise in warm place 1-1½ hours. Preheat oven to 400°. Bake 20 minutes. While hot, invert onto waxed paper.

Moravian Sugar Bread:

½ recipe potato ice box roll dough
butter, softened
½ cup butter, melted
1 cup light brown sugar
2 teaspoons cinnamon

Grease two 9x9 cake pans. Divide dough in half; pat into pans. Spread with softened butter. Cover; let rise in warm place until doubled, about 1 hour. With index finger, punch indentions at 1 inch intervals in dough. Pour melted butter over bread. Combine brown sugar and cinnamon; sprinkle over bread. Preheat oven to 350°. Bake 15-20 minutes.

To test for yeast freshness, even after expiration date, sprinkle 1 t sugar on yeast dissolved in water. Fresh yeast will produce a foam.

PORTUGUESE SWEET BREAD

"This bread bakes into a peak and is beautiful in appearance and texture."

2 packages active dry yeast
½ cup lukewarm water
1 cup milk, scalded
½ cup butter
2 teaspoons salt
6 eggs
1½ cups sugar
8-9 cups plain flour
melted butter

Sprinkle yeast on water; stir to dissolve. Add butter and salt to scalded milk; cool. Combine eggs and sugar in large bowl of electric mixer; beat until light. Add milk mixture. Stir in yeast. Gradually beat in 3 cups flour. Continue to add flour until a soft dough that leaves the sides of the bowl forms. Knead dough 10 minutes on a lightly floured surface, or process with a dough hook 4-5 minutes or until dough becomes elastic. Transfer to greased bowl; cover, let rise in warm place 1½-2 hours or until doubled. Punch down; allow to rest 10 minutes. Divide into thirds. Shape into smooth balls. Grease three 9 inch cake pans; flatten dough into pans. Cover; let rise in warm place 1 hour. Preheat oven to 350°. Bake 30 minutes. Brush with melted butter while bread is hot. Cool on wire racks. Allow to cool before slicing.

MONKEY BREAD

2 packages active dry yeast
1 cup lukewarm water (115°)
4 tablespoons sugar
1 teaspoon salt
½ cup butter, melted
3½-4 cups plain flour, sifted

Dissolve yeast in lukewarm water. Stir in sugar, salt and butter. Add flour; beat well. Let rise, covered, in warm place until almost doubled. Punch down. Roll out to ⅓ inch thickness on lightly floured surface. Cut in 2 inch rounds with floured cutter. Dip each round in melted butter and place in 9 inch tube pan. overlapping slightly. When all rounds have been placed, cover; let rise in warm place until doubled. Preheat oven to 400°. Bake 25 minutes or until golden brown. Remove from oven to a wire rack. Cool 10 minutes. Invert onto a wire rack and then turn upright onto a serving plate. To serve, allow guests to pull off desired amount.

Variation: 1. To serve as an appetizer, instead of cutting dough into 2 inch circles, roll dough into cylinders 2 inches long and ½ inch thick. Bake as above. To serve, fill center of ring with a small bowl of hot chili. Guests pull off bread and dip it into chili.

2. For a delicious coffee cake, dip dough pieces in melted butter, roll in cinnamon-sugar and place in pan as directed.

REFRIGERATOR ROLLS

¾ cup shortening
1 cup milk, scalded
2 eggs, beaten
¾ cup sugar
2 teaspoons salt
1 cup cold water
3 packages active dry yeast
½ cup lukewarm water
7½ cups plain flour, sifted
butter, melted

Add shortening to scalded milk. Stir until shortening is melted. Set aside. Combine eggs, sugar and salt; beat in cold water. Stir yeast into lukewarm water to dissolve. Add to egg-sugar mixture; stir well. Add cooled milk and shortening. Mix well. Stir in flour to form soft dough. Cover with waxed paper. Chill in refrigerator overnight. Two hours before serving, remove dough from refrigerator. Roll out on lightly floured surface to ½ inch thickness. Cut with 2 inch biscuit cutter. Fold biscuits to form Parker House rolls; place on well greased baking sheets. Brush with melted butter. Cover; let rise in warm place 1½ hours. Preheat oven to 375°. Bake 10 minutes. Yields: 6-8 dozen rolls.

"This dough will keep in refrigerator 4-5 days."

SALLY LUNN

"Elegant served on your best cake stand with butter balls or curls."

4 cups plain flour
3 tablespoons sugar
2 teaspoons salt
1 package active dry yeast
½ cup shortening
½ cup butter
1 cup milk, lukewarm
3 eggs, separated

In large mixing bowl, combine flour, sugar, salt and yeast. Melt shortening in saucepan; cool. Warm milk to lukewarm. Separate eggs. Beat yolks thoroughly. Beat egg whites until stiff; set aside. Add cooled shortening to beaten egg yolks. Add to flour mixture along with lukewarm milk. Mix well; fold in stiffly beaten egg whites. Beat thoroughly; set in warm place, covered, until double in bulk, about 3 hours. Beat down. Grease a 10 inch tube or bundt pan, turn batter into prepared pan. Set in warm place; let rise until doubled, 2-3 hours. Preheat oven to 325°. Bake 25 minutes, increase temperature to 375°, bake 20 minutes longer. Remove from oven; cool 10 minutes. Remove from pan and serve.

GIFT OF THE MAGI BREAD

½ cup butter or margarine
1 cup sugar
2 eggs
1 teaspoon vanilla extract
2 cups plain flour
1 teaspoon soda
pinch of salt
3 large bananas, mashed
11 ounces mandarin orange segments, drained
6 ounces semi-sweet chocolate chips
1 cup coconut
⅔ cup almonds, sliced and divided
½ cup maraschino cherries, chopped
½ cup dried figs or dates, chopped
confectioners' sugar

Preheat oven to 350°. Cream butter and sugar until light and fluffy. Add eggs, one at the time, beating well after each. Add vanilla. Sift flour, soda and salt. Add to creamed mixture alternately with mashed bananas. By hand, stir in orange segments, chocolate chips, coconut, ½ cup almonds, cherries and dried figs or dates. Grease two 7½x3¾ pans. Line with waxed paper and grease paper. Pour into pans. Sprinkle remaining almonds on top. Bake 1-1¼ hours. Cool 5-10 minutes. Turn out onto wire racks; cool completely. Sprinkle tops with sifted confectioners' sugar.

Bread has risen enough when 2 finger tips pressed lightly in top leave the indentations.

High humidity days require more flour in bread recipes.

To make 1 c self-rising flour from plain flour, mix 1 c plain flour, 1 t baking powder, and ½ t salt.

CINNAMON BUNS

"This bread requires no kneading."

1 cup powdered milk
2 cups lukewarm water
2 packages active dry yeast
½ cup sugar
½ cup butter, melted and cooled
4 cups plain flour, divided
1 teaspoon salt
½ teaspoon baking powder
½ teaspoon baking soda

Filling:
½ cup butter, softened
¾ cup sugar
2-3 tablespoons cinnamon

Icing:
2½ cups confectioners' sugar, sifted
1 tablespoon butter, melted
¼ cup half and half
2 tablespoons rum, (optional, for delicious rum buns)

Combine powdered milk, water, yeast, sugar, melted butter and 2 cups flour. Beat well. Allow to stand at room temperature 1½ hours, covered. Add 2 cups flour, salt, baking powder and soda. Mix, adding more flour if necessary to make a firm dough. Divide in half. Roll each half to a 10x18 rectangle. Spread with softened butter, sprinkle with combined sugar and cinnamon. Roll as for jelly roll from 18 inch side. Cut in 1 inch pieces. Place rolls close together on greased baking sheets. Cover; let rise in warm place 1 hour. Preheat oven to 350°. Bake 30 minutes. Drizzle with icing while warm. Yields: 36 buns.

Variation: For dinner rolls, roll to ½ inch thickness. Let rise 1 hour on greased baking sheets. Bake 12-15 minutes.

ZUCCHINI-NUT BREAD

"So good served warm with coffee for breakfast."

2 cups zucchini, grated
4 large eggs
2 cups sugar
1 cup oil
3½ cups plain flour, unsifted and divided
4 teaspoons baking powder
1½ teaspoons salt
2 teaspoons cinnamon
2 teaspoons wheat germ
1 cup pecans or walnuts, chopped
1 cup raisins
1½ teaspoons vanilla extract

Preheat oven to 350°. Grate zucchini; set aside. In large bowl of electric mixer, beat eggs until thick. Gradually beat in sugar and oil. In a separate bowl, sift 3¼ cups flour, baking powder, salt and cinnamon. On low speed, add dry ingredients to egg mixture alternately with zucchini and wheat germ. Combine remaining ¼ cup flour with nuts and raisins. Fold, by hand, into batter. Stir in vanilla. Spoon batter into 2 greased and waxed paper lined 9x5 loaf pans. Bake 55-60 minutes. Cool 10 minutes. Turn onto wire racks to cool.
Note: This bread may be frozen tightly wrapped.

CRANBERRY BREAD

"A delicious tart treat perfect for Christmas gift giving."

3 cups plain flour, sifted
3 teaspoons baking powder
1 teaspoon salt
½ teaspoon baking soda
½ cup shortening
1½ cups sugar
2 large eggs
¾ cup fresh orange juice
1½ tablespoons orange rind, grated
¾ cup nuts, chopped
2¼ cups fresh cranberries, coarsely chopped

Preheat oven to 350°. Sift flour, baking powder and salt. Set aside. Add soda to shortening. Cream, gradually adding sugar. Beat in eggs, one at a time. Alternately add flour mixture and orange juice to shortening mixture. By hand, stir in orange rind, nuts and cranberries. Grease and line with waxed paper three 8x4 loaf pans. Spoon batter into prepared pans. Bake 45-55 minutes. Cool 10 minutes. Remove from pans. Peel off waxed paper. Cool on wire racks.
"Enjoy this bread year round by buying cranberries while in season and freezing them in plastic bags."

BANANA-NUT BREAD

½ cup shortening
1 cup brown sugar (or ½ cup white sugar and ½ cup honey)
3 medium ripe bananas, mashed
1 teaspoon vanilla extract
2 eggs, beaten
1½ cups whole-wheat flour
½ cup wheat germ
2 teaspoons baking powder
½ teaspoon salt
½ teaspoon cinnamon
½ cup walnuts, chopped (optional)

Preheat oven to 325°. Cream shortening and sugar until light. Add bananas, vanilla and eggs. Beat until smooth. Combine remaining ingredients in separate bowl. Add to creamed mixture by hand, mixing just enough to moisten thoroughly. Grease a 9x5 loaf pan well. Line pan with waxed paper and grease again to insure no sticking. Bake 1 hour and 10 minutes until well browned and crusty. Cool 10-15 minutes. Remove from pan, remove waxed paper and cool on wire rack.

SOUR CREAM TWIST

"A delicious flaky pastry."

4 cups plain flour
1 teaspoon salt
1 cup butter
1 package active dry yeast
¼ cup warm water
1 cup sour cream
1 egg, beaten
2 egg yolks, beaten
1 teaspoon vanilla extract
flour
sugar

Preheat oven to 375°. Sift flour and salt into large bowl. Cut in butter until the consistency of corn meal. Dissolve yeast in warm water. Stir into flour mixture along with sour cream, egg, egg yolks and vanilla. Mix well, using hands if necessary. Cover dough completely with damp cloth; place in refrigerator for 2 hours or in freezer for 10 minutes. Dough will keep in refrigerator up to 2 weeks at this point. Remove ½ of dough; roll out on board sprinkled with flour and sugar into a 8x16 rectangle. Fold the dough toward center overlapping completely. Sprinkle dough with sugar and roll again to a 8x16 rectangle. Fold ends in again, sprinkle with sugar. Roll dough to ¼ inch thickness. Cut into 1x4 strips. Holding the strips by the ends, twist in opposite directions to form a tightly twisted roll. Place on ungreased cookie sheets; let rest 15 minutes. Bake 15 minutes. Cool on wire racks. Serve hot or cold. Yields: 4-5 dozen.

BEEHIVE COFFEE CAKE

"A marvelously different coffee cake that's good enough to be served as a dessert."

1¼-1¾ cups plain flour, divided
2 tablespoons sugar
¼ teaspoon salt
1 teaspoon lemon peel, grated
1 package active dry yeast
⅓ cup milk
¼ cup water
2 tablespoons margarine
1 egg

Coconut Topping:
⅔ cup coconut
¼ cup sugar
4 tablespoons margarine
1 tablespoon almonds, slivered
2 tablespoons honey
1 tablespoon milk
⅛ teaspoon almond extract

Vanilla Cream Filling:
3½ ounces vanilla pudding mix
1½ cups milk
½ cup whipping cream

In large mixing bowl, mix ½ cup flour, sugar, salt, lemon peel and yeast. Combine milk, water and margarine. Heat over low heat until very warm. Margarine does not have to melt. Gradually add dry ingredients; beat 2 minutes on medium speed of electric mixer. Add egg and ½ cup flour. Beat at high speed 2 minutes. Stir in remaining flour to make a soft dough. Cover; let rise in warm place until doubled, about 30 minutes.

Prepare coconut topping by combining all ingredients. Stir batter down. Grease 8 inch square pan. Spread batter in pan. Cover; let rise in warm place until doubled, about 30 minutes. Carefully spread coconut topping over batter. Preheat oven to 350°. Bake 30 minutes. Remove from pan. Cool on wire rack.

Prepare vanilla cream filling by combining all ingredients in a saucepan. Cook over medium heat, stirring constantly, until pudding comes to a full boil. Pour into a bowl; cover directly with plastic wrap. Chill until firm.

When cake and filling are cooled, split cake horizontally. Fill with vanilla cream, replace top. Serve at once or refrigerate until serving. Yields: 9 squares.

BUDAPEST COFFEE CAKE

3 cups plain flour, sifted
1½ teaspoons baking powder
1½ teaspoons baking soda
½ teaspoon salt
¾ cup butter
2 teaspoons vanilla extract
1½ cups sugar
3 eggs
2 cups sour cream

Filling:
¾ cup dark brown sugar, packed
1 tablespoon cinnamon
1 tablespoon cocoa
2-3 tablespoons raisins
1 cup pecans, finely chopped

Glaze:
2 cups confectioners' sugar
1 teaspoon vanilla extract
2-3 tablespoons hot milk

Preheat oven to 375°. Combine all filling ingredients; set aside. Sift flour, baking powder, soda and salt. With electric mixer, cream butter well. Add vanilla and sugar; beat 2 minutes. Add eggs, one at a time, beating thoroughly after each addition. On low speed, add dry ingredients and sour cream alternately beginning and ending with dry ingredients. Beat only until smooth after each addition. Grease 10 inch bundt or tube pan thoroughly, even if it is Teflon, it *must* be greased. Spread a thin layer of batter on bottom of pan. Sprinkle with ⅓ of filling. Continue to layer so there are 4 batter layers and 3 filling layers. The top layer should be batter. For best results in spreading batter, drop small spoonfuls over filling and spread with the back of a spoon. Bake 50-60 minutes. Remove from oven and cool 5 minutes, no longer. Invert on large piece of waxed paper.
To make glaze, combine sugar and vanilla. Add 2 tablespoons hot milk. Very gradually add more milk until glaze is the consistency of a thick cream sauce. While cake is hot, quickly pour glaze over. Do not try to spread it. When cool, cover and refrigerate until ready to serve.

Lightly oil measuring cup before filling with honey, molasses or corn syrup & liquid will pour easily.

Bread is easier to slice if knife is dipped in hot water.

When bread is rising, grease top of dough to prevent drying out.

FILLED COFFEE RING

2 packages active dry yeast
½ cup warm water
1½ cups lukewarm milk
½ cup sugar
2 teaspoons salt
2 eggs, beaten
½ cup oil
6½-7½ cups plain flour

Dissolve yeast in warm water; set aside 5 minutes. Combine milk, sugar and salt; stir in yeast mixture, eggs and oil. Add enough flour to form a soft but slightly sticky dough; mix well. Cover; let rise in warm place 1 hour or until double in bulk. Turn dough onto floured surface; knead 5 minutes. Return to clean, greased bowl. Cover; let rise in warm place 40 minutes or until double in bulk.

Filling:
¼ cup butter, melted
2 tablespoons cinnamon
½ cup sugar
6 tablespoons maraschino cherries (red or green), chopped
6 tablespoons pecans, chopped

Place dough on floured surface. Roll into a 21x12 rectangle. Spread with melted butter. Sprinkle with cinnamon, sugar, cherries, and pecans. Starting at long edge, roll jelly roll fashion; pinch to seal edge. Place roll on a greased 15 inch pizza pan; form into a ring. Pinch to seal ends. Cut with scissors at 1 inch intervals ⅔ of way through roll. Gently pull slices out and twist, overlapping slightly. Cover; let rise in warm place 1-1½ hours or until double in bulk. Preheat oven to 350°. Bake 20-25 minutes or until done.

Creamy Frosting:
1 cup whipping cream
1 cup sugar
1 teaspoon almond extract

Combine all ingredients in saucepan. Cook, stirring constantly, over low heat until mixture reaches 230°. Pour into bowl of electric mixer; beat at high speed until thick and creamy. Drizzle frosting over hot ring. Yields: 16-20 servings.

BEST EVER COFFEE CAKE

3 cups plain flour, sifted
3 teaspoons baking powder
1 teaspoon salt
1 cup shortening
1 cup sugar
2 eggs, beaten
1 cup milk
1 teaspoon vanilla extract

Filling:
1½ cups brown sugar
3 tablespoons plain flour
2½ tablespoons cinnamon
¾ cup butter, melted
1 cup raisins, rinsed in hot water
1½ cups walnuts, chopped

Preheat oven to 350°. Sift together first 3 ingredients. With electric mixer, cream shortening and sugar. Add eggs; beat 4 minutes. Add dry ingredients alternately in fourths with milk to which vanilla has been added. Set aside. Combine brown sugar, flour and cinnamon for filling. Grease two 8x8 pans. In bottom of each pan, spread a layer of batter, top with a layer of filling and drizzle with melted butter. Repeat. Bake 50 minutes. Yields: 16-20 servings.

DANISH PUFF

"An interesting and different accompaniment for morning coffees. Best eaten the day it is made."

½ cup butter or margarine
½ cup plain flour
2 tablespoons water

Preheat oven to 350°. Cut butter into flour. Sprinkle with water. Mix; shape into a ball and divide in half. On ungreased baking sheet, pat each half into a strip about 12x3. These strips should be about 3 inches apart on the baking sheet. Set aside.

½ cup butter or margarine
1 cup water
1 teaspoon almond extract
1 cup plain flour
3 eggs

Heat butter or margarine with 1 cup water to a rolling boil. Remove from heat; add almond extract and flour. Stir vigorously over low heat until mixture forms a ball, about 1-3 minutes. Remove from heat; beat in eggs until smooth and glossy. Spread this mixture evenly over the two strips. Bake 45-60 minutes or until top is crisp and brown. Allow to cool slightly. Glaze.

1 cup confectioners' sugar
2 tablespoons margarine
½ teaspoon vanilla extract
1-2 tablespoons warm water
chopped pecans (optional)

Combine all but pecans. Blend well, adding more warm water if necessary. Spread over cooled strips. Sprinkle with chopped pecans if desired. Cut into 1½x3 strips. Yields: 10-18 servings.

SOUTHERN PANCAKE SPECIAL

"For a delectable brunch, serve with fresh orange juice, Canadian bacon and scrambled eggs."

½ cup plain flour
½ cup milk
2 eggs, lightly beaten
pinch of grated nutmeg
4 tablespoons butter
2 tablespoons confectioners' sugar
½ lemon, juiced

Preheat oven to 425°. In mixing bowl combine flour, milk, eggs, and nutmeg. Beat lightly, leaving batter a little lumpy. Melt butter in 12 inch oven-proof skillet. When pan is very hot, pour in batter. Bake 15-20 minutes, or until pancake is golden brown. Remove from oven and sprinkle with sugar. Return to oven for 2-3 minutes. Remove and sprinkle with lemon juice. Serve with jelly or jam, if desired. Yields: 2-4 servings.

BUTTERMILK-BRAN WAFFLES

¾ cup plain flour
1 teaspoon baking powder
½ teaspoon baking soda
¼ teaspoon salt
¼ cup sugar
1 cup bran cereal or bran buds
2 eggs, separated
1 cup buttermilk or sour milk
6 tablespoons margarine, melted

Preheat waffle iron. Sift together dry ingredients, add bran cereal. Add egg yolks, buttermilk and margarine. Stir until well blended. Beat egg whites stiff. Fold into batter. Bake in waffle iron until golden brown. Yields: 8 waffles.

COLLECTION OF TAR HEEL POTPOURRI

North Carolina — named for King Charles I (Rex Carolus)
Raleigh — capital, named for Sir Walter Raleigh
Largest County — Sampson
Smallest County — Chowan
Most Populated County — Mecklenburg
Least Populated County — Tyrrell
Total Square Miles — 52,712
Distance North to South — 203 miles
Distance East to West — 522 miles
Geographical Center — town of Gulf in Chatham County
Highest Point of Elevation — Mt. Mitchell; 6,684 feet (highest point east of Mississippi)
Rank in Size — 28th
Rank in Population — 12th
Average Temperature — 56°
Highest Recorded Temperature — 109°, Albermarle in 1940
Lowest Recorded Temperature — Mt. Pisgah, -29° in 1967
Average Rainfail — 48″
Population — 5½ million
Jockey's Ridge — tallest sand dune in eastern America
Cape Hatteras — tallest light house in America
N.C. has more different kinds of trees than all of Europe
N.C. has more than 300 different kinds of minerals — has been called "Nature's Jewel Box"
New River — 500 million years old; 2nd oldest river in world; 2nd to Nile
Original Siamese Twins became naturalized citizens and settled in Surry County where they became prosperous land owners. Eng (Right) and Chang (Left) Bunker
World's largest man lived in N.C. in early part of 19th Century. Miles Darden, 7½ feet tall weighed 1,000 pounds
Five sets of twins born in succession to the Curtis Jones family in Cumberland County. Medical records show no other such rarity.
Wild ponies, descendants of horses shipwrecked on the islands 100s of years ago may still be seen on the outerbanks.
U.S.S. North Carolina — most popular tourist attraction in N.C.
Raleigh — most visited city in N.C.

cakes

THE CAROLINA COLLECTOR'S CONCOCTIONS

. . . Make cake in rectangular pan. When done, pierce all over with fork; pour 3 ozs. jello mixed with 1½ c hot water over cake; pour over 2 pkgs. instant vanilla pudding & 3½ c. milk. Refrigerate overnight.

. . . A quick honey frosting is 2 T butter, 3 ozs. cream cheese, ½ c confectioners' sugar, 2 T honey & dash salt mixed until smooth.

. . . Cut a ½" slice pound cake; spread with honey & top with coconut.

. . . Top an unfrosted layer cake with a mint sauce made with 4 T butter, 1 c confectioners' sugar, 1 beaten egg & ½ c orange juice, & 3 T finely chopped mint leaves.

. . . Add coconut flavor to a pound cake mix.

. . . Split angel food cake into ⅓ s crosswise; spread each layer with any preserves & frost with whipped cream.

. . . Substitute beets for carrots in a carrot cake for a surprise.

. . . Frost a 3 layer 9 inch cake with Maple Frosting. Soften and blend thoroughly 1 stick butter, 3 oz. cream cheese, 1½ c conf. sugar, ⅓ c dark corn syrup, 2 t maple flavoring, 2 t lemon flavoring and 1 t vanilla.

. . . Add a little honey to strained Jr. fruits for delicious sauces to top cakes or ice cream.

BISHOP'S CAKE

"A pretty make-ahead dessert to be served during the holidays."

17 ounces white angel food cake mix
3-4 pints lemon ice cream, slightly softened
⅓ cup crème de menthe (green)

Prepare angel food cake mix and bake in a 10 inch tube pan as label directs. Cool; remove from pan, wash pan, replace cake into it. Hollow out cake, leaving shell about ¾ inch thick. Spoon ⅓ of ice cream into bottom of hollow. Pour ½ of crème de menthe over ice cream. Spoon ⅓ of ice cream over crème de menthe, covering it. Pour rest of crème de menthe over ice cream and top with remaining ice cream. With a thin knife, cut through ice cream to marble crème de menthe through it. Replace top of cake. Freeze. Wrap cake, then freeze up to 2 weeks.

Glaze:
1 cup evaporated milk
dash salt
12 ounces semi-sweet chocolate chips
2 teaspoons vanilla extract

In a small saucepan, bring evaporated milk and salt to a boil. Remove from heat, stir in chocolate pieces and vanilla until smooth. Let stand 5-10 minutes to thicken slightly. Remove cake from freezer; unwrap, invert to wooden board or piece of foil. Quickly spread top and sides with glaze. Refreeze cake. When ready to serve, transfer cake to serving plate. Cut slices with a sharp knife.
Hint: Use lemon custard ice cream or substitute another flavor.

An 8″ cake serves 10-14.

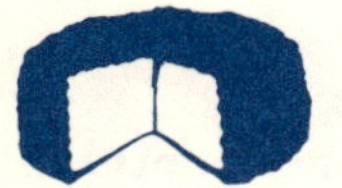

A 9″ cake serves 12-16.

A 9x13 cake serves 15-18.

A serrated knife cuts angel or chiffon cakes best.

LEMON-ORANGE ANGEL CAKE

1 large angel food cake
4 eggs
1½ cups sugar
¼ cup fresh lemon juice
½ cup fresh orange juice
1½ teaspoons lemon rind, grated
2½ teaspoons orange rind, grated
2 cups whipping cream, whipped
1 teaspoon vanilla extract

Slice 1 inch layer off top of cake; reserve. Carefully hollow out cake, leaving 1 inch shell. Cut cake that is removed into small pieces. Beat eggs with 1 cup sugar. Add juices and rinds. Cook over hot water until very thick. Chill. When cold, fold in 1 cup of whipped cream and cake pieces. Pour into the cake shell and chill until firm. Replace reserved cake top. Frost with remaining whipped cream to which remaining sugar and vanilla have been added.

CARROT-PINEAPPLE CAKE

1 cup butter, softened
2 cups sugar
3 eggs
2½ cups plain flour
½ teaspoon salt
2 teaspoons cinnamon
2 teaspoons baking soda
2 teaspoons vanilla extract
1 cup carrots, grated
1 cup crushed pineapple, drained
1 cup flaked coconut
1 cup pecans, chopped

Preheat oven to 325°. Grease 9 inch tube pan, line with waxed paper and grease paper. Cream butter and sugar. Add eggs, one at a time, beating well after each addition. Sift together dry ingredients; add gradually to butter mixture. Add vanilla, carrots, pineapple, coconut and pecans. Pour into pan. Bake 1 hour 15 minutes. Cool on wire rack 10 minutes before turning out of pan. Frost with Sour Cream and Orange Sauce.

Sour Cream and Orange Sauce:
2 tablespoons butter
1 cup light brown sugar
1 tablespoon light corn syrup
½ cup fresh orange juice
1 teaspoon baking soda
½ cup sour cream
½ cup pecans, chopped (optional)

Combine all ingredients except sour cream. Cook over low heat until dissolved. Bring to a boil; cook 5 minutes. Stir in sour cream. Remove cake from pan while still warm and prick the top with a fork. Pour hot sauce over cake; sprinkle with pecans.

OLD-FASHIONED CARAMEL CAKE

½ cup butter or margarine
1½ cups sugar
2 eggs
2 cups plain flour, sifted
1 cup buttermilk
1 tablespoon vinegar
1 teaspoon soda

Preheat oven to 350°. Cream margarine and sugar together until light and fluffy. Add eggs, one at a time, and continue beating. Add flour alternately with buttermilk. Blend well. Stir in soda which has been dissolved in vinegar. Pour into 2 greased and floured 8 or 9 inch pans. Bake 35 minutes.

Caramel Icing:
½ cup butter
1 cup dark brown sugar, packed
¼ cup milk
1¾-2 cups confectioners' sugar, sifted

Melt butter in large saucepan. Add brown sugar. Boil over low heat 2 minutes, stirring constantly. Add milk; bring to a boil, stirring constantly. Take off heat; beat about 5 minutes. Gradually add confectioners' sugar. Beat until thick enough to spread. If too thick, add milk. This amount ices two 8 inch layers or a 13x9 sheet cake.
"Good on Spice Cake too!"

MOUNTAIN APPLE CAKE

3 eggs
1½ cups oil
2 cups sugar
3 cups plain flour
1 teaspoon salt
1 teaspoon soda
2 teaspoons cinnamon
2 teaspoons vanilla extract
3 cups apples, chopped
1½ cups pecans, chopped

Preheat oven to 350°. Mix eggs, oil, and sugar; blend well. Sift flour, salt, soda and cinnamon; add to egg mixture. Add vanilla, apples and nuts. Pour into greased 8 inch tube or bundt pan. Bake 1 hour. While cake is still hot, pour hot topping over it in pan; let cool. When completely cool, remove from pan.

Topping:
1 cup brown sugar
¼ cup milk
½ cup butter
1 teaspoon vanilla

Combine all ingredients; cook 2½ minutes. Pour immediately over cake in pan.

CHEESECAKE WITH SOUR CREAM TOPPING

"Make ahead dessert."

Crust:

1½ cups graham crackers, crushed
5 tablespoons butter, melted
1 tablespoon sugar

Combine all ingredients. Press into 9x13x2 baking pan.

Filling:

24 ounces cream cheese, softened
5 eggs
1 cup sugar
1½ teaspoons vanilla extract

Preheat oven to 300°. Cream the cheese with eggs, adding one at a time. Stir sugar and vanilla in slowly. Pour over crust. Bake 1 hour.

Topping:

3 cups sour cream
½ cup sugar
1½ teaspoons vanilla extract

Preheat oven to 350°. Combine all ingredients. Spread over cooked filling; let stand 3 minutes. Bake 5 minutes. Chill overnight in refrigerator.

ELEGANT CHOCOLATE CHEESECAKE

8 ounces cream cheese, softened
1½ cups sugar
6 tablespoons unsweetened cocoa
1 teaspoon vanilla extract
4 large eggs
4 cups sour cream

Beat cream cheese until smooth. Mix sugar, cocoa, and vanilla. Add eggs, one at a time, beating after each. Add sour cream. Pour into chocolate crust-lined 9 inch springform pan. Bake at 350° 1 hour 20 minutes or until edge is set and dull in color, while 4 inch center is glossy looking. When cool, remove pan rim and set on serving plate. Pile cream topping in center of cake. Grate semi-sweet chocolate over cream.

Chocolate Crust:

2 cups chocolate wafer cookie crumbs, finely crushed
¼ cup sugar
¼ teaspoon cinnamon
7 tablespoons butter, melted

In 9 inch springform pan, blend 2 cups finely crushed crumbs with sugar, cinnamon and butter. Using spoon, press crumbs over bottom and up sides of pan 3 inches.

Cream Topping:

3 ounces cream cheese, softened
½ cup whipping cream
¼ cup confectioners' sugar
3-4 tablespoons crème de cacao (or to taste)
semi-sweet chocolate

Cream the cream cheese until soft. Gradually add whipping cream. Mix at high speed on mixer until consistency of stiffly whipped cream. Blend in confectioners' sugar and crème de cocoa. Cover; chill until ready to serve.

For a higher and fluffier cake, allow all ingredients to come to room temperature.

FROZEN BLUEBERRY RIPPLE CHEESECAKE

¾ cup graham cracker crumbs
2 tablespoons sugar
3 tablespoons butter, melted
1 cup sugar
⅓ cup water
⅛ teaspoon cream of tartar
3 egg whites
16 ounces cream cheese, softened
½ cup sour cream
2 teaspoons vanilla extract
1 tablespoon grated lemon rind
½ cup blueberry preserves
½ cup whipping cream, whipped
1 cup unsweetened blueberries, fresh or frozen

Combine crumbs, sugar and butter in a small bowl. Press firmly into bottom of 8 inch springform pan. Chill. In saucepan, combine sugar, water and cream of tartar. Bring to a rapid boil. Reduce heat to low; continue to cook to 236° on candy thermometer. In large bowl of electric mixer, beat egg whites until stiff peaks form. Pour hot syrup in a thin stream over egg whites, beating constantly. Continue beating until very stiff peaks form. Cool about 15 minutes. Beat cream cheese and sour cream until light and fluffy. Beat in vanilla and lemon rind. Add ¼ of meringue to cheese mixture and stir. Fold remaining meringue into cheese mixture until no streaks remain. Spoon about ¼ of cheese mixture into prepared pan; drizzle part of blueberry preserves over. Continue layers. Freeze overnight or until firm. Decorate with whipped cream and blueberries.

CAROLINA SUPREME CHOCOLATE CAKE

1 cup unsweetened cocoa, unsifted
2 cups boiling water
2¾ cups plain flour, sifted
2 teaspoons baking soda
½ teaspoon salt
½ teaspoon baking powder
1 cup butter, softened
2½ cups sugar
4 eggs
1½ teaspoons vanilla extract

Preheat oven to 350°. Grease and flour three 9 inch pans. In medium bowl combine cocoa and water. Mix until smooth; cool completely. Sift flour, soda, salt and baking powder together. On high speed, cream butter, sugar, eggs and vanilla 5 minutes. On low speed, beat in flour (in fourths) alternately with cocoa mix (in thirds). Divide in pans. Bake 25 minutes. Cool in pans 10 minutes. Remove and cool on racks.

Frosting:
6 ounces semi-sweet chocolate chips
½ cup half and half
1 cup butter
2½ cups confectioners' sugar, sifted

In medium saucepan, mix chocolate pieces, cream, and butter. Stir until smooth over medium heat. Remove from heat. With wisk beat in confectioners' sugar. Transfer to bowl over ice; beat until frosting holds shape.

Filling:
1 cup whipping cream
¼ cup confectioners' sugar
1 teaspoon vanilla extract

Beat all together. Place between layers and frost top and sides of cake with frosting.

Cakes spring back when touched lightly if done.

Cakes are done if they separate from sides of pan.

Test cake for doneness by listening for a singing sound when pan is held to ear — no sound if done.

1 c plain flour minus 2 T equals 1 c sifted cake flour.

DUTCH MOCHA CAKE

3 cups cake flour, sifted
1 teaspoon baking soda
½ teaspoon salt
¾ cup unsweetened cocoa
2¾ cups sugar
1 cup hot coffee (instant may be used)
1 cup butter
1 cup sour cream
2 teaspoons vanilla extract
5 egg whites

Preheat oven to 350°. Grease three 9 inch layer cake pans, line with waxed paper and grease paper. Combine flour, baking soda and salt. Sift these 3 times. Combine cocoa, ½ cup of sugar and hot coffee. Cool. Cream butter and 1½ cups sugar until light and fluffy. Add cocoa mixture, sour cream and vanilla. Add flour mixture, stirring until smooth. Beat egg whites with remaining sugar until stiff. Fold into batter. Pour into prepared pans and bake 25-30 minutes or until done. Cool in pan 5 minutes before turning out onto wire racks.

Filling:
½ cup plain flour
pinch of salt
½ cup sugar
1 cup hot milk
3 egg yolks
1 cup whipping cream, whipped
1 teaspoon vanilla extract

Mix flour, salt and ¼ cup of sugar. Stir in hot milk and place in top of double boiler over boiling water. Cook until smooth and thickened, stirring constantly. Combine egg yolks with remaining sugar; add to mixture and continue cooking 3 minutes. Cool. Fold in whipped cream and vanilla. Spread between cake layers.

Frosting:
1⅔ cups confectioners' sugar
3 ounces unsweetened chocolate, melted
dash of salt
1 tablespoon hot coffee
3 egg yolks
4 tablespoons butter, softened
1 teaspoon vanilla extract

Sift sugar and add to melted chocolate. Add salt and coffee; beat well. Add yolks, one at a time, beating well after each addition. Add butter and vanilla; beat well. Spread on top and sides of cake.

CHOCOLATE CHERRY CAKE

1½ cups plain flour, sifted
1 cup sugar
½ cup butter
⅔ cup buttermilk
½ teaspoon salt
1 teaspoon baking soda
1 egg
1 ounce unsweetened chocolate, melted with 1 tablespoon water
2 tablespoons juice from jar of maraschino cherries
½ cup maraschino cherries, halved
½ cup pecans, chopped

Preheat oven to 350°. Grease an 8x8x2 pan, line with waxed paper and grease paper. In mixing bowl, combine all above ingredients except cherries and nuts. Beat on medium speed several minutes. Add cherries and nuts; mix well. Pour into prepared pan. Bake 35-40 minutes or until cake tests done. Cool in pan on wire rack. When cool, turn out and strip off paper. Ice with Chocolate Frosting and decorate with additional cherries.

Variation: Substitute light brown sugar for white sugar and hot water for buttermilk. Increase chocolate to 2 ounces and bake in well greased and floured 9x13 pan 25-30 minutes or until it tests done. Remove from oven and immediately arrange 12 halved marshmallows cut side down on top of cake. Cut cake in small squares with a marshmallow in center of each. Place a spoonful of Chocolate Frosting on top of each marshmallow.

Chocolate Frosting:

1 ounce unsweetened chocolate
2 tablespoons butter
1 tablespoon milk
1 cup confectioners' sugar, sifted
½ teaspoon vanilla extract

Melt chocolate and butter with milk. Stir in sugar. Add more milk if necessary. Place a spoonful of frosting on top of each marshmallow.

MISSISSIPPI MUD CAKE

"Don't let the name fool you! This is delicious."

1 cup margarine
4 eggs
2 cups sugar
1½ cups plain flour
¼ teaspoon salt
½ cup cocoa
1 teaspoon vanilla extract
1 cup pecans, chopped
10½ ounces miniature marshmallows

Preheat oven to 350°. Melt margarine in 9x13 pan; cool. Beat eggs and add sugar. Sift flour, salt and cocoa together. Add to egg mixture. Add melted margarine, vanilla and nuts. Pour into pan that margarine was melted in. Bake 35 minutes. Place miniature marshmallows on top. Return to oven for 5 minutes or until melted. Spread with following icing.

Icing:
16 ounces confectioners' sugar, sifted
½ cup margarine, melted
½ cup evaporated milk
⅓ cup cocoa

Beat until smooth. Spread on top of hot cake.

CHOCOLATE CAKE WITH FROSTING AND GLAZE

½ cup butter, softened
1¾ cups cake flour, sifted
2 teaspoons baking powder
½ teaspoon baking soda
1½ cups sugar
½ teaspoon salt
1 cup sour cream
3 large eggs, separated
1½ teaspoons vanilla extract
2 ounces unsweetened chocolate, melted

Preheat oven to 350°. Grease a 9 inch tube pan, line with waxed paper and grease paper. Cream butter. Sift flour, baking powder, soda, sugar and salt. Add to creamed butter with sour cream; mix until flour is just dampened. Beat on medium speed 2 minutes. Add egg yolks, vanilla and melted chocolate. Beat egg whites until stiff; fold into batter. Pour into prepared pan. Bake 45 minutes. When cool, remove from pan.

FROSTING:
½ cup butter, melted
1 cup light brown sugar
1⅓ cups shredded coconut
⅓ cup half and half (or evaporated milk)

Combine all ingredients; let stand 10 minutes. Spread onto top of cake. Broil under broiler until lightly brown and bubbly; *do not burn.* Cool.

GLAZE:
½ cup semi-sweet chocolate pieces
2 tablespoons corn syrup
1 teaspoon water

Combine; cook over hot water until chocolate is melted and pour over frosting.

SOUR CREAM CHOCOLATE LAYER CAKE

3 ounces unsweetened chocolate
½ cup boiling water
2 cups cake flour, sifted
1½ teaspoons baking powder
1 teaspoon baking soda
¼ teaspoon salt
¾ cup butter
2 teaspoons vanilla extract
1 cup granulated sugar
⅔ cup light brown sugar, firmly packed
3 eggs
1 cup sour cream

Preheat oven to 350°. Grease 2 round 9 inch layer cake pans. Line with waxed paper and grease paper. Melt chocolate with boiling water. Cool. Sift together flour, baking powder, baking soda and salt. Cream butter in large bowl of electric mixer. Add vanilla, granulated sugar and light brown sugar; beat well. Beat in eggs, one at a time, beating well after each addition. Stir sour cream and cooled chocolate together until smooth; add to batter. Beat only until mixed. On lowest speed, add sifted dry ingredients; scrape bowl and beaters with spatula. Beat only until smooth. Pour into prepared pans. Spread top smooth and then run batter up on the sides a bit, leaving batter slightly lower in the center. Bake 35 minutes or until top springs back when lightly touched. Cool in pan 5 minutes. Invert and remove pan. Invert again to finish cooling right side up. Frost with Chocolate Sour Cream Frosting or your favorite.

Chocolate Sour Cream Frosting:

3 ounces unsweetened chocolate
2 tablespoons butter
¾ cup sour cream
1 teaspoon vanilla extract
¼ teaspoon salt
16 ounces confectioners' sugar, sifted

Melt chocolate and butter. Cool completely. Beat sour cream, vanilla and salt. Gradually beat in sugar. When smooth, add cooled melted chocolate. Beat at high speed ½ minute, until very smooth. Frost top and sides of a 9 inch layer cake.

BROWNIE CUPCAKES

"A must for chocolate lovers – almost like candy."

4 ounces unsweetened chocolate
1 cup butter
1½ cups pecans, finely chopped
1¾ cups sugar
1 cup plain flour, sifted
4 eggs
1 teaspoon vanilla extract

Preheat oven to 325°. Melt chocolate and butter over very low heat. Add pecans; stir until coated. Combine sugar, flour, eggs and vanilla. Mix well until blended but do not beat. Add chocolate mixture; stir carefully. Pour into paper cup lined muffin tin. Bake 25-30 minutes or until just done. Do not overcook. Frost with chocolate icing. Yields: 24.

Chocolate Icing:
½ cup margarine
½ cup evaporated milk
1 cup sugar
6 ounces semi-sweet chocolate chips

Combine first 3 ingredients; bring to a boil, boiling 2 minutes. Remove from heat and add chocolate chips. Stir. Beat well to spreading consistency.

Unfrosted cakes freeze best & will keep 4 mos.

ITALIAN CREAM CAKE

½ cup margarine
½ cup shortening
2 cups sugar
2 cups self-rising flour
1 teaspoon soda
1 cup buttermilk
5 egg yolks
5 egg whites
3½ ounces coconut, flaked
1 cup pecans, chopped
1 teaspoon vanilla extract

Preheat oven to 350°. Cream margarine, shortening and sugar. Combine flour and soda; add alternately with mixture of buttermilk and egg yolks. Add coconut. Beat egg whites; fold in. Add pecans and vanilla. Pour into 4 greased and lined 8 or 9 inch layer cake pans. Bake 25 minutes or until done.

Filling:
16 ounces cream cheese, softened
16 ounces confectioners' sugar, sifted
7 tablespoons butter
1 teaspoon vanilla extract
1 cup pecans, chopped

Combine all ingredients. Milk may be added if needed for right consistency. Spread between layers and on top and sides of cake.

COCONUT CAKE WITH BOURBON FILLING

18 ounces yellow cake mix

Preheat oven to 350°. Bake cake in 2 greased and floured 8 inch pans according to package directions. Split each layer to make 4 layers.

Filling:
½ cup margarine
3 eggs
1½ cups sugar
¼ cup bourbon
1 cup pecans, chopped
1½ cups coconut (fresh or frozen)
1 pint whipping cream, whipped

Melt margarine. Add eggs, sugar and bourbon. Cook until thick. Remove from heat; add nuts and 1 cup coconut. Fill layers. Ice cake with whipped cream and reserved coconut.

Keep boiled frosting from becoming hard by adding ⅓ t vinegar.

A little flour or cornstarch sprinkled on top of cake keeps icing from running off.

4-DAY COCONUT SOUR CREAM CAKE

"This must be made ahead."

18½ ounces buttered-flavored cake mix
2 cups sugar
16 ounces sour cream
12 ounces frozen coconut, thawed
1½ cups frozen whipped topping, thawed

Prepare cake mix according to package directions, making two 8 inch layers. When completely cooled, split layers. Combine sugar, sour cream and coconut; blend well. Chill. Reserve 1 cup sour cream mixture for frosting; spread remainder between layers of cake. Combine reserved sour cream mixture with whipped topping; blend until smooth. Spread on top and sides of cake. Seal cake in air-tight container. Refrigerate 3 days before serving.

DATE-NUT CAKE

1 cup dates, chopped
1 cup water
2½ cups cake flour
1 teaspoon baking powder
1 teaspoon baking soda
½ teaspoon salt
½ cup butter, softened
1½ cups sugar
3 large eggs
1 cup pecans, chopped
1 cup buttermilk
1 teaspoon vanilla extract

Preheat oven to 325°. Grease well a 9 inch tube pan. Cook dates in water until thick. Sift flour, baking soda, baking powder and salt. Cream butter, gradually add sugar; beat until well blended. Add eggs, one at a time, beating well after each addition. Add date mixture, pecans and dry ingredients alternately with buttermilk. Add vanilla. Pour into prepared pan. Bake 60 minutes. When partially cool, remove from pan.

Topping:
¾ cup pecans, chopped
½ cup light brown sugar
5 tablespoons butter
3 tablespoons evaporated milk

Combine ingredients; cook 3 minutes. Spread on top of cake while topping is hot. Broil 4 inches from broiler 1 or 2 minutes. Be careful not to burn. Cool on wire rack.

To "plump" dried fruit for fruitcake, sprinkle with water and place covered in preheated oven 10-15 minutes.

REFRIGERATOR FRUIT CAKE

½ pound regular marshmallows
1 cup evaporated milk
⅓ cup orange juice (or port wine)
2 cups golden raisins
1 cup dates, finely chopped
1½ cups pecans, chopped
⅔ cup candied cherries, chopped
⅔ cup candied pineapple, chopped
1½ cups mixed candied fruit, chopped
½ teaspoon cinnamon
½ teaspoon nutmeg
¼ teaspoon ground cloves
8½ cups graham cracker crumbs

Cut marshmallows finely with scissors. Pour milk and orange juice or wine over marshmallows; set aside. Prepare remaining ingredients and add to marshmallow mixture. Blend well until all crumbs are moistened. Line 2 loaf pans with waxed paper. Press firmly into pans. Chill 2 days before turning out and cutting. Use sharp knife to slice.

HOLIDAY FRUIT CAKE

½ pound dried apricots, chopped
½ pound dates, chopped
½ pound red and green candied cherries, chopped
½ pound red and green candied pineapple, chopped
½ pound golden raisins
½ pound almonds, blanched, toasted and chopped
½ pound pecans, broken into pieces
2 cups plain flour
1 cup butter, softened
¾ cup light brown sugar
¾ cup granulated sugar
6 large eggs
½ teaspoon ground cloves
1 teaspoon cinnamon
½ teaspoon mace
¾ teaspoon baking soda
½ teaspoon salt
2 tablespoons rum, light or dark
2 tablespoons Curacao
2 tablespoons brandy
1 orange, juice and rind
1 lemon, juice and rind

Preheat oven to 300°. Thoroughly grease two 8x5x3 loaf pans. Dredge fruit and nuts with ½ cup flour; set aside. Cream butter and sugar. Add eggs, one at a time, beating well after each addition. Sift remaining flour with spices, baking soda and salt. Add to creamed mixture alternately with flavorings and juices. Fold floured fruit and nuts into batter. Pour into prepared loaf pans; place pans in large pan of water and bake about 2½ hours.

Set hot layer cake pans on damp cloth as soon as they are removed from oven & cake will easily slip out.

LEMON-YOGURT CAKE

3 cups cake flour (or 2¾ cups plain flour)
1 teaspoon baking soda
¼ teaspoon salt
6 large eggs, separated
2 cups sugar, divided
1 cup butter, softened
2 teaspoons grated lemon peel
2 tablespoons fresh lemon juice
1 cup plain yogurt

Preheat oven to 350°. Grease well a 10 inch tube or fluted tube pan. Sift flour, soda and salt together. Beat egg whites until soft peaks form. Gradually add ½ cup sugar, beating until stiff but not dry. Beat butter with remaining 1½ cups sugar, egg yolks, lemon peel and juice until fluffy. Stir flour mixture alternately with yogurt into creamed butter mixture. Gently fold into egg white mixture. Pour into prepared pan. Bake 50-60 minutes or until pick inserted in center comes out clean. Cool in pan 10 minutes before turning out on rack to finish cooling.

SWEET POTATO CAKE

"Great for the holidays but delicious anytime."

1½ cups oil
2 cups sugar
4 eggs, separated
4 tablespoons hot water
2½ cups cake flour
3 teaspoons baking powder
¼ teaspoon salt
1 teaspoon ground cinnamon
1 teaspoon ground nutmeg
1½ cups uncooked sweet potatoes, grated
1 cup pecans, finely chopped
1 teaspoon vanilla extract

Preheat oven to 350°. Grease three 8 inch cake pans. Combine oil and sugar; beat until smooth. Add egg yolks; beat well. Stir in hot water. Combine dry ingredients; blend into sugar mixture. Stir in potatoes, pecans and vanilla, blending thoroughly. Beat egg whites until stiff; fold gently into batter. Spoon into prepared pans. Bake 25-30 minutes. Remove from pans. Cool on rack. Spread Coconut Filling between layers and on top of cake.

Coconut Filling:
13 ounces evaporated milk
1 cup sugar
½ cup butter
3 tablespoons plain flour
1 teaspoon vanilla extract
1⅓ cups flaked coconut

Combine all ingredients, except coconut, in saucepan. Cook over medium heat, stirring constantly, until thickened (about 12 minutes). Remove from heat; stir in coconut. Beat until thickened and cooled.

HONEY CAKE

2½ cups plain flour, sifted
1 cup oil
1 cup honey
1 cup sugar
3 eggs
½ teaspoon allspice
½ teaspoon cinnamon
½ teaspoon ground cloves
½ teaspoon nutmeg
1 teaspoon salt
1 teaspoon vanilla extract
½ teaspoon baking soda
½ cup water, boiling

Preheat oven to 325° (300° for glass pan). Sift flour, measure, and sift again. Add spices and salt. Combine oil, honey, sugar and eggs; beat well. Add vanilla and soda; beat in flour and water, starting with flour and ending with flour. Pour into a greased 9x3x3 loaf pan. Bake 1 hour. Cool on wire rack 15 minutes before removing from pan.

"Freezes well."

PINEAPPLE MERINGUE TORTE

2 cups plain flour
1 tablespoon baking powder
½ teaspoon salt
½ cup shortening
1⅓ cups sugar
1 teaspoon vanilla extract
1 cup pineapple juice
3 egg whites

Sift flour, baking powder and salt together. Cream shortening and sugar; beat until light and fluffy. Add sifted ingredients alternately with vanilla and pineapple juice. Beat until smooth. Beat egg whites until stiff but not dry; fold into batter. Pour into two 9 inch cake pans which have been greased, lined with waxed paper and paper greased. Cover batter with meringue topping mixture.

Meringue Topping:
3 egg whites
¼ teaspoon salt
⅔ cup sugar
1 teaspoon vanilla extract
¾ cup pecans, chopped

Preheat oven to 350°. Beat egg whites and salt until stiff but not dry. Add sugar gradually. Add flavoring and nuts. Bake 35-40 minutes or until cake springs back when touched; cool in pan on wire rack 10 minutes. Remove from pan as you would any other cake. Meringue may crack some but frosting will cover.

Pineapple Cream Frosting:
½ pint whipping cream, chilled
2 teaspoons confectioners' sugar
1 cup crushed pineapple, drained
¼ teaspoon vanilla extract

Whip cream; fold in sugar, pineapple and vanilla extract. Place cake, meringue side down, on serving plate; spread with 1-1½ cups pineapple cream frosting. Place second layer on top of frosting with meringue side up; spread with remaining frosting. Do not frost sides.
"This cake can be refrigerated for several hours before serving."

In using glass pans, lower oven temperature by 25°.

Dip knife in hot water & wipe dry to prevent icing from sticking to knife when cutting cake.

ORANGE-PINEAPPLE FANTASY CAKE

"Simple to prepare; elegant to serve."

18½ ounces Duncan Hines Butter Cake mix
4 eggs
½ cup oil
11 ounces canned mandarin oranges, drained

Preheat oven to 350°. Grease and flour four 8 inch cake pans. Mix all the above ingredients. Pour batter into prepared pans. Bake 10-15 minutes or until cake tests done. Let layers cool 5 minutes before turning onto wire racks to cool completely.

Frosting:
9 ounces Cool Whip
4½ ounces instant vanilla pudding
8¼ ounces crushed pineapple, drained
¾ cup coconut, shredded

Mix Cool Whip, vanilla pudding and crushed pineapple. Spread between layers and on top and sides of cake. Sprinkle coconut on top.
Note: This cake must be refrigerated.

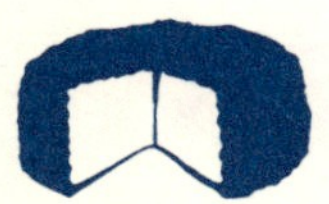

For a fine textured cake, add a few drops of boiling water to butter and sugar when you cream them.

BROWN SUGAR POUND CAKE

"This makes a wonderful gift at Christmas."

16 ounces light brown sugar
1 cup granulated sugar
½ cup shortening
1 cup butter or margarine
5 large eggs
3 cups plain flour
1 teaspoon baking powder
½ teaspoon salt
1 cup milk
1 teaspoon vanilla extract
2 cups pecans, chopped and divided

Preheat oven to 325°. Cream sugars, shortening and butter. Add eggs, one at a time, beating well after each. Sift all dry ingredients together; add to creamed mixture, mixing well. Add milk and vanilla. Stir in 1 cup pecans. Pour into greased and floured 10 inch tube pan. Sprinkle 1 cup pecans over batter, pressing down lightly. Bake 1½ hours.
Note: Cover top of pan with foil to prevent over browning of pecans after 1 hour. This cake freezes well.

POUND CAKE

1 cup butter, softened
16 ounces confectioners' sugar, sifted
1 teaspoon vanilla extract
5 eggs
½ cup milk
2 cups plain flour, sifted
1 teaspoon baking powder

Preheat oven to 350°. Cream butter and sugar and add vanilla. Add eggs one at a time, beating well after each. Add milk and beat. Add sifted flour and baking powder, beat well. Pour into 10 inch greased tube pan, dropping pan 5 or 6 times on counter top. Bake 45 minutes. Remove; place on wire rack for 1 hour. Turn cake out on plate.

Dress-up cakes with Gum Drop Roses — shave colored gum drops very thin. Place on iced cake. They will curl & look like small roses.

BLACK AND WHITE POUND CAKE

2 cups butter
1 tablespoon vanilla extract
3⅓ cups sugar
10 eggs
4 cups plain flour, sifted
½ teaspoon almond extract
¼ teaspoon baking soda
2 tablespoons instant coffee
¾ cup chocolate syrup

Preheat oven to 350°. Grease a 10 inch tube pan and line with waxed paper. Grease and dust with flour. Cream butter. Beat in vanilla and gradually add sugar. Beat on medium speed 3 minutes. Add eggs, two at a time, beating well after each addition. On lowest speed, gradually add flour and beat only until flour is incorporated. Remove half of batter; set aside. Mix almond extract into remaining batter; pour into prepared pan. Level the top. Return the other half of batter to mixer bowl. Add baking soda, instant coffee and chocolate syrup. Beat on low speed only until smooth. Pour evenly on top of white batter. Level top by rotating pan briskly back and forth. Cover top of pan with aluminum foil. Bake 30 minutes. Remove foil quickly. Continue to bake 1 hour and 20 minutes or until cake tester comes out dry. Remove from oven. Cool in pan 15 minutes. Cover with rack and invert. Invert again so cake can finish cooling right side up. Let stand overnight before serving.

COCONUT POUND CAKE

6 eggs
1 cup shortening
½ cup margarine
3 cups sugar
½ teaspoon almond extract
½ teaspoon coconut extract
3 cups cake flour, sifted
1 cup milk
2 cups fresh coconut, grated

Preheat oven to 300°. Separate eggs. Let whites warm to room temperature. Beat yolks with shortening and margarine until well blended. Add sugar, beating until light and fluffy. Add extracts. On low speed, beat in flour alternately with milk, beginning and ending with flour. Add coconut; beat until well blended. Beat egg whites until stiff peaks form. Fold into batter (use wire whisk) until well combined. Pour into greased 10 inch tube pan. Bake 2 hours.

Note: Slices better the second day.
Freezes well.
Fresh coconut is best but you may substitute frozen in same amount.

DR. BYRD'S POUND CAKE

3 cups cake flour
2 cups sugar
1 teaspoon salt
1 teaspoon baking soda
1 teaspoon cinnamon
1½ cups Crisco oil
3 eggs
8¼ ounces canned crushed pineapple, undrained
2 cups ripe bananas, diced
1 cup pecans, chopped

Preheat oven to 325°. Sift all dry ingredients together. Add oil, eggs and pineapple. Blend well with a spoon. Do *not* use mixer! Add bananas and pecans. Mix well; pour into a greased and floured 9 inch tube pan. Bake 1½ hours.

Icing:
½ cup whipped margarine (do not use stick margarine)
8 ounces cream cheese
1 teaspoon vanilla extract
16 ounces confectioners' sugar, sifted

Soften margarine and cream cheese. Add vanilla and mix *with a spoon.* Work in small amounts of the sugar at a time. Do *not* use electric mixer. Icing will be stiff. Cool cake before icing.

PEACH BRANDY POUND CAKE

3 cups sugar
1 cup butter or margarine, softened
6 eggs
3 cups plain flour, sifted
¼ teaspoon soda
pinch salt
1 cup sour cream
2 teaspoons rum
1 teaspoon orange extract
¼ teaspoon almond extract
½ teaspoon lemon extract
1 teaspoon vanilla extract
½ cup peach brandy

Preheat oven to 325°. Combine sugar and butter; cream until light and fluffy. Add eggs, one at a time, mixing well after each addition. Combine dry ingredients; add to creamed mixture alternately with sour cream, beating well after each addition. Stir in remaining ingredients. Pour into a well greased and floured 10 inch bundt or tube pan. Bake 1 hour and 20 minutes or until cake tests done.

Frost the cake as soon as it is thoroughly cool. Frosting protects the cake — keeps it fresh and moist. To prevent the cake from becoming soggy, both frosting and/or filling should be cool.

PINEAPPLE POUND CAKE

½ cup vegetable shortening
1 cup butter
2¾ cups sugar
6 large eggs
3 cups plain flour, sifted
1 teaspoon baking powder
¼ cup milk
1 teaspoon vanilla extract
20 ounces crushed pineapple, divided
4 tablespoons butter, softened
1½ cups confectioners' sugar, sifted

Cream shortening, butter, and sugar very well. Add eggs, one at a time, beating thoroughly after each addition. Add flour sifted with baking powder, a spoonful at a time, alternately with milk. Add vanilla; stir in ¾ cup undrained crushed pineapple, saving the remainder for the glaze; blend well. Pour batter into well-greased 10 inch tube pan. Place in *cold* oven. Turn oven to 325°. Bake 1½ hours or until done. Let stand a few minutes in pan. Run knife around edge and remove to rack. Combine butter, confectioners' sugar and remainder of pineapple, well drained. Pour over cake while hot.

SOUR CREAM SURPRISE CAKE

3 cups plain flour, sifted
¼ teaspoon baking soda
¼ teaspoon salt
1 cup butter or margarine
3 cups sugar
6 eggs
1 cup sour cream
¼ teaspoon vanilla extract
pecans, coarsely chopped
ground nutmeg or mace

Preheat oven to 300°. Combine flour, soda, and salt. Cream together butter and sugar; add eggs, one at a time, beating well after each addition. Beginning and ending with dry ingredients, add dry ingredients to creamed mixture alternately with sour cream. Add vanilla extract. Generously grease a 10 inch tube pan. Cover bottom of pan with pecans. Spoon batter over pecans and sprinkle generously with nutmeg or mace. Bake 1½ hours. Remove from oven and remove from pan immediately. Cool on cake rack.

BUTTER RUM CAKE

"A very flavorful and delicious cake."

1 cup butter
2 cups sugar
4 eggs
3 cups plain flour
1 teaspoon salt
1 teaspoon baking powder
½ teaspoon baking soda
1 cup buttermilk
2 teaspoons vanilla extract

Preheat oven to 325°. Grease bottom only of a 10 inch tube pan. Cream butter and sugar well. Add eggs, one at a time, beating well after each addition. Sift together flour, salt, baking powder, and soda. Add flour mixture and buttermilk alternately in small amounts to creamed mixture beating well after each addition. Stir in vanilla. Pour batter into prepared pan. Bake 60-65 minutes or until done. Ten minutes before cake is done, prepare sauce.

Rum Sauce:

1 cup sugar
¼ cup water
½ cup butter
2 tablespoons rum or 1 tablespoon rum extract
2 tablespoons confectioners' sugar

Place sugar, water and butter in pan; heat until butter is melted (do not boil). Remove from heat; stir in rum. When cake is done, remove and prick top with fork. Pour on warm sauce. Cool cake thoroughly before removing from pan. Sprinkle with confectioners' sugar.

FRUIT AND SPICE CAKE

½ cup dried apricots
1 cup orange juice
½ cup butter
1 cup sugar
2 large eggs
2 cups plain flour, sifted
1 teaspoon baking powder
1 teaspoon baking soda
½ teaspoon salt
1½ teaspoons cinnamon
¾ teaspoon nutmeg
¼ teaspoon ground cloves
¾ teaspoon ginger
1½ cups buttermilk
1 cup dried prunes, cooked and finely chopped
1 cup pecans, finely chopped

Preheat oven to 350°. Grease two 8 inch layer cake pans. Line with waxed paper and grease paper. Soak apricots in orange juice 1 hour. Drain; purée with a little of the orange juice in a blender. Cream butter and sugar. Beat in eggs until mixture is light. Sift all dry ingredients; add to butter mixture alternately with buttermilk. Stir in apricot purée, prunes and nuts. Turn into prepared pans. Bake 40-45 minutes or until done. Cool in pan 5 minutes. Turn onto wire rack to cool completely. Frost with cream cheese frosting.

Cream Cheese Frosting:
6 ounces cream cheese, softened
1 egg, separated
1 teaspoon vanilla extract
dash salt
3-3½ cups confectioners' sugar, sifted

Cream cheese until light. Beat in egg yolk, vanilla and salt. Add sugar gradually until smooth. Frost cake. Wrap in plastic wrap and foil. Store in refrigerator 2 days. Remove wrapping while cake is still cold.

PLUM SPICE CAKE

2 cups self-rising flour, measured after sifting
2 cups sugar
1 teaspoon cinnamon
1 teaspoon ground cloves (or allspice)
1 cup salad oil
3 large eggs
9½ ounces strained baby food plums
1 cup pecans, chopped

Preheat oven to 325°. Combine flour, sugar and spices. Add oil, eggs and plums; mix well. Add pecans. Pour into greased and floured 9 or 10 inch tube pan. Bake 1 hour and 15 minutes or until cake tests done. Cool 5 minutes and remove from pan. Use either Sherry Glaze *or* Caramel Icing over cake.

Sherry Glaze:

1 cup confectioners' sugar, sifted
4 tablespoons sherry

Mix and pour over cake.

Caramel Icing:

1 cup sugar
½ cup buttermilk
½ cup butter or margarine
1 tablespoon light corn syrup
½ teaspoon baking soda
½ teaspoon vanilla extract

Mix and boil 2 minutes. Pour over warm cake.

BANANA SPICE CAKE

"Make ahead cake."

½ cup butter
1 cup sugar
2 eggs
2 cups plain flour, sifted
1 teaspoon cinnamon
½ teaspoon nutmeg
½ teaspoon ground cloves
1 teaspoon baking powder
1 teaspoon baking soda
½ teaspoon salt
1 cup buttermilk
1 medium banana, mashed
1 teaspoon vanilla extract
½ cup pecans, chopped (optional)

Preheat oven to 350°. Cream butter and sugar. Add eggs, one at a time, and beat until light. Sift together flour, spices, baking powder, soda and salt. Combine buttermilk with mashed banana and vanilla. Add flour mixture alternately with buttermilk mixture. Add pecans. Pour into 2 waxed paper lined 8 inch layer pans. Bake 35-40 minutes. Let cake cool in pan 5 minutes. Turn out onto wire racks to cool completely before frosting. Frost with Penuche Icing. Wrap cake tightly with plastic wrap and foil. Let stand at room temperature for at least 1 day, preferably 2-3.
Note: Can be baked in a 13x9x2 baking pan 40-45 minutes or until done.

Penuche Frosting:

1 cup butter
2 cups light brown sugar
½ cup milk
4 cups confectioners' sugar, sifted
1 cup pecans, chopped

In a saucepan melt butter; stir in brown sugar and bring to a boil. Reduce heat, simmer 2 minutes. Add milk and bring to a boil, stirring constantly; remove from heat. Let mixture cool. Gradually beat in confectioners' sugar until frosting is of spreading consistency. Frost cake and sprinkle with pecans.

OATMEAL CAKE

1⅓ cups boiling water
½ cup butter or margarine
1 cup uncooked rolled oats
1 cup sugar
1 cup light brown sugar, firmly packed
2 eggs
1½ cups plain flour, sifted
1 teaspoon baking soda
1 teaspoon ground cinnamon
½ teaspoon salt
½ teaspoon ground nutmeg
Coconut Topping (recipe below)

Preheat oven to 350°. Grease and flour a 13x9x2 pan. Combine boiling water, butter and oats. Cover; let stand 20 minutes. Beat sugar and eggs into oat mixture. Beat in flour, baking soda, cinnamon, salt and nutmeg. Pour batter into prepared pan. Bake 30-35 minutes or until cake tests done. Make Coconut Topping. Increase oven to 550° and/or broil. Spread Coconut Topping over hot cake. Broil 4 inches from heat until topping is golden, about 2 minutes.

Coconut Topping:
1 cup light brown sugar, firmly packed
1 cup pecans, chopped
1 cup flaked coconut
½ cup butter or margarine
3 tablespoons milk

Mix all ingredients in saucepan. Cook over medium heat, stirring constantly, until butter melts.

RUM PUMPKIN CAKE

34 ounces pound cake mix
16 ounces canned pumpkin
1½ teaspoons pumpkin pie spice

Preheat oven to 325°. Prepare pound cake mix according to directions, decreasing milk to a total of ⅔ cup. Add pumpkin and pie spice. Turn into well greased and floured tube or bundt pan. Bake 1 hour 20 minutes. Cool in pan 10 minutes. Cool on rack 20 minutes.

Frosting:
1 cup sugar
1 cup orange juice
1 two inch stick cinnamon
¼ cup rum

Using a long fork, punch holes around cake at one inch intervals. In saucepan combine sugar, orange juice and cinnamon stick. Bring to a boil; remove cinnamon stick. Add rum. Spoon mixture over cake very slowly until all is absorbed. Chill until serving.

PECAN RUM CAKES

2¼ cups cake flour, sifted
1½ cups sugar
1 teaspoon salt
3½ teaspoons baking powder
½ cup butter, softened
¾ cup milk
1½ teaspoons vanilla extract
4 egg whites
½ teaspoon rum extract
¼ cup rum

Preheat oven to 350°. Sift flour, sugar, salt and baking powder. Add butter, milk and vanilla. Beat on low speed until blended. Beat at medium speed 2 minutes. Add unbeaten egg whites, rum extract and rum; beat 2 minutes longer. Pour into a 13x9x2 pan that has been greased, floured and lined with waxed paper. Bake 35 minutes or until it tests done. Let cake cool.

Icing:
½ cup butter, softened
3 cups confectioners' sugar
4 tablespoons milk
1½ teaspoons vanilla extract
pecans, finely chopped

Cream butter and sugar. Stir in milk; beat until very fluffy. Add vanilla. Cut cake into small squares. Pour a generous teaspoon of rum on each square. Spread icing on all sides and roll in chopped pecans.
Variation: Fresh or frozen coconut can be used instead of pecans.

CHOCOLATE ICING

½ cup margarine
½ cup evaporated milk
1 cup sugar
6 ounces semi-sweet chocolate chips
1 teaspoon vanilla extract

Combine first 3 ingredients; bring to a boil, boiling 2 minutes. Remove from heat; add chocolate chips. Stir. Beat well to spreading consistency. This will frost and fill a 9 inch 2 layer cake.

FLUFFY WHITE FROSTING

2 cups confectioners' sugar, sifted
½ cup shortening
1 egg white
Pinch of salt
2 tablespoons plain flour
2 tablespoons milk
½ teaspoon vanilla extract

Combine all of the above ingredients and beat together 10-15 minutes, or until fluffy.

COLLECTION OF MOUNTAIN ATTRACTIONS

"The Land Of The Sky" was the name given this region in 1876 by author Christian Reid. Below are many of its attractions but more than anything else, the N.C. mountains are a place where uncommon beauty is not uncommon at all.

Appalachian Trail — 200 miles of the wilderness route from Maine to Georgia

Beech Mountain, Banner Elk, Boone — Snow skiing resorts

Biltmore House & Gardens — Largest house in America — 365 rooms — built by George Vanderbilt; Asheville

Blowing Rock — unique rock formation where air currents return light objects and cause snow to fall upside down. The unusual phenomenon is caused by strong updrafts resulting from steady vertical wind movements along the southern face of the cliff. And in the winter, falling snow caught in the updrafts really appears to be falling "upside down."

Brevard Music Center — "Summer Music Capitol of Southeast"; Brevard

Cherokee Indian Reservation — Home of eastern band of Cherokees; Cherokee

Chimney Rock — Unique rock formation overlooking Lake Lure; Chimney Rock

Cowee Valley — Ruby fields open to "rock hounds"; near Franklin

Flatrock Playhouse — N.C.'s state theatre; Flatrock

Fontana Dam — Highest of TVA dams; Fontana Village

Frontierland — Frontier Village; near Cherokee

Ghost Mountain — Frontier Village overlooking Maggie Valley

Grandfather Mountain — Some of the oldest known rock formations in the world, dating back a billion years, have been found here; near Linville

Land of Oz — A journey along the Yellow Brick Road with Dorothy and her friends; Beech Mountain

Linville Caverns — Unusual stalactites and stalagmites in lighted cavern; Linville

Mount Mitchell — Highest point east of Mississippi River; off Blue Ridge Parkway

Oconaluftee Indian Village — Recreated Cherokee Village of 200 years ago; Cherokee

Tweetsie Railroad — Scenic train, frontier village; near Blowing Rock

cookies
and
candies

THE CAROLINA COLLECTOR'S CONCOCTIONS

. . . Boil 1 c each butter, brown sugar, pecans for 2 min.; spread on graham crackers. Bake 5 min. at 400°.

. . . Pat mix of ½ lb. butter, ½ c sugar, 3 c flour onto cookie sheet; bake 30 min. at 350°. Cut in squares.

. . . Energy candy is ½ c honey, ½ c peanut butter, 1½ c dry milk, kneaded and shaped into rolls. Roll in nuts, raisins & wheat germ.

. . . Surprise your guests at a tea with mincemeat and pound cake sandwiches.

. . . Make quick brownies with a pkg. of brownie mix & bake 15 minutes. Sprinkle with 1 c miniature marshmallows & a pkg. quick fudge mix. Cool.

. . . Easy pralines. Boil 1⅓ c sugar, 1 c butter, ½ c light corn syrup 15 min. Add 1 t vanilla extract & pour mixture over popcorn, pecans & almonds.

. . . A quick & pretty popcorn ball is made with 1 c light corn syrup & ½ c sugar brought to a boil; add 3¼ oz. jello dissolved in liquid; pour over popcorn & nuts. Shape into any shape.

. . . Add herb seeds to basic sugar cookies before baking; glaze with beaten egg white & press in seeds such as anise, coriander, sesame, caraway & fennel seeds.

. . . Add wheat germ to your favorite cookie mix for a nutritious treat.

. . . Add mincemeat to a basic brownie recipe and spinkle all with confectioners' sugar.

ALMOND SHORTBREAD COOKIES

1 cup plain flour
½ cup cornstarch
½ cup confectioners' sugar
1 cup almonds, finely chopped
¾ cup butter or margarine, softened

Preheat oven to 300°. Combine flour, cornstarch, and confectioners' sugar. Stir in nuts. Add butter; blend with a wooden spoon until a soft dough forms. Shape dough into small balls. Place on ungreased cookie sheet; flatten each ball with a lightly floured fork. Bake 15-25 minutes or until edges are lightly browned. Cool before storing. Yields: 3 dozen.
Note: Using butter will yield a flatter crisper cookie.

Substitution for 1 t baking powder — ½ t cream of tartar and ¼ t baking soda.

CHOCOLATE CUP COOKIES
"Delicious!"

¾ cup butter, softened
½ cup sugar
2 cups plain flour, sifted
¼ teaspoon salt
1 teaspoon vanilla extract

Preheat oven to 350°. Thoroughly grease bottom and sides of 3 dozen very small tart shells or small muffin tins. Cream butter and sugar well. Gradually add flour, salt and vanilla. Press dough into tins.

Brownie Nut Filling:
2 eggs
¼ teaspoon salt
½ cup sugar
1 cup semi-sweet chocolate pieces, chopped
¾ cup pecans, chopped

Beat eggs until thick; add salt and sugar. Mix in chocolate and nuts. Fill each shell with a rounded teaspoonful of filling. Bake 20 minutes.

Topping: (optional)
1 cup whipping cream, whipped
2 tablespoons confectioners' sugar
½ teaspoon vanilla extract

Mix together. Place a dollop on each cookie. Yields: 3 dozen.

CHOCOLATE COVERED BUTTER COOKIES

½ cup butter, softened
½ cup brown sugar
1 egg yolk, beaten
1 cup plain flour, sifted
½ teaspoon vanilla extract
14 ounces Hershey's milk chocolate bars
½ cup pecans, chopped

Preheat oven to 350°. Cream butter and brown sugar; add egg yolk, flour and vanilla. Mix well. Spread on an ungreased 10x15 pan about ¼ inch thick. Bake 15 minutes. Unwrap chocolate bars while cookies are baking. Remove from oven; lay chocolate bars on baked layer. Return to oven 1-2 minutes, or until chocolate melts. Remove; quickly spread chocolate evenly. Sprinkle with pecans. Place in freezer. When frozen, break into uneven sized pieces with the point of a knife. Return to freezer in airtight container. Serve semi-frozen. Yields: approximately 4 dozen pieces.

When making rolled cookies use confectioners' sugar on a pastry board & rolling pin instead of flour.

CHOCOLATE CREAM STICKS

"This treat melts in your mouth."

3 ounces unsweetened chocolate
¾ cup butter
1½ cups sugar
3 eggs
¾ cup plain flour
¾ cup pecans, chopped

Preheat oven to 350°. Melt chocolate and butter over low heat; add other ingredients, blending well. Spread evenly in a greased and floured 9x13 pan. Bake 20 minutes. Cool completely.

6 tablespoons butter, softened
3 cups confectioners' sugar
3 tablespoons milk
½ teaspoon vanilla extract

Mix; spread evenly and chill. Top with:

4 ounces semi-sweet chocolate
4 tablespoons butter

Melt together. Spread on top. Refrigerate until firm. Cut into finger-like sticks. Keep refrigerated. Yields: approximately 4 dozen.

CHERRY DATE PINWHEELS

"These are a must for the Christmas holidays."

1 cup dates, chopped finely
⅔ cup plus 1 tablespoon plain flour, sifted
3 large eggs
¾ cup sugar
½ teaspoon baking powder
½ teaspoon salt
½ cup pecans, chopped finely
1 teaspoon vanilla extract
20 whole maraschino cherries, drained
confectioners' sugar

Preheat oven to 325°. Line a 15x10 jellyroll pan with greased waxed paper. Sprinkle dates with 1 tablespoon flour. Beat eggs until thick; add sugar, beating constantly. Fold in dry ingredients, pecans, vanilla and dates. Spread batter evenly in prepared pan. Arrange 10 cherries across each end about ½ inch from edge of pan. Bake 25-35 minutes. Remove from oven and immediately turn cake out onto waxed paper sprinkled with confectioners' sugar. Remove paper, trim edges of cake and cut across into 2 rectangles 7½x10. Beginning with cherry end, roll each rectangle tightly. Wrap in waxed paper and cool before frosting.

Frosting:
1½ cups confectioners' sugar
2 tablespoons evaporated milk
½ teaspoon vanilla extract
chopped pecans, enough to cover outside of both cookie rolls

Mix together all ingredients, except pecans, until smooth. Spread cooled roll thinly with frosting and roll in pecans. Chill 24 hours or more and slice ½ inch thick.

PRALINE BROWNIES

"Tastes as if you spent many hours in preparation. A favorite from our old cookbook."

22½ ounces brownie mix (or your favorite brownie recipe)
¾ cup pecans, chopped
3 tablespoons margarine, melted
¾ cup light brown sugar

Preheat oven to 350°. Prepare brownies according to package direction. (Do not add nuts.) Place in a greased 9x13x2 pan. Combine pecans, margarine and brown sugar. Sprinkle over batter. Bake 25-30 minutes. Yields: 24.

FUDGE NUT SQUARES

1 cup butter, softened
2 cups light brown sugar
2 eggs
3 teaspoons vanilla extract
2½ cups plain flour
1 teaspoon baking soda
½ teaspoon salt
3 cups rolled oats
1 cup pecans, chopped

Preheat oven to 350°. Grease a 10x16 pan. Cream together the butter and brown sugar. Add eggs and vanilla. Beat well. Sift together flour, baking soda and salt; add to the butter-sugar mixture. Blend in oats and nuts. Press two-thirds of this mixture into prepared pan.

Filling:
12 ounces chocolate chips
15 ounces sweetened condensed milk
3 tablespoons butter
¾ cup pecans, chopped
1 teaspoon vanilla extract

Melt chocolate, condensed milk and butter in a double boiler over hot water. Add pecans and vanilla. Pour onto cookie mixture. Sprinkle remaining cookie mixture over filling and bake 20-25 minutes. Do not overbake. Cut into small squares. Yields: 32-40.

Be sure that cookie sheets are at least 2 inches narrower and shorter than the oven rack so that heat can circulate evenly.

BLACK-EYED SUSANS

"Delicious served with coffee or hot tea."

1 cup butter, softened
1 pound sharp cheese, grated
3 cups plain flour, sifted
1 teaspoon salt
½ teaspoon red pepper
1 pound Dromedary dates, pitted
pecan halves
confectioners' sugar

Preheat oven to 325°. Mix butter, cheese, flour, salt and pepper together. Shape dough into a ball and chill slightly. Divide chilled dough and roll out on a lightly floured pastry sheet. Cut into circles using a 2½ inch cookie cutter or glass. Stuff each date with a pecan half. Put stuffed date in the center of a cheese round. Fold dough over to the center from 2 sides and press together. The other 2 ends will remain open. Bake 12-15 minutes or until slightly brown. When cool, sprinkle with confectioners' sugar. Store in a tin box. Yields: 7 dozen.

ORIENTAL TREASURE COOKIES

"Pass these for dessert after your next Chinese meal."

1⅔ cups plain flour
1½ teaspoons baking powder
½ teaspoon soda
½ cup brown sugar, firmly packed
½ cup sugar
½ cup shortening
1 egg
1 tablespoon soy sauce
½ teaspoon almond extract
½ cup slivered almonds
2 teaspoons sugar
1 teaspoon soy sauce

Preheat oven to 350°. In large bowl of electric mixer, combine first 9 ingredients and blend well. Using a rounded teaspoon of dough, shape into balls. Combine almonds, sugar and 1 teaspoon soy sauce; blend well. Dip top of cookies into mixture. Place on ungreased cookie sheets. Bake 12-15 minutes. Yields: 46-50 cookies.

BUSY DAY BARS

graham crackers, broken on lines, to fill bottom of 10x15 pan
sliced almonds
¾ cup brown sugar, packed
1 cup margarine

Preheat oven to 350°. Place crackers on bottom of 10x15 pan. Cover with sliced almonds. Bring brown sugar and margarine to boil; boil 3 minutes. Spoon over crackers and nuts. Bake 8 minutes. When cool, cut on lines where crackers were broken. Yields: 48.

CINNAMON CRUNCH SQUARES

"An instant success!"

¾ cup butter
1 cup sugar
1 cup plain flour
1 egg, separated
1 teaspoon vanilla extract
½ teaspoon cinnamon
1 cup pecans, finely chopped

Preheat oven to 325°. Cream butter; add sugar, flour, egg yolk, vanilla and cinnamon. Mix well. Spread with moistened fingers on lightly greased 10x15 cookie sheet. Brush slightly beaten egg white over batter. Pour on nuts and spread. Bake 30-40 minutes or until dark tan in color. Cut while warm into squares. Remove from pan after cooling. Yields: 6 dozen.

BROWNED BUTTER YULE COOKIES

1 cup margarine or butter
½ cup sugar
2 teaspoons vanilla extract
2 teaspoons lemon extract
2 teaspoons almond extract
2 cups plain flour, unsifted
1 teaspoon baking powder
50 pecan halves (or almonds)

Preheat oven to 325°. Melt margarine or butter; brown lightly. Pour into mixing bowl; cool. Beat in sugar and stir in flavorings. Add flour and baking powder; mix well. Chill dough a short time. Shape dough into small balls (about 1 teaspoonful each). Top each with a pecan half. Bake on ungreased cookie sheet 15-20 minutes. Yields: 50.

Shredded coconut can be freshened by soaking in ½ c milk before using.

FAYETTEVILLE ORANGE BLOSSOMS

"A favorite from our old cookbook."

1¼ cups cake flour, sifted
¼ teaspoon salt
1 teaspoon baking powder
¼ teaspoon soda
¼ cup butter
½ cup sugar
1 egg
1 tablespoon orange rind, grated
½ cup pecans, chopped
½ cup fresh orange juice
Orange Syrup

Preheat oven to 375°. Sift together flour, salt, baking powder and soda. Cream butter until light, gradually adding sugar. Beat in egg. Stir in orange rind and pecans. Add dry ingredients alternately with orange juice, mixing very quickly. Grease tiny muffin pans. Fill ⅔ full. Bake 8-12 minutes. Remove from pan; cool. Using a long tined fork, dip cakes into hot Orange Syrup. Allow excess syrup to drain. Place on wire rack. When cool, store in airtight containers. Yields: 3-4 dozen.

Orange Syrup:
½ cup fresh orange juice
1 cup sugar
1 teaspoon orange rind, grated

Mix and stir over low heat until sugar is dissolved. Increase heat; boil rapidly 5 minutes or until candy thermometer registers 230°.

CRACKLE COOKIES

1 cup margarine or butter, softened
1½ cups sugar
2 egg yolks
¼-½ teaspoon salt
1 teaspoon soda
1 teaspoon cream of tartar
2 cups plain flour
1 teaspoon almond extract

Preheat oven to 325°. Cream margarine and sugar; add egg yolks. Sift dry ingredients; mix with sugar mixture. Add almond extract; mix well. Make small balls and roll in granulated sugar. Space 2 inches apart on cookie sheet. Bake 10-12 minutes. Will be soft when removed from oven but will firm up. Yields: 4 dozen.

HOLIDAY FRUITCAKE BARS

1 cup mixed candied fruits, diced
1 cup candied cherries, halved
1 cup candied pineapple, diced
2 cups raisins
¾ cup sweet white wine
chopped nuts (optional)
1⅓ cups plain flour
1 cup light brown sugar, packed
6 tablespoons butter or margarine, softened
2 eggs
1 teaspoon cinnamon
1 teaspoon ground cloves
¼ teaspoon baking soda
¼ teaspoon salt

Mix fruits and wine; let stand overnight. Preheat oven to 350°. Grease and flour a 15x10 pan. Mix remaining ingredients at low speed. Stir in fruit mixture and nuts. Spread in prepared pan. Bake 30 minutes or until toothpick comes out clean. Cool completely; cut into bars. Yields: 4 dozen.

HEATH BAR COOKIES

1 cup butter
⅔ cup confectioners' sugar
2⅔ cups plain flour
1 teaspoon almond extract
1½ cups Heath Bars, coarsely crushed

Preheat oven to 325°. Cream butter and sugar until fluffy. Add flour and almond extract; mix well. Add crushed Heath Bars. Form into small balls and place on ungreased cookie sheets. Flatten with bottom of glass dipped in sugar. Bake 10-15 minutes or until done. Yields: 3-4 dozen.

LEMON COCONUT BARS

1½ cups plain flour, sifted
1½ cups sugar
½ cup butter or margarine, softened
2 tablespoons plain flour
½ teaspoon baking powder
½ teaspoon salt
2 eggs
1 teaspoon vanilla extract
1 cup walnuts, coarsely chopped
4 ounces sweetened shredded coconut

Preheat oven to 350°. Grease well a 13x9x2 pan. In a large bowl mix together flour and 1 cup of sugar. Using a pastry blender or 2 knives, cut butter into flour and sugar until the mixture has the appearance of coarse corn meal. Turn into prepared pan; spread evenly and pat down firmly. Bake 10 minutes. Meanwhile in a small bowl, mix remaining ½ cup sugar with the 2 tablespoons of flour, baking powder and salt. In a medium bowl, slightly beat eggs with the vanilla; beat in sugar mixture and blend well. Stir in the nuts and coconut. After the bottom layer has baked 10 minutes, immediately spread coconut mixture over top; continue to bake 20-25 minutes or until lightly browned. Let cool completely in pan; spread with lemon icing. When set, cut into bars. Yields: 24.

Lemon Icing:
1 tablespoon butter, softened
1 cup confectioners' sugar, sifted
2 tablespoons lemon juice

Place softened butter in a small bowl. Using a wooden spoon, gradually stir in confectioners' sugar and lemon juice. Blend well.

CRISP LEMON THINS

½ cup butter, softened
¾ cup brown sugar, packed
1 egg
¾ cup plain flour, sifted
½ cup almonds, finely chopped
¼ cup quick cooking rolled oats
1 tablespoon lemon rind, grated
½ teaspoon lemon extract

Preheat oven to 350°. Cream butter and sugar; blend in unbeaten egg. Add flour and mix thoroughly. Stir in almonds, oats, lemon rind, and lemon extract. Drop by ½ teaspoonfuls at least 3 inches apart onto greased baking sheets. Flatten each cookie with moist fingers. Bake 7-10 minutes or until edges are golden brown. Remove from baking sheet immediately. Yields: 3 dozen.

LEMON FROSTED CARROT BARS

4 eggs, well beaten
2 cups sugar
¾ cup vegetable oil
1½ cups cooked carrots, mashed (or 13½ ounces baby food carrots)
2 cups plain flour, sifted
2 teaspoons baking soda
1 teaspoon salt
2 teaspoons cinnamon
4 tablespoons butter, softened
3 ounces cream cheese, softened
16 ounces confectioners' sugar
½ teaspoon vanilla extract
juice of 1 lemon

Preheat oven to 350°. In large bowl combine eggs, sugar, oil and carrots. Sift dry ingredients and add to egg mixture. Mix well. Pour into 2 greased 9x13 pans. Bake 20-30 minutes and cool. Cream 4 tablespoons butter, cream cheese and confectioners' sugar. Add vanilla and lemon juice. Ice cakes. Cut into squares. Yields: 60-70.
Variation: Substitute 16 ounces canned pumpkin for the mashed carrots.

Baked cookies and cookie dough, tightly wrapped in foil, may be stored frozen 9 to 12 months.

LEBKUCHEN
"Soft and spicy."

1 quart molasses
1 tablespoon soda
1 pound brown sugar
6 eggs
4 egg whites
½ pound citron
1 pound dates
1 pound figs
8 ounces seedless raisins
3 cups plain flour
1 tablespoon ground cloves
1 tablespoon ground ginger
1 tablespoon ground cinnamon
1 tablespoon ground allspice
5 cups plain flour
½ pound almonds, finely chopped
½ pound pecans, finely chopped
½ lemon, juice and rind
½ cup peach brandy
1 pound confectioners' sugar
4 egg whites

Preheat oven to 350°. Mix molasses and soda; add sugar and lightly beaten eggs. Run fruits through a meat grinder. Carefully dredge fruit in 3 cups of flour. Mix spices with 5 cups of flour; combine with the fruit mixture. Add molasses mixture, nuts, lemon juice and rind, and brandy. Drop by scant teaspoonfuls onto greased cookie sheets. Bake until they spring back when touched. Cool and ice with mixture of confectioners' sugar and 4 egg whites, beaten until smooth. Yields: hundreds.

MARZIPAN CUPCAKES

5½ tablespoons butter (no substitute), softened
¼ cup confectioners' sugar
1 egg, separated
¼ teaspoon almond extract
1 cup plain flour

Preheat oven to 375°. Cream butter and sugar well in bowl of electric mixer; add egg yolk and almond extract; mix well. Blend in flour. Chill dough 1 hour or more for easier handling. Pinch off marble-sized pieces of dough and press into bottom and sides of tiny ungreased muffin tins. Bake 7-8 minutes.

5½ tablespoons butter (no substitute), softened
4 ounces almond paste
½ cup granulated sugar
2 eggs
½ teaspoon almond extract

Preheat oven to 350°. Cream butter with almond paste until well blended; beat in sugar thoroughly. Blend in eggs and almond extract. Spoon into each baked shell; bake 20 minutes.

Frosting:
¾ cup confectioners' sugar
orange or lemon juice
¼ teaspoon almond extract

While tarts bake, prepare frosting by combining ¾ cup sugar with orange or lemon juice and about ¼ teaspoon almond flavoring. Drizzle over outer edges of warm cakes. Yields: 36 cupcakes.
"These cupcakes can be prepared in advance and frozen. The recipe easily doubles to serve a cocktail party for 20."

CAROLINA MERINGUE COOKIES

1 egg white
¼ teaspoon salt
1 cup brown sugar, firmly packed
1 cup pecans, chopped
1 tablespoon plain flour
½ teaspoon vanilla extract

Preheat oven to 275°. Beat egg white until stiff; add salt. Add brown sugar gradually. Chop nuts and sprinkle with flour, add to egg white mixture. Add vanilla; drop by teaspoonfuls onto greased cookie sheet. Bake 20 minutes. Allow to cool 1 minute before removing from cookie sheet. Yields: 2 dozen.

OLD-FASHIONED GINGER COOKIES

¾ cup butter or margarine, softened
1 cup light brown sugar, firmly packed
1 egg
⅓ cup molasses
2¼ cups plain flour, sifted
2 teaspoons soda
¼ teaspoon salt
¾ teaspoon ground cloves
1½ teaspoons cinnamon
1½ teaspoons ginger

Preheat oven to 325°. Cream butter and sugar thoroughly; add egg and molasses. Sift all dry ingredients together. Add to creamed mixture; blending well. Chill 2 hours or until easy to handle. Roll into walnut sized balls. Dip tops in granulated sugar. Place sugar side up 3 inches apart on greased cookie sheets. Sprinkle each cookie with 2-3 drops of water to produce a crackled surface. Bake 9-10 minutes or until set. Yields: about 4 dozen.
Note: For a crisper cookie, cook a few minutes longer.

Shiny cookie sheets make browner cookies.

PEANUT BLOSSOMS

"The children can't resist this cookie-candy treat."

½ cup butter, softened
⅓ cup peanut butter
½ cup sugar
½ cup light brown sugar
1 large egg
1 teaspoon vanilla extract
1¾ cups plain flour, sifted
1 teaspoon baking soda
½ teaspoon salt
1 egg white
sugar
chocolate candy kisses, 1 for each cookie

Preheat oven to 375°. Grease cookie sheet well. Cream butter and peanut butter. Add sugar, egg, vanilla and dry ingredients. Shape dough into walnut-size balls, using about 1 tablespoonful for each ball. Dip each ball in egg white, then roll lightly in sugar and place on cookie sheet about 1 inch apart. Bake 8 minutes. Remove from oven and top each cookie with a candy kiss and press firmly into cookie. Return to oven and bake 2-5 minutes longer or until golden brown. Candy will not melt but will soften. After removing from oven, you may press each kiss with a knife to flatten. Yields: 3½ dozen 2 inch cookies.
Note: If these should soften before the last one is eaten, you may crisp them up by heating in a slow oven for about 15 minutes.

PEANUT BUTTER STICKS

"You won't believe how really good this is."

thick slices of bread
peanut butter
oil

Preheat oven to 225°. Trim crust from bread. Cut bread into finger like strips. Place strips and crusts on a cookie sheet; bake until thoroughly dry, approximately 1 hour. Mix peanut butter with enough oil to make a soupy mixture. Make fine crumbs from the dry crust. Dip strips into peanut butter and roll in crumbs.

ICE BOX PECAN COOKIES

½ cup butter, softened
1 cup light brown sugar
1 egg
1½ cups plain flour
½ teaspoon soda
¼ teaspoon salt
1 cup pecans, chopped

Mix all ingredients thoroughly. Place in refrigerator to harden. When relatively hard, remove, mold into a long roll. Cover with wax paper; refrigerate overnight. Preheat oven to 400°. Cut thin slices from roll. Bake 10 minutes. Yields: 2-3 dozen.

PECAN PIE COOKIES

1 cup butter or margarine
½ cup sugar
½ cup dark corn syrup
2 eggs, separated
2½ cups plain flour, unsifted
Pecan Filling

Stir butter or margarine and sugar on low speed in large bowl of electric mixer. Add corn syrup and egg yolks; beating until thoroughly blended. Stir in flour gradually. Chill dough several hours. Prepare Pecan Filling.

Pecan Filling:
½ cup confectioners' sugar
¼ cup butter or margarine
3 tablespoons dark corn syrup
½ cup pecans, chopped

Combine sugar, butter or margarine and corn syrup in saucepan. Stir to combine. Cook over medium heat until mixture reaches a full boil. Remove from heat; stir in pecans. Chill. When dough is thoroughly chilled, preheat oven to 375°. Beat egg white slightly. Using one tablespoonful of dough for each cookie, roll into balls. Brush very lightly with egg white. Place 2 inches apart on greased cookie sheets. Bake 5 minutes. Roll ½ teaspoon of chilled Pecan Filling into a ball; repeat with all of filling. Remove cookies from oven, press 1 ball into the center of each cookie. Bake an additional 5 minutes. Cool 5 minutes; remove to wire racks. Yields: 48.

GOLDEN PECAN TASSIES

"Perfect to serve anytime."

6 ounces cream cheese, softened
1 cup margarine, softened
2 cups plain flour
¾ cup pecans, chopped

Blend cream cheese and margarine with a wooden spoon or at lowest speed on mixer. Add flour. Mix well, chill in refrigerator 2-3 hours. Roll into 1 inch balls and press into tiny muffin tins, forming shells. Sprinkle a few chopped pecans into bottom of each shell (approximately ½ teaspoon).

2 eggs, slightly beaten
1½ cups light brown sugar, firmly packed
2 tablespoons butter, melted
⅛ teaspoon salt
1 teaspoon vanilla extract

Preheat oven to 350°. Mix eggs, sugar, butter, salt and vanilla. Spoon this sticky mixture into shells, filling about ⅔-¾ full. Sprinkle a few chopped pecans over tops. Bake 15-17 minutes. Reduce temperature to 250° and continue to bake 10 minutes or until set. Yields: 48 tassies.

Make sure cookies are baked on sheets without sides to ensure even baking. Remove from sheets to cooling racks immediately as cookies continue baking.

POUND CAKE DELIGHTS

"Pound cake flavor baked in a cookie."

2½ sticks butter (no substitution), softened
1 cup sugar
2 egg yolks
3 cups plain flour, sifted
1 teaspoon vanilla extract
Candied cherry halves or pecans

Preheat oven to 350°. Cream butter and add sugar gradually. Add egg yolks one at a time. Add flour gradually; mix well. Add vanilla. Drop by teaspoonfuls on ungreased cookie sheet or form in small balls and flatten in palms of hands. Place cherry or pecan in center of each cookie. Bake 12-15 minutes. Yields: 5-6 dozen.

RISE 'N SHINERS

"Great to serve for morning meetings."

½ pound bacon
½ cup butter
¾ cup sugar
1 egg
1 cup plain flour
¼ teaspoon baking soda
2 cups corn flakes
½ cup raisins

Preheat oven to 350°. Cook bacon until crisp; drain well and break into ½ inch pieces. Beat butter and sugar together until fluffy; add egg and beat. Combine flour and soda; stir into butter mixture. Stir in bacon, corn flakes and raisins. Drop by rounded tablespoons 2 inches apart on ungreased cookie sheets. Bake 15-18 minutes. Cool 1 minute. Remove to racks; cool. Yields: 2 dozen.

LENA'S SUGAR COOKIES

"An all-time favorite."

1½ cups self-rising flour
1 cup sugar
1 egg, beaten
½ cup butter (no substitute), softened
1 teaspoon vanilla extract

Preheat oven to 325°. Sift flour and sugar together. Add other ingredients; mix well. Make a small ball of dough and place on greased cookie sheet. Flatten with bottom of glass that has been dipped in granulated sugar. Bake 8-12 minutes or until lightly browned. Yields: 5 dozen.

Note: The smaller and thinner you can make these cookies, the better they will be.

DELICATE PASTEL SUGAR COOKIES

"You choose the color of this cookie to go with your party colors."

¾ cup butter, softened
½ cup sugar
3 ounces gelatin, any flavor
2 eggs
1 teaspoon vanilla extract
2½ cups plain flour, sifted
1 teaspoon baking powder
1 teaspoon salt

Preheat oven to 375°. Cream butter; add sugar and gelatin gradually. Beat in eggs and vanilla. Blend in sifted dry ingredients; chill. Shape into 1 inch balls; roll in granulated sugar. Place 2 inches apart on lightly greased cookie sheets. Flatten with bottom of glass that has been dipped in granulated sugar. Bake 5-10 minutes. Do not brown. Yields: 7½ dozen.

WINNIE'S PRALINE COOKIES

½ cup butter, softened
½ cup sugar
½ cup dark brown sugar, packed
1 large egg, well beaten
½ cup plain flour, measured after sifting
1 cup nuts, chopped
1 teaspoon vanilla extract

Preheat oven to 350°. Cream together butter and sugars until light and fluffy. Add egg and gradually blend in flour. Stir in nuts and vanilla. Drop from teaspoon onto a greased cookie sheet and bake 10 minutes. Loosen while warm and cook on wire rack. Yields: 2½-3 dozen.

YANKEE QUAKERS

2 cups light brown sugar
1 cup shortening
2 eggs, beaten
2 cups plain flour, sifted
1 cup oatmeal
1½ teaspoons baking soda
1 teaspoon salt
2 teaspoons vanilla extract
sugar

Preheat oven to 375°. Cream sugar and shortening. Add eggs, flour, oatmeal, baking soda, salt, and vanilla. Roll dough into small balls and then roll in sugar. Bake about 10 minutes. Yields: 80.

Store softened cookies in a tight container with a piece of orange, apple or bread.

Store crisp cookies in a jar with a loose top — crisp limp ones in a 300° oven for 5 min.

RAISIN CLUSTERS

1 cup semi-sweet chocolate chips
1 cup raisins
½ cup sliced Brazil nuts (or other nuts)

Melt chocolate chips in top of double boiler over hot (not boiling) water. Remove; add raisins and nuts. Drop by spoonfuls on waxed paper. Cool.

CHOCOLATE CHERRIES

"Elegant served on a silver tray or box them and give as a gift."

7¼ ounces vanilla wafers, finely crushed
½ cup confectioners' sugar
½ cup walnuts, finely chopped
¼ cup boiling water
2 tablespoons margarine
1 tablespoon light corn syrup
2 teaspoons instant powdered coffee
30 maraschino cherries with stems
12 ounces semi-sweet chocolate chips
flaked coconut (optional)
multi-colored sprinkles (optional)
chocolate sprinkles (optional)
nuts, chopped (optional)

Mix vanilla wafer crumbs, confectioners' sugar, and walnuts. Combine water, butter, corn syrup and instant coffee; add to first mixture. Shape approximately ½ tablespoonful of mixture around each cherry. Cover and refrigerate at least 1 hour. Melt chocolate over warm water. Holding stem, dip coated cherries into chocolate, coating carefully and completely. Place on waxed paper. After 5 minutes, garnish with coconut, sprinkles or nuts if desired. Refrigerate until chocolate has hardened. Yields: 30.

Substitution for 1 oz. unsweetened chocolate — 3 T cocoa & 1 T butter.

VANILLA CARAMELS

2 cups sugar
2 cups half and half, warmed
1 cup corn syrup
½ teaspoon salt
5 tablespoons butter
1 teaspoon vanilla extract
½ cup nuts, broken

Mix sugar, 1 cup of the cream, corn syrup and salt in large saucepan. Cook, stirring for about 10 minutes. Add remaining cream very slowly so mixture does not stop boiling. Cook 5 minutes longer. Stir in butter, 1 teaspoon at a time. Cook slowly, stirring, until 248° registers on candy thermometer. Remove from heat; add vanilla and nuts and mix gently. Pour into buttered 8x8 pan and cool. Turn out on board and mark off ¾ inch squares and cut. Wrap in waxed paper. Yields: 2 pounds.

Variation: Chocolate caramels – add 3 or 4 ounces unsweetened chocolate to mixture before cooking.

NEW ORLEANS CREAM PRALINES

1 pound light brown sugar
⅛ teaspoon salt
¾ cup evaporated milk
1 tablespoon butter (no substitution)
2 cups pecan halves
½ teaspoon vanilla extract

In a 2 quart saucepan, combine sugar, salt, milk and butter. Cook and stir over low heat until sugar dissolves. Add pecans and continue cooking and stirring over low heat to soft ball stage of 234° on candy thermometer. Remove from heat; stir in vanilla; cook 5 minutes. Meanwhile cover a large baking sheet with aluminum foil or place large sheet of foil on flat surface. Cook and stir mixture until it begins to thicken and coats pecans lightly. Remove from heat and beat until creamy. Drop rapidly from tablespoon onto foil to form patties. If candy becomes too stiff to handle, stir in few drops of hot water. Let patties stand until cool and set. Yields: 20 patties.

FUDGE

2 cups sugar
½ teaspoon salt
2 ounces unsweetened chocolate
2 tablespoons light corn syrup
⅔ cup milk
1 tablespoon butter
1 teaspoon vanilla extract

Combine sugar, salt, chocolate, syrup, and milk in saucepan. Mix well and boil 5-10 minutes on medium heat, stirring constantly. Cook until candy thermometer reads 234°. Add butter and vanilla; beat well. Pour into buttered 8x8 pan. Cut when practically cooled. Yields: 25 pieces.

CREAMY HOLIDAY FUDGE

"A favorite from our old cookbook."

2 cups sugar
⅔ cup evaporated milk
12 marshmallows
½ cup butter
pinch of salt
6 ounces chocolate chips
1 cup pecans, chopped
1 teaspoon vanilla

Mix sugar, milk, marshmallows, butter, and salt in heavy saucepan. Cook over medium heat until mixture comes to full boil, stirring constantly. Remove from heat. Stir in chocolate chips; continue to cook and stir for five minutes. Add nuts and vanilla; pour into a buttered 8x8 pan. Cool and cut into squares.

ENGLISH TOFFEE

"Everyone will fight for the last one."

1 cup sugar
1 cup butter (no substitute)
3 tablespoons water
1 teaspoon vanilla extract
¾ cup pecans, chopped (optional)

Place first 4 ingredients in heavy saucepan. Cook over medium heat, stirring constantly, until 280° registers on candy thermometer or turns deep tan in color. Pour into greased 9x9 pan. Sprinkle pecans on top if desired. When cool, break in bite size pieces. Store in tight container.

GRAHAM CRACKER BONBONS

1 cup margarine, melted
1 teaspoon vanilla extract
⅓ pound graham crackers, crushed
1 cup nuts, chopped
3½ ounces coconut
6 ounces peanut butter
confectioners' sugar
⅕ pound paraffin wax
6 ounces chocolate chips

Mix all ingredients except confectioners' sugar, paraffin wax and chocolate chips. Add enough confectioners' sugar so that balls can be made of mixture. Melt chocolate chips and paraffin in top of double boiler. Dip walnut-size balls into chocolate mixture; place on waxed paper to harden. Yields: 50.

CANDIED GRAPEFRUIT PEEL

"An old-time holiday candy."

2 or 3 grapefruit
1 cup sugar, per grapefruit
½ cup water, per grapefruit

Remove pulp and inner skin from grapefruit. Cut peel into long strips ½ inch wide. Soak peel 24 hours in water to cover, changing water several times. Put peel in fresh cold water and boil 5 minutes; repeat twice. The third time, boil peel until tender. (It can be easily pierced with a fork.) Drain and let rest. Make heavy syrup using sugar and water per grapefruit. Cook syrup until 238° registers on candy thermometer. Add grapefruit; simmer until most of syrup has evaporated (about ½ hour). Watch pan to prevent grapefruit from sticking. Drain in sieve. Roll the peel, few pieces at a time, in sugar. Cool and store in covered containers. Flavor improves after 1 week.

MINTS

½ cup butter
½ cup cold water
1 envelope plain gelatin
2-3 pounds confectioners' sugar
5 drops oil of peppermint

Mix until smooth butter, gelatin softened in water, confectioners' sugar and oil of peppermint. Add as much confectioners' sugar as mixture will take. Place in refrigerator for several hours. Then roll out small amount of mixture and cut in shapes with small cutter.

PECAN BRITTLE

1½ cups pecans, coarsely broken
1⅛ cups sugar
1 cup butter

Place aluminum foil on cookie sheet. Spread pecans on top and set aside. Mix sugar and butter in large saucepan. Using long handled wooden spoon, heat and stir constantly until mixture turns the color of a brown paper bag. Match the sack color exactly. Pour over pecans and spread. Cool and break into pieces. Yields: 1 pound.

Successful candy cannot be made on rainy and/or humid days.

OLD-TIME PENUCHE

4½ cups brown sugar, firmly packed
1 cup evaporated milk
½ cup butter or margarine
¼ teaspoon salt
1 teaspoon vanilla extract
2 cups walnuts, chopped

In large saucepan mix sugar, milk, butter, and salt. Cook, stirring until sugar dissolves. Continue cooking until 238° registers on candy thermometer, or until small amount of mixture dropped into cold water forms soft ball. Remove from heat and let stand until 170° registers on candy thermometer. Add vanilla and walnuts. Beat until mixture is thick and loses its gloss. Pour into buttered 9x9 square pan. When firm cut into squares. Yields: 3 pounds.

COLLECTION OF PIEDMONT ATTRACTIONS

Typical of the new South is the stretch of forested, gently rolling hills which separate N.C.'s coastal and mountain regions. Native Tar Heels call this the Piedmont. Do not pass too quickly on the modern thoroughfares when you visit the midlands for there is much to see and do in this region which links old and new.

Carowinds — outstanding theme park which sits astride the North and South Carolina state line; outside Charlotte

Chinqua — Penn Plantation — priceless collection of art and furnishings; Reidsville

Duke University Chapel — 210 foot Gothic cathedral spire; Durham

Gaddy's Wild Goose Refuge — winter home of Canada geese; Ansonville

Historic Hillsboro — former colonial capital, museum

Andrew Johnson's Birthplace — birthplace of 17th U.S. President; Raleigh

Mint Museum of Art — museum in former U.S. Mint; houses a permanent collection of paintings, porcelain and sculpture; Charlotte

Morehead Planetarium — scientific exhibits; UNC at Chapel Hill

Lake Norman — state's largest man-made lake; between Charlotte and Statesville

N.C. Museum of Art — Raleigh

N.C. Museum of History — Raleigh

N.C. Museum of Life & Science — Durham

N.C. Capital — built in 1833; Raleigh

N.C. State Legislative Building — home of General Assembly; Raleigh

N.C. State Museum — natural history museum; Raleigh

N.C. State Zoo — features natural confinement areas for animals from every continent; Asheboro

Nuclear Reactor Building — N.C. State University campus; Raleigh

Old Salem — restored 18th century Moravian town; Winston-Salem

Pottery Centers — near Seagrove and Sanford

Research Triangle Park — industrial-governmental research area; Raleigh

Reynolda House — estate of late R.J. Reynolds containing outstanding collection of American art; Winston-Salem

The Sandhills — year-round resort towns of Pinehurst and Southern Pines located here; winter golfing capital of the mid-south

World Golf Hall of Fame — contains memorabilia of interest to golfers and golf lovers; Pinehurst

desserts

THE CAROLINA COLLECTOR'S CONCOCTIONS

. . . To make sweetened condensed milk, use 1 c instant dry milk, ⅔ c sugar, ⅓ c boiling water, 3 T melted margarine. Combine in blender until smooth. Store in refrigerator. Yields 14 oz.

. . . To make almond paste, grind 1½ c blanched almonds fine; mix with 1 egg white, 1 t almond extract, ¼ t salt, & 1½ c confectioners' sugar. Work until stiff & refrigerate.

. . . For granola ice cream, mix 2 c whipped cream with 1 can prepared frosting & 2 c granola. Freeze.

. . . For lemon snow, freeze 4 c water, 2 c sugar, 1 c lemon juice & rind until slushy; serve.

. . . To make frozen yogurt, mix 3 oz. jello, 1 c boiling water, 8 oz. yogurt & ½ T honey. Freeze.

. . . A quick mousse — in blender, blend 2 min., 6 oz. chocolate chips, 2 eggs, ¾ c scalded milk, 3 T strong hot coffee, 1 T rum. Chill only 2-3 hrs.

. . . Coat baking cups with melted chocolate chips & chill. Fill with ice cream, custard or fresh fruit.

. . . Make blender applesauce by mixing 4 apples cut in ⅛'s, ¼ c orange juice, ¼ c sugar & ¼ t cinnamon. Blend well.

. . . Pour powdered expresso coffee over vanilla ice cream; pour 2 T Scotch whiskey over this & serve.

. . . Place a caramel in bottom of custard cup before baking & when inverted you have a caramel sauce.

. . . Sauté bananas in butter & sugar 5 min.

. . . Quick ice cream — mix 56 oz. any carbonated beverage & 2 cans condensed milk. Freeze in electric freezer.

. . . Cook 1 c instant cocoa & 1 T milk until smooth; add 1 T peanut butter & stir until mixed. Serve over ice cream.

. . . Pour hot caramel sauce over split bananas & sprinkle with peanuts.

. . . Make a speedy cheesecake with 8 oz. cream cheese, 2 c milk & instant lemon pudding. Pour in graham cracker crust & chill 1 hour.

GREAT SMOKEY MOUNTAIN APPLES WITH NUTS

1 cup sugar
3 cups water
6 baking apples, cored and peeled
1½ cups pecans, chopped
½ pint whipping cream, whipped

Combine sugar and water; boil over medium high heat until it forms a moderately thick syrup. Place apples in syrup. Cook until tender, but not to pieces. Remove apples. When syrup is thick, remove pan from heat. Dip apples in syrup; roll in pecans. Place in two quart serving dish and place briefly in oven to brown (use broiler but put apples on low rack in oven). When nicely browned, remove to individual serving dishes; cool slightly. Serve with whipped cream. Yields: 6 servings.

DELICIOUS APPLE DESSERT

"A quick dessert for a busy day."

40 ounces apple pie filling (or fresh apples peeled and sliced)
¾ cup margarine, softened
18.5 ounces Duncan Hines white cake mix
2 cups nuts, chopped

Preheat oven to 350°. Lightly grease 3 quart casserole. Place apples in casserole. Combine margarine, cake mix and nuts; sprinkle over apples. Bake until topping browns. Yields: 8-10 servings.
Note: Excellent served topped with ice cream or Cool Whip.

COLD BANANA PUDDING

3 boxes instant vanilla pudding, 3¾ ounces each
5 cups milk
8 ounces sour cream
9 ounces Cool Whip
1 pound vanilla wafers
3-4 large bananas

Mix pudding and milk; add sour cream and ½ of Cool Whip. Line 3 quart round casserole with wafers. Top with layer of sliced bananas and ½ of pudding. Repeat layers. Top with remaining Cool Whip. Chill. Yields: 10-12 servings.

CARAMEL PRALINE SOUFFLÉ

1 tablespoon unflavored gelatin
1½ cups cold water, divided
35 caramels
2 tablespoons sugar
5 eggs, separated
¼ teaspoon salt
1 cup whipping cream, whipped

Soften gelatin in ½ cup water. Melt caramels and sugar with remaining water in double boiler, stirring occasionally, until sauce is smooth. Stir small amount into egg yolks; return to hot mixture. Cook 3 minutes over low heat, stirring constantly. Stir in gelatin. Cool to room temperature. Beat egg white with salt until foamy; continue beating until stiff peaks form. Fold egg whites and whipped cream into caramel mixture. Wrap a 3 inch collar of aluminum foil around top of 1 or 1½ quart soufflé dish and secure with tape. Pour mixture into dish; chill until firm. Remove foil collar before serving. Garnish with topping.

Topping:
2 tablespoons sugar
¼ cup pecans, well chopped and toasted

Melt sugar in skillet over low heat (will take fairly long to do this) until clear and caramel-colored. Add nuts; stir until well coated. Spoon onto greased cookie sheet. Immediately separate nuts with 2 forks. Cool, break into small pieces, and sprinkle over soufflé before serving. Yields: 6-8 servings.

SAUCY CHERRY DESSERT

"A rich, delicious winter dessert."

Pudding:
1¼ cups sugar
1 cup plain flour
1 teaspoon cinnamon
1 teaspoon baking soda
½ teaspoon salt
1 cup pecans, chopped
16½ ounces dark sweet pitted cherries, drained and juice reserved
1 egg, beaten
2 tablespoons butter, melted

Sauce:
reserved cherry juice
1 tablespoon plain flour
½ cup sugar
2 tablespoons butter, melted
whipping cream, whipped, for garnish

Preheat oven to 350°. Combine all pudding ingredients; beat well. Pour into 8 inch spring form pan. Bake 40 minutes. While torte is baking, combine sugar and flour in saucepan. Slowly stir in juice and butter. Cook over medium heat, stirring constantly, until thick. Remove from heat; keep warm. Cool torte 15 minutes before cutting into wedges. Spoon sauce over; top with whipped cream. Yields: 6-9 servings.

BRANDY ALEXANDER SOUFFLÉ

2 envelopes unflavored gelatin
2 cups cold water
1 cup sugar
4 egg yolks
8 ounces cream cheese, softened
6 tablespoons crème de cacao
6 tablespoons brandy
4 egg whites
1 cup whipping cream, whipped

Soften gelatin in 1 cup water. Stir over low heat to dissolve; add remaining water. Remove from heat and blend in ¾ cup sugar and beaten egg yolks. Return to heat and cook 2-3 minutes until thickened. Gradually add to softened cream cheese, mixing until well blended. Stir in crème de cacao and brandy. Chill until slightly thickened. Beat egg whites until soft peaks form. Gradually add remaining ¼ cup sugar, beating until meringue is stiff. Fold egg whites and whipped cream into dessert. Wrap a 3 inch collar of foil around top of 1½ quart soufflé dish. Secure with tape. Pour mixture into dish. Chill until firm. Remove foil collar before serving. Yields: 8-10 servings.

CHOCOLATE DELIGHT

"This is a nice, light, fancy dessert."

4 ounces Baker's German Sweet Chocolate
3 tablespoons water
1 or 2 teaspoons cognac
½ cup pecans, chopped
1 pint whipping cream, whipped
additional whipped cream or whipped topping, for garnish
slivered pecans, for garnish
shaved bitter chocolate, for garnish

Stir chocolate in water over low heat until melted. Remove from heat; allow to cool until thickened. Add cognac and nuts. Whip cream; fold into chocolate mixture. Pour into individual ramekins. Chill 2 hours. Before serving, top with additional whipped cream or topping, slivered pecans, and shaved bitter chocolate. Yields: 4-6 servings.

CHOCOLATE VELVET CREAM

Crust:

1½ cups plain chocolate wafers, crushed
6 tablespoons margarine, melted

Preheat oven to 325°. Combine wafers and margarine. Press into bottom of 9 inch square pan. Bake for 10 minutes.

Filling:

8 ounces cream cheese, softened
½ cup sugar, divided
1 teaspoon vanilla extract
2 eggs, separated
6 ounces semi-sweet chocolate pieces, melted
1 cup whipping cream, whipped
¾ cup pecans, chopped
additional whipping cream, whipped, for garnish
additional semi-sweet chocolate, shaved, for garnish

Combine cream cheese, ¼ cup sugar and vanilla. Mix until well blended. Beat 2 egg yolks; add to cheese, along with melted chocolate pieces. Beat egg whites until soft peaks form, gradually beat in remaining ¼ cup sugar. Fold into chocolate mixture. Fold in whipped cream and pecans. Pour over crumb crust and freeze. Remove from freezer 10 minutes before serving. Cut into squares and garnish with additional whipped cream and chocolate, if desired. Yields: 9 servings.

Substitute cream with 3 T butter and ⅞ c milk per cup of cream.

QUICK AND EASY BLENDER CHOCOLATE MOUSSE

6 ounces semi-sweet chocolate
2 tablespoons Kahlua
1 tablespoon orange juice
2 whole eggs
2 egg yolks
1 teaspoon vanilla extract
¼ cup sugar
1 cup whipping cream
additional whipped cream, for garnish
semi-sweet chocolate, shaved, for garnish

Melt chocolate in Kahlua and orange juice over low heat. Set aside. Put eggs and yolks in blender; add vanilla and sugar. Blend 2 minutes at medium-high. Add cream; blend 30 seconds. Add melted chocolate mixture; blend until smooth. Pour into bowl or small individual cups. Refrigerate. Serve topped with whipped cream and shaved chocolate. Yields: 4-6 servings.

WINTER DATE PUDDING

¾ cup boiling water
1 cup pitted dates, cut up
2 tablespoons butter
1 egg, beaten
½ cup brown sugar, firmly packed
1 cup lemon or orange marmalade
1¾ cups plain flour
½ teaspoon salt
1 teaspoon soda
½ cup pecans, chopped
hard sauce or whipped cream (optional)

Preheat oven to 350°. Grease an 11x7 baking dish. Pour water over dates and butter. Combine egg, brown sugar and marmalade; stir into date mixture. Sift dry ingredients; stir into date mixture. Add nuts. Pour into greased baking dish. Bake about 30 minutes. Cut in squares and serve warm with hard sauce or sweetened whipped cream. Yields: 8 servings.

EGGNOG VELVET

1 tablespoon gelatin
¼ cup cold water
½ cup boiling water
2 eggs, separated
¾ cup sugar
½ cup milk
½ cup whiskey, brandy, or wine (use less for milder taste)
1 cup whipping cream, whipped
½ teaspoon vanilla extract

Dissolve gelatin in ¼ cup cold water. Add boiling water to softened gelatin; let cool. Beat egg yolks in separate bowl. Gradually add sugar, milk and liquor to egg yolks. Beat egg whites in separate bowl until fluffy; fold into egg yolk mixture. Whip cream. Add gelatin and vanilla to whipped cream. Fold into egg yolk mixture. Congeal in sherbet dishes. Yields: 8 servings.

LEMON CAKE TOP PUDDING

"Each serving will contain lemon custard at bottom, spongecake at top!"

2 tablespoons butter, softened
1½ cups sugar
⅓ cup plain flour
¼ teaspoon salt
½ cup fresh lemon juice
1 teaspoon lemon peel, grated
3 eggs, separated
1¼ cups milk

Preheat oven to 375°. Mix butter and sugar together. Add flour, salt, lemon juice and lemon peel. Beat egg yolks; add milk. Combine these 2 mixtures. Stiffly beat 3 egg whites; fold into batter. Pour into a 1½ quart rectangular dish. Set dish in pan of water. Bake 45 minutes. Yields: 6 servings.
"May be served warm or refrigerated and served cold."

DESSERT CREPES

Basic Dessert Crepe:

4 eggs
½ cup milk
½ cup water
½ teaspoon salt
2 tablespoons butter or margarine, melted
2 teaspoons sugar
1 teaspoon vanilla extract
1 cup plain flour

Combine all ingredients except flour in large mixing bowl. Beat with electric mixer on medium speed, gradually adding flour, until all ingredients are combined. If small lumps appear, pour batter through a strainer before using. Cook according to manufacturer's directions for type of crepe utensil being used. Use immediately or stack between sheets of waxed paper, secure in plastic bag and freeze. Allow about 1 hour for frozen crepes to thaw before using. Yields: 12-15 crepes.

Lemon Dream Crepes:

½ cup butter
1 teaspoon lemon peel, grated
½ cup fresh lemon juice
⅛ teaspoon salt
1½ cups sugar
3 egg yolks, beaten
3 eggs, beaten
1 cup whipping cream, whipped and divided
12-15 basic dessert crepes

In saucepan melt butter; add lemon peel, lemon juice, salt and sugar. Stir in beaten egg yolks and whole eggs. Cook over very low heat, beating constantly with a whisk, until mixture is shiny and thick. Cool. Fold one-half of whipped cream into lemon mixture. Spread cooked crepes with lemon cream; roll. Crepes may be served immediately or refrigerated, covered, for 4-5 hours. Serve with remaining whipped cream.

Brandied Peach Crepes with Almond Cream Sauce:

3 or 4 large fresh or home frozen peaches, peeled and sliced
¾ cup sugar, divided
2 tablespoons peach brandy (or to taste)
¼ teaspoon salt
2 tablespoons cornstarch
2 cups half and half
2 egg yolks, beaten
1 tablespoon butter or margarine
½ teaspoon almond extract
10-12 basic dessert crepes
¼ cup slivered almonds, toasted

Combine peaches, ¼ cup sugar and peach brandy. Set aside. In heavy saucepan, combine remaining ½ cup sugar, salt and cornstarch. Stir well. Gradually add half and half. Cook over medium heat, stirring constantly, until mixture thickens. Remove from heat; gradually stir part of hot mixture into beaten egg yolks. Return egg mixture to saucepan. Simmer 1 minute, stirring frequently. Remove from heat. Stir in butter or margarine and almond extract. To serve, spoon sliced peaches into cooked crepe, fold. Spoon warm almond cream over crepe and sprinkle with toasted almonds. Serve immediately.

Fudge Sundae Crepes:

½ cup butter
1 cup sugar
⅛ teaspoon salt
1 teaspoon instant coffee powder
2 tablespoons rum
⅓ cup cocoa
1 cup whipping cream
1 teaspoon vanilla extract
15-18 basic dessert crepes
15-18 small scoops vanilla ice cream
whipped cream (optional)

Melt butter in saucepan. Blend in sugar, salt, coffee powder, rum and cocoa. Add cream. Simmer about 5 minutes, stirring occasionally. Remove from heat; add vanilla. Fill each crepe with one scoop vanilla ice cream. Fold. Spoon hot fudge sauce over filled crepes. Serve topped with whipped cream if desired. Serve immediately.

One T brandy or your favorite liqueur added to the basic crepe batter makes a delicious variation.

SPICY ORANGE SUNDAE

4 medium oranges
¾ cup sugar
1 teaspoon cornstarch
¾ teaspoon ground ginger
½ teaspoon cinnamon
2 tablespoons raisins
1½ pints (approximately) vanilla ice cream

Halve oranges making zig-zag edges around top of each cup half. Remove and retain pulp. Rinse scooped out shells, dry and put in freezing compartment. Meanwhile, strain pulp to remove seeds and fibrous material. Put remaining pulp in saucepan with mixture of sugar, cornstarch, ginger and cinnamon. Bring to boil. Add raisins and boil gently about 12 minutes or until it begins to thicken. Chill before serving. Remove orange shells from freezer. Fill each with a scoop of vanilla ice cream. Cover with foil. Return to freezer. To serve, put each filled orange in small dish and pour spicy syrup over them. Yields: 8 servings.

"Delicious and pretty to look at as well. Can be made several days ahead. Just place sauce in jar in refrigerator and allow to come to room temperature before serving."

ORANGE DELIGHT

"An interesting, though tart, dessert."

1 cup orange juice
juice of 1 lemon
rind of 2 oranges, grated
½ cup sugar
4 tablespoons plain flour
4 eggs, separated
½ cup butter, softened
1 cup confectioners' sugar
2 packages lady fingers, without filling
whipping cream, whipped

Cook first five ingredients in saucepan, stirring with wooden spoon until mixture begins to thicken. Add 4 egg yolks, one at a time; cook until very thick. Set aside to cool. Cream butter and powdered sugar; add to cold custard. Fold in stiffly beaten egg whites: Line bottom and sides of 2 quart mold or dish with lady fingers; pour in mixture. Chill several hours. Serve covered with whipped cream. Yields: 8-10 servings.

Melt chocolate in coffee instead of water when making chocolate sauce.

LAFAYETTE FRENCH MERINGUES

"These are so nice to pass after a buffet meal."

Base:
3 egg whites
1 cup sugar
15 saltine cracker squares, crushed
1 cup nuts, chopped
1 teaspoon vanilla extract

Topping:
1 cup butter, softened
2 cups confectioners' sugar
4 ounces bitter chocolate, melted and cooled
3 egg yolks
1 egg
¾ teaspoon mint extract
2 teaspoons vanilla extract

Preheat oven to 350°. Beat egg whites until stiff. Add sugar, crushed saltine crackers and nuts. Mix well. Add vanilla. Put 1-2 teaspoons of mixture in 2 inch cup cake liners placed in muffin tins. Spread evenly over bottom with back of spoon. Bake 10-15 minutes, or just until lightly browned. Set aside to cool before adding topping.

For topping, combine butter and sugar with mixer and beat on medium speed for 5 minutes. Blend in melted chocolate. Add egg yolks, one at a time, beating well after each; then add whole egg. Continue to beat. Add mint and vanilla. Put mixture on top of cup cakes and freeze. Yields: 36 tarts.

Note: 1. These can be made well ahead, frozen, and thawed about 10 minutes before serving.

2. For variety, substitute 1 teaspoon almond extract for mint. To make mocha tarts, combine 3 teaspoons instant coffee granules with ½ teaspoon water, instead of mint extract.

FOUR SEASONS FROZEN LEMON SOUFFLÉ

8 egg whites, beaten
1¼ cups sugar
8 lemons, juice and grated rind
1 pint whipping cream, whipped
½ teaspoon lemon extract
1-2 drops yellow food coloring
12 large frozen strawberries, for garnish

While beating whites, gradually add sugar, lemon juice and rind. To whipped cream, add lemon extract and food coloring. Add this mixture to egg white mixture. Pour into 6 inch soufflé mold. Chill in freezer for a minimum of 6 hours. Garnish with fresh strawberries, if desired. Yields: 12 servings.

GARDEN CLUB DESSERT

2 cups Rice Chex Cereal
½ cup slivered almonds
½ cup coconut
½ cup butter, melted
½ cup light brown sugar, packed
1 quart vanilla ice cream, softened
¼ cup Smuckers or Evans butterscotch sauce

Preheat oven to 225°. Crumble, with hands, the cereal; set aside. Toast almonds and coconut until lightly browned. Mix together butter, brown sugar, Rice Chex, coconut and almonds. Stir until well mixed, cool slightly, set aside. Press 1 quart vanilla ice cream in 8x8 dish. Dribble butterscotch sauce over ice cream evenly, spread with crumb mixture. Put in freezer. Remove 20 minutes before serving. Yields: 8-12 servings.

"Absolutely marvelous to fix for meetings. Fix anytime after the date is set and it keeps if nobody knows it's there. The real advantage is that you can fix it when you don't know how many are coming! It should be taken from freezer about 20 minutes before serving, cut in squares, and can be placed on plates or served on a large tray."

PINEHURST PEACH TRIFLE

"A wonderful way to use fresh peaches."

12 ladyfingers, unfilled
½ cup peach preserves
2 tablespoons sherry
2 cups peaches, fresh or frozen
4½ ounces instant vanilla pudding
2 tablespoons sugar
½ pint whipping cream, whipped
slivered almonds

Split ladyfingers and spread with peach preserves. Reassemble and arrange on bottom of 1½ quart casserole. Sprinkle with sherry. Arrange peaches on top of ladyfingers. Mix pudding according to package directions; pour on top of peaches. Combine sugar and whipping cream; whip until stiff. Spread on top of trifle and sprinkle with almonds. Refrigerate several hours before serving. Yields: 6-8 servings.

Note: *This would be even more delicious with homemade pudding or sauce.*

When cooking use less sugar as fruits sweeten during cooking.

SHERRY CREAM DESSERT

2 tablespoons unflavored gelatin
⅓ cup cold milk
5 eggs, separated
1 cup sugar
½ cup milk
¼ teaspoon salt
¼ teaspoon nutmeg
½ cup sherry
1 pint whipping cream, divided
1 angel food cake (10 or 12 ounce)
bitter chocolate, shaved
toasted almonds

Soften gelatin in milk. Beat egg yolks slightly in top of double boiler. Add sugar and milk to egg mixture; cook slowly and stir until thick; remove from heat. Add gelatin mixture, salt and nutmeg. Add sherry *slowly*. Place in refrigerator to set. When cooled and beginning to set (but before it becomes congealed), remove from refrigerator. Whip ½ pint whipping cream. Beat 5 egg whites in a separate bowl. Fold whipped cream and beaten egg whites into custard mixture. Break angel food cake into small pieces. Grease a 9 or 10 inch tube pan. Alternate layers of cake and layers of cream mixture. Place in refrigerator to set. When set, run knife around edges of pan and unmold cake onto serving platter. Whip remaining ½ pint whipping cream and ice cake. Yields: 20-24 servings.

"May garnish with shaved bitter chocolate or toasted almonds, if desired; but it is delicious just as is."

CHAMPION PERSIMMON PUDDING

1 cup white sugar
1 cup brown sugar
3 egg yolks
½ cup butter, melted
2-2½ cups persimmon pulp
2 cups flour
1 teaspoon soda
1 teaspoon baking powder
1 teaspoon nutmeg
1 teaspoon cinnamon
1 teaspoon vanilla extract
3 cups milk
3 egg whites

Preheat oven to 350°. Mix sugar and egg yolks, add melted butter and persimmon pulp. Add flour, soda, baking powder, nutmeg and cinnamon with the milk and vanilla. Beat egg whites until stiff; fold in batter. Pour in 2 quart rectangular casserole and bake 1 hour. Serve with whipped cream. Freezes well. Yields: 8-10 servings.

Add honey instead of sugar to whipped cream. It helps stabilize cream & keeps it firm longer.

CHADBOURN STRAWBERRY DELIGHT

1 cup plain flour
½ cup butter, melted
¼ cup brown sugar
⅔ cup pecans, finely chopped
24 regular marshmallows
⅔ cup milk
½ pint whipping cream, whipped
6 ounces strawberry flavored gelatin
2 cups hot water
16 ounces frozen, sliced strawberries, partially thawed

Preheat oven to 350°. Mix flour, butter, brown sugar, and pecans together well. Press, like a crust, into a 9x13x2 baking pan, lightly greased. Bake 15 minutes. Cool. Melt marshmallows with milk in a double boiler. *Cool* well. Fold in whipped cream; spread over crust. Chill until *set*. Dissolve gelatin in hot water. Add partially frozen strawberries. Chill 15 minutes before gently pouring strawberry mixture over completely set first 2 layers. Entire dessert must be chilled at least 3 hours, preferably overnight, before serving. Yields: 8 servings.

"A delicious dessert, but success depends upon cooling and setting mixture properly."

STRAWBERRY AND CHOCOLATE MERINGUE CAKE

Meringue:

5 egg whites, at room temperature
¼ teaspoon cream of tartar
¼ teaspoon salt
½ teaspoon vanilla extract
1¼ cups sugar

Filling and Frosting:

6 ounces semi-sweet chocolate chips
3 tablespoons water
1½ teaspoons unflavored gelatin
3 tablespoons cold water
⅓ cup sugar
1 teaspoon vanilla extract
3 cups whipping cream, whipped
3 cups fresh strawberries, sliced (reserve 8 whole strawberries for decoration)

Preheat oven to 250°. To make meringue layers, grease and flour baking sheets to hold 3 meringue layers. Draw three 8 or 9 inch circles using plate as guide. Combine egg whites, cream of tartar, salt, and vanilla. Beat until egg whites hold soft peaks. Gradually add sugar, a tablespoon at a time. Continue beating until meringue is very stiff and dull. Spread meringue evenly over circles. Meringue should be dried rather than baked. Bake 45 minutes. *Do not allow meringues to brown.* After 45 minutes of baking, turn oven off and allow meringue to dry out in oven 1 hour longer. Do not open oven door. They will be crisp and easily removed from pan with spatula. Wrap in plastic wrap when completely cool. (If you should break one, don't worry — no one will know once the cake is assembled.) The meringue layers will keep nicely for a week or more at room temperature if wrapped in plastic wrap. To assemble cake (2-6 hours before serving, or cake can be completely assembled and frozen), melt chocolate in 3 tablespoons water over boiling water. Soften gelatin in 3 tablespoons cold water. Stir over low heat until gelatin dissolves and looks clear. Beat dissolved gelatin, sugar, and vanilla into cream just as it begins to thicken. Place a meringue layer on serving plate and drizzle some melted chocolate over it. Spread with a thick layer of whipped cream and top this with a layer of sliced strawberries. Place another meringue layer on top, drizzle with more chocolate and spread with more whipped cream and layer with rest of strawberries. Top with last layer of meringue. Drizzle rest of chocolate over and cover top and sides with last of whipped cream. Decorate with 8 reserved strawberries. Freeze for 2-6 hours before serving, or freeze cake and when frozen, wrap air-tight and freeze for up to 6 weeks. Serve frozen. Yields: 15 servings.

Note: Strawberries may be folded into whipped cream instead of layering them. Gelatin and water may be omitted (gelatin keeps cream from running).

STRAWBERRY MERINGUE ROLL

"This is a beautiful jelly roll type dessert for special occasions. It is a springtime specialty for those who don't mind spending a little effort."

Cake:

4 egg yolks
¾ cup sugar, divided
½ teaspoon vanilla extract
4 egg whites
¾ cup cake flour
¼ teaspoon salt
1 teaspoon baking powder

Preheat oven to 375°. Line a 15x10 baking sheet pan with waxed paper. Beat egg yolks until thick and lemon colored. Gradually add ¼ cup sugar and vanilla. Beat egg whites until almost stiff and gradually add remaining sugar. Beat very stiff. Fold in egg yolk mixture, then sifted dry ingredients. Bake in prepared pan 12 minutes. Turn onto tea towel dusted with confectioners' sugar. Remove paper. Trim edges of cake. Top with fresh waxed paper, cut the size of cake. Quickly roll lengthwise with waxed paper on inside. Wrap in sugared cloth. Put on cake rack to cool. When cool, unroll, remove paper and spread with filling.

Strawberry Filling:

¾ cup whipping cream
2 tablespoons sugar
1 cup strawberries, sliced

Add sugar to cream and whip; fold in strawberries. Spread on cake, roll up again, cover loosely with cloth and chill. Frost with meringue.

Strawberry Meringue:

¾ cup strawberries, sliced
½ cup sugar
1 egg white
⅛ teaspoon salt

Combine above ingredients, and beat with electric mixer until very stiff, 7-10 minutes. Meringue will be a delicate pink. Decorate with whole stemmed strawberries. Yields: 12-14 servings.

To soften hardened sugar, place in warm oven 10-15 min.

Butter springform pan well & ladyfingers will stay in place.

FROSTY STRAWBERRY SQUARES

"A beautiful, light dessert. Perfect way to use fresh strawberries."

1 cup plain or self-rising flour, sifted
¼ cup brown sugar
½ cup pecans or walnuts, chopped
½ cup margarine, melted
2 egg whites
1 cup granulated sugar
2 cups fresh strawberries, sliced (or 20 ounces frozen strawberries, thawed and drained)
2 tablespoons lemon juice
1 cup whipping cream, whipped
fresh whole strawberries, for garnish

Preheat oven to 350°. Stir together first four ingredients; spread evenly in shallow baking pan. Bake 20 minutes, stirring occasionally. (Mixture should be light brown.) Sprinkle ⅔ of crumbs in a 13x9x2 baking dish. Combine egg whites, sugar, berries and lemon juice in large bowl of electric mixer. Beat at high speed until stiff peaks form, about 15-20 minutes. Fold in whipped cream. Spoon over crumbs; top with remaining crumbs. Freeze 6 hours or overnight. Cut in squares to serve, and top with fresh whole strawberries. Yields: 10-12 servings.

"This dessert will keep indefinitely and remain delicious. Each square may be topped with additional cream and whole berry, if desired."

RASPBERRY CREAM SWIRL

¾ cup graham cracker crumbs
2 tablespoons butter, melted
2 tablespoons sugar
3 eggs, separated
8 ounces cream cheese, softened
1 cup sugar
⅛ teaspoon salt
1 cup whipping cream, whipped (or Cool Whip)
10 ounces frozen raspberries, partially thawed

Preheat oven to 375°. Combine graham cracker crumbs, butter and 2 tablespoons sugar; pat in 7x11 dish. Bake 8 minutes. Cool. Beat egg yolks until thick. Mix cream cheese, salt and 1 cup sugar, separately, until smooth. Combine eggs with cheese mixture. Beat egg whites until stiff. Fold egg whites and whipped cream into cheese mixture. Blend raspberries in blender until smooth. Pour ½ of raspberries into cheese mixture. Put cheese mixture on crust. Pour remaining berries on top and swirl with a knife. Place in freezer, covered, until firm. Yields: 8 servings.

Note: A thin layer of yellow sponge cake may be substituted for crust. Strawberries or blueberries may be substituted for raspberries.

BUTTER PECAN ICE CREAM

14 ounces sweetened condensed milk
14 ounces water
1 cup dark brown sugar
dash salt
5 eggs, beaten
1 pint half and half
milk to "fill" mark on freezer
1 teaspoon vanilla extract (or to taste)
1 drop maple flavoring
1 teaspoon butter flavoring
1 cup toasted pecans, chopped

Combine condensed milk, water and brown sugar in top of double boiler. Cook over simmering water until heated. Beat with rotary beater until smooth. Add a little hot mixture to beaten eggs and return to milk in boiler. Cook over simmering water, stirring constantly, until slightly thickened. Remove from heat and cool completely. Toast pecans with 1 tablespoon margarine and a *little* salt in aluminum pan at 300° until toasted. In freezer can, combine cooled mixture, half and half, vanilla, maple and butter flavorings and enough milk to "fill" line. Freeze until slightly mushy; add chopped pecans. Freeze, pack and let mellow for several hours.

BUTTERFINGER ICE CREAM

5 pints half and half
2½-3 cups sugar
2 teaspoons vanilla extract
12 Butterfinger candy bars, crushed

Combine all ingredients in container of ice cream freezer. Freeze according to manufacturer's directions. When frozen, pack in ice or transfer container to freezer compartment of refrigerator to mellow for 2-3 hours before serving. Yields: 5 quarts.

ORANGE-PINEAPPLE SHERBET

60 ounces orange crush drink, chilled
28 ounces sweetened condensed milk
15 ounces crushed pineapple, drained

Mix all ingredients in freezing container and freeze according to manufacturer's directions. Yields: 1 gallon.

FOUR FRUIT SHERBET

1 cup fully-ripe bananas, mashed
⅔ cup sugar
½ teaspoon orange peel, grated
⅓ cup orange juice
1 tablespoon lemon juice
1 cup cranberry juice cocktail
6 drops red food coloring
1 egg white, stiffly-beaten

Combine mashed banana, sugar, orange peel, orange juice and lemon juice. Beat until mixture is smooth. Stir in cranberry juice cocktail and food coloring. Put into a 4-cup refrigerator tray; freeze until firm. Break mixture into chunks; turn into chilled mixer bowl. With chilled beaters, beat mixture until smooth. Fold in beaten egg white; return mixture to cold refrigerator tray. Freeze until firm. Let stand at room temperature a few minutes before serving. Yields: 6 servings.

Note: This keeps well in the freezer and is good with pineapple slices for a quick salad.

STRAWBERRY PATCH SHERBET

"Ice cream parlor taste."

4 quarts or less fresh strawberries, sliced
4 cups sugar
2⅔ cups milk
⅔ cup orange juice
⅛ teaspoon ground cinnamon

Mix strawberries and sugar; let stand until juicy (about 1½ hours). Mash or purée in blender (strain for a seedless sherbet). Add milk, orange juice and cinnamon. Mix well. Pour into 1 gallon freezer can and freeze. Yields: 1 gallon.

FRUITED VELVET ICE CREAM

1½ quarts half and half
5-6 eggs, well beaten
1½ cups sugar
1 teaspoon vanilla extract
½ cup pecans, chopped
½ cup bananas, diced
½ cup maraschino cherries, chopped
½ cup crushed pineapple, well drained
½ cup strawberries, sliced
¼ cup sugar
½ teaspoon salt

Cook milk, eggs and sugar over low heat until thick. Add vanilla. Set aside to cool. Mix fruits with sugar and salt. Let set 5 minutes. Add to cool custard. Pour into 5 quart ice cream freezer and freeze according to manufacturer's directions. Yields: 30 single scoops.

"Can be made up to 48 hours ahead, placed in freezer after churning, and left to harden. Remove from freezer the morning of serving and scoop out with a ball ice cream scoop into muffin papers in colors of party decor. Place attractively on silver platter and place in freezer until serving time. This makes ice cream serving simple, but elegant, and no last minute mess."

BUTTERSCOTCH SAUCE

¾ cup brown sugar (light or dark)
⅓ cup light corn syrup
2 tablespoons butter
½ cup whipping cream

In saucepan, mix together brown sugar, corn syrup and butter. Cook, stirring constantly, until well blended (at least 5 minutes). Cool. Add whipping cream and beat well. Yields: 1⅓ cups.

CRUNCHY CHOCOLATE SYRUP

1 cup chocolate chips
½ cup butter or margarine
1 cup pecans, chopped

Melt butter, add chocolate chips. Stir over medium-low heat until melted. Remove from heat and add nuts. Yields: 1⅓ cups.
"When sauce cools on ice cream, it forms a firm, smooth coating – similar to ice-cream-on-a-stick chocolate. A most delectable flavor."

BUTTERED RUM SAUCE

½ cup sugar
4 teaspoons cornstarch
⅛ teaspoon salt
1 cup hot water
2 tablespoons butter, at room temperature
2 tablespoons whipping cream
1 teaspoon vanilla extract
2 tablespoons dark rum
raisins, optional

Mix sugar, cornstarch, and salt in small, heavy saucepan. Gradually stir in water. Cook over moderate heat, stirring gently and constantly, about 5 minutes or until mixture is thick and clear. Remove from heat. Add butter; stir until melted. Add cream, vanilla, and rum. Serve warm, at room temperature or cold. Yields: 1⅓ cups.

COLLECTION OF COASTAL ATTRACTIONS

Where is eastern North Carolina? Ask a mountain man or a resident of the midlands and he'll tell you, "Down Yonder." "Down Yonder" is roughly one-third of N.C. and covers a broad sweep of beaches and islands, rivers and fields and friendly people.

Historic Bath — N.C.'s oldest town; incorporated in 1705

Beaufort — 18th century seaport; historic dwellings

Bentonville Battleground — site of largest Civil War battle in N.C.; Johnston County

Blockade Runner Museum — artifacts from sunken blockade runners; Wilmington

Calabash — known for delicious seafood; Calabash

Edenton — colonial town; several 18th century buildings

Fort Raleigh — historic drama "The Lost Colony" presented here; near Manteo

Hope Plantation — restoration of old mansion; near Windsor

Kitty Hawk — site of Wright Brothers first powered flight; December 17, 1903; Kitty Hawk

Lake Mattamuskeet — state's largest natural lake; famous for hunting and as a refuge

Nags Head — Largest of outer banks resort areas

Ocracoke — Blackbeard's Hideout: It was no secret that Blackbeard, the notorious pirate whose real name was Edward Teach, once used the remote island of Ocracoke as his base of operations. Blackbeard made his home in Bath and was killed near Ocracoke in 1718. The night before he died, one of his crew asked if Blackbeard's wife knew where his treasure was buried. "Nobody but me and the devil knows," Blackbeard replied, "and the longest liver will take all."

Orton Plantation — 18th century rice plantation famous for gardens; Wilmington

Tryon Palace — restored colonial governor's residence; first state capital; furnished with antiques, formal gardens; New Bern

U.S.S. N.C. Battleship — World War II battleship berthed in Cape Fear River; Wilmington

Murfreesboro — restoration program underway to preserve 70 mid-1850 Victorian homes

eggs and cheese

THE CAROLINA COLLECTOR'S CONCOCTIONS

. . . For a new twist, poach an egg in tomato juice or tomato soup.

. . . An easy soufflé is made with 6 beaten egg yolks & 6 stiffly beaten egg whites with ¼ t cream of tartar. This may be folded into any can of cream soup plus Swiss, Cheddar or Gruyere cheese, cooked meat or vegetables & spices such as basil, curry, nutmeg or dill.

. . . Add fried onion, hamburger, avocado & chili powder to an omelet.

. . . Add chutney, onion rings, curry powder & chicken to make an extra special omelet.

. . . Add drained fruit, cinnamon & cottage cheese or cream cheese to an omelet for a refreshing taste.

. . . Serve poached eggs on a nest of croutons & top with brandy laced cream sauce.

. . . Scramble eggs with diced cooked bacon & potatoes.

. . . Serve poached eggs on hearts of palm slices & top with buttered spinach & hollandaise sauce.

. . . Cut a round out of bread & fry; fry egg in the circle.

. . . For a real lift to a cheese omelet, crumble a few rose geranium leaves in the omelet.

. . . Add a thin slice or 2 of raw apple to a cheese sandwich.

. . . Make a turnover filling of sausage, hard cooked eggs & chives. Pour a mushroom sauce over all.

. . . Cook 1 can spaghetti in tomato sauce with 1 can corn with peppers; top with sliced cheese. Heat 10 min.

BACON GOURMET

1 egg yolk
1 teaspoon mustard
2 teaspoons Worcestershire sauce
5 strips bacon
dry bread crumbs

Preheat oven to 250°. Combine egg yolk, mustard and Worcestershire sauce in a small bowl. Dip bacon in mixture to coat and then in dry bread crumbs. Lay on wire rack placed on baking sheet. Bake 25 minutes. Yields: 2 servings.

CAMP-STYLE EGGS AND CORN

"Excellent cooked on outdoor grill or indoors."

½ pound bulk sausage
16 ounces canned cream style corn
6 eggs
minced onions
minced green peppers

Brown sausage in skillet; pour off fat. Add corn. Beat eggs. Add eggs to corn-sausage mixture. Cook as for scrambled eggs. Add onions and green peppers, stirring gently. Yields: 6 servings.

DEVILED EGGS AND SHRIMP

"Wonderful with a green salad for supper before or after the theatre."

1 pound shrimp, cooked and cleaned
6 hard-cooked eggs
1 tablespoon anchovy paste
1 teaspoon onion juice
6 tablespoons butter
salt and pepper
¼ cup plain flour
1 cup milk
½ cup whipping cream
2 tablespoons sherry
Parmesan cheese, grated

Mash egg yolks and combine with anchovy paste, onion juice and 2 tablespoons butter. Season with salt and pepper. Use mixture to stuff egg whites. Place eggs in 2 quart casserole. Make a cream sauce with 4 tablespoons of butter, flour, milk and cream. Season with salt. Stir in shrimp and then sherry. Pour over eggs and sprinkle generously with grated Parmesan cheese. Heat in medium-hot oven until bubbly. Yields: 4-6 servings.

BRUNCH SPECIAL

"This is an egg-vegetable filled crepe that is ideal for entertaining."

Sauce:

2 tablespoons cooking oil
4 medium onions, thinly sliced
2 green peppers, thinly sliced
½ pound fresh mushrooms, thinly sliced
1 clove garlic, minced
6 medium tomatoes, peeled, seeded and chopped
½ teaspoon salt
½ teaspoon seasoned salt
⅛ teaspoon pepper
½ teaspoon fine herbs

Heat oil in large saucepan; add onions and peppers. Sauté until tender. Stir in mushrooms, garlic, tomatoes, salt, seasoned salt, pepper and fine herbs. Cover; cook 5 minutes. Uncover; cook over medium heat several minutes, stirring several times.

Filling:

8 eggs
¼ teaspoon salt
⅛ teaspoon pepper
2 tablespoons butter

Beat eggs, salt and pepper. Heat butter in large skillet. Pour in egg mixture; stir with fork or wooden spoon until eggs are set, but still creamy. Stir in the sauce. Remove egg mixture from heat.

24 cooked crepes
Hollandaise Sauce, see Index for recipe
avocado slices

Spoon about 3 tablespoons filling into the center of each crepe. Fold over; place in two 9x13 baking pans. Crepes may be frozen at this point. When ready to serve, thaw, cover and bake at 350° 10-15 minutes. Spoon hollandaise sauce over each crepe and top with an avocado slice at serving time. Yields: 24 crepes.

Crepes:

4 eggs
¾ cup cold water
¾ cup cold milk
½ teaspoon salt
2 cups flour
4 tablespoons butter

Place all ingredients in blender and blend 1 minute at medium speed. Refrigerate 2 hours.

EGGS BENEDICT HOLIDAY SPECIAL

3 English muffins, split and toasted
6 thin slices country ham, cooked
6 eggs, poached

Split English muffins and toast lightly. Place thin slice ham on each piece. Place 1 poached egg on top of ham. Spoon hollandaise sauce over eggs. Serve at once. Yields: 3 servings.

Hollandaise Sauce:
2 egg yolks
½ cup margarine, melted
1 tablespoon lemon juice
½ teaspoon salt

Place top of double boiler over lukewarm water on low heat. Stir egg yolks in top pan until thick and lemon colored. Add ⅓ of the melted butter, a little at a time, beating constantly. Slowly add remainder of the butter, alternately with lemon juice, continuing to beat constantly. Season with salt.
"This is a good use for leftover ham and great for brunch or supper."

2 egg yolks plus 1 T water may be substituted for 1 egg.

EGGS ENTERALLIS

4 tablespoons butter
4 tablespoons plain flour
2 cups milk
1 pound sharp Cheddar cheese, grated
1 garlic clove, crushed
¼ teaspoon thyme
¼ teaspoon marjoram
¼ teaspoon basil
2 tablespoons parsley, chopped
18 eggs, hard-cooked and thinly sliced
½ pound bacon, fried and crumbled
bread crumbs, buttered

Preheat oven to 350°. Melt butter in saucepan. Stir in flour; brown slightly. Slowly add milk; cook until mixture begins to thicken. Add cheese and seasonings. Heat and stir until cheese melts. Pour ½ of cheese sauce into a 2 quart, buttered casserole. Add sliced eggs, then bacon crumbs and remainder of cheese sauce. Sprinkle with bread crumbs. Bake 20 minutes. Yields: 10 servings.
"Serve with tossed fruit salad or fried apples."

EGG AND SAUSAGE CASSEROLE

6-8 slices bread, trimmed
2 pounds pork sausage
1 teaspoon prepared mustard
6 ounces Swiss cheese, sliced
3 eggs, slightly beaten
1¼ cups milk
¾ cup half and half
½ teaspoon salt
dash of pepper
dash of nutmeg
1 teaspoon Worcestershire sauce

Place bread in bottom of 3 quart oblong casserole. Use enough bread to cover the bottom. Brown and drain sausage. Mix sausage and mustard. Spread over bread. Cover with cheese slices. Mix remaining ingredients; pour over bread, sausage and cheese. Cover; refrigerate overnight. Cook from room temperature in a 350° oven 25-30 minutes or until puffed like a soufflé and set. Yields: 6 servings.
"This may be made up to 2 days before serving. It is great to make ahead for a company breakfast and serve with broiled grapefruit and biscuits."

If egg cracks during boiling, add a bit of vinegar to keep white from escaping.

QUICHE LORRAINE

"Great luncheon or supper dish that can be varied in many ways."

1 deep-dish or 10 inch pie shell
½ pound bacon, fried and crumbled
1 medium onion, minced and sautéed
1½ cups Swiss cheese, grated
4 eggs
1 cup milk (or half and half)
dash of salt and pepper
dash of nutmeg
½ cup Parmesan cheese, grated

Preheat oven to 400°. Bake pie shell 5-8 minutes. Reduce heat to 375°. Place bacon, onion and cheese in bottom of pie shell. Combine eggs, milk and seasonings in a bowl. Stir with a wire whisk. Pour over other ingredients in shell. Top with Parmesan cheese. Bake 30-35 minutes. It will rise slightly and be golden brown on the surface. Yields: 6 servings.

Variations: One-half pound browned sausage, tuna, crab, salmon, ground round or shrimp may be used as the meat base. Sharp Cheddar cheese and 3 hard cooked eggs, chopped, are especially good with sausage or ground round. A variety of vegetables may be added such as tomatoes, mushrooms, peppers or cooked and drained spinach. Sherry may also be used in place of some of the milk.

BUFFET CHEESE RING

"Wonderful way to serve 2 vegetables and a tasty cheese dish all on one platter."

3 eggs, well beaten
½ cup sugar
1 teaspoon salt
¼ teaspoon dry mustard (or 1 tablespoon prepared mustard)
1 cup milk
1 tablespoon butter, melted
½ cup cider vinegar
1 pound sharp Cheddar cheese, grated
2 ounces pimento, chopped
1 cup saltine cracker crumbs
16 ounces peas (or mushrooms or lima beans), drained
14½ ounces asparagus (or 16 ounces broccoli), drained

Preheat oven to 325°. Using a heavy pan or double boiler, combine eggs, sugar, salt, mustard, milk and butter. Add vinegar last. Cook over medium heat until thickened and smooth, stirring constantly. Remove from heat. Add grated cheese, pimentos and cracker crumbs; beat until well blended. Grease an 8 inch ring mold; lightly dust with cracker crumbs. Pour in the cheese mixture. Bake 1 hour. Remove pan from oven; let stand 20-30 minutes. Invert warm cheese ring onto serving platter. Garnish with pimento. Serve with peas in the middle and asparagus around the outside *or* place mushrooms or lima beans in the middle and broccoli around the outside. Yields: 8-10 servings.

Hints: 1. Do not use processed cheese. The ring will be runny instead of firm.
2. This may be made ahead and kept, uncooked, in refrigerator 24 hours or uncooked in freezer until needed.

CHEDDAR PIE

"Serve this for brunch with cold baked ham or Canadian bacon."

1 cup Cheddar cheese, grated
1 cup fresh bread crumbs
1 cup milk
2 eggs, beaten
½ teaspoon salt
½ teaspoon paprika

Preheat oven to 350°. Grease 9 inch pie plate. Mix all ingredients; pour into prepared pan. Bake 20 minutes or until set. Cut into wedges to serve. Yields: 3-4 servings.

"This may be made early in the day, kept refrigerated and baked at serving time."

SWISS FONDUE

"This is a nice hors d'oeuvre or late supper dish."

1 clove garlic
1 pound imported Swiss cheese, grated
¼ teaspoon salt
¼ teaspoon monosodium glutamate
⅛ teaspoon pepper
2 cups Neuchâtel wine
2 tablespoons cornstarch
2 tablespoons kirsch
1 pound loaf French bread

Rub chafing dish with cut surface of garlic clove. Place cheese, salt, monosodium glutamate and pepper in chafing dish. Refrigerate. At serving time, pour wine over this mixture; heat. Mix together cornstarch and kirsch; blend into cheese mixture when cheese is melted. Stir until bubbly. Cut bread into bite size pieces, each with a crusty side. Dip bread; lifting out of fondue with a twirling motion so you won't lose any of the cheese. Yields: 2½ cups.
Note: Do not *use a metal chafing dish.*

To keep a cheese soufflé high, use quick tapioca instead of flour to thicken. (3 egg soufflé — 3 T tapioca & 1 c milk.)

CHEESE MUSHROOM SOUFFLÉ

5 tablespoons butter
5 tablespoons plain flour
1 teaspoon salt
1½ cups milk
¾ cup Parmesan cheese, grated
6 egg yolks, beaten
¼ pound fresh mushrooms, finely chopped
8 egg whites
¼ teaspoon cream of tartar

Preheat oven to 375°. Make a 3 inch foil collar around a 1½ quart soufflé dish, letting collar extend 2 inches above rim. Oil inside surface of collar and dish. Melt butter. Add flour and salt. Stir until bubbly. Add milk gradually, stirring constantly until smooth and thick. Add Parmesan cheese. Mix in beaten egg yolks and mushrooms. Beat egg whites and cream of tartar until stiff. Mix about ¼ beaten egg whites into cheese mixture. Fold cheese mixture into remaining egg whites. Pour into soufflé dish. Bake 50 minutes. Serve at once. Yields: 6 servings.

MOCK CHEESE SOUFFLÉ

5 slices white bread
butter
¾ pound sharp Cheddar cheese, grated
2 cups milk
1 teaspoon dry mustard
dash cayenne pepper
1 teaspoon salt
½-¾ teaspoon Worcestershire sauce
4 eggs, beaten

Remove crust from bread. Butter bread; cut into cubes. Alternate bread cubes and cheese in 2 quart buttered casserole. Mix milk, dry mustard, pepper, salt and Worcestershire sauce. Add to beaten eggs. Mix; pour over cheese and bread. Cover; refrigerate overnight or up to 3 days. Bake at 350° one hour. If browning too quickly, cover with aluminum foil. Serve immediately! Yields: 6 servings.
"For a milder soufflé, omit mustard and Worcestershire sauce."

HAM AND CHEESE STRATA

16 slices white bread, crust removed
8 slices ham (or Canadian bacon)
8 slices American cheese
6 eggs
3 cups milk
½ teaspoon salt
½ teaspoon dry mustard
potato chips, crushed
4 tablespoons butter, melted

Preheat oven to 350°. Make 8 sandwiches using ham and cheese. Place sandwiches in a greased 3 quart casserole. Mix the remaining ingredients; pour over sandwiches. Sprinkle with potato chips and drizzle with butter. Bake, uncovered, 1 hour and 15 minutes. Yields: 8 servings.

NATURAL EGG DYES

"Eggs take longer to dye this way but are much prettier!"

red cabbage — turns eggs robin's egg blue
onion skins — turns eggs gold
curry powder — turns eggs light yellow
beet juice — turns eggs red
boiling water

Pour boiling water over ingredients; steep 30 minutes. The longer it steeps, the more intense the color. Strain off dye. Dip hard-cooked eggs into it for several minutes.

COLLECTION OF STATE HISTORIC SITES

Alamance Battleground — Pre-revolutionary battleground. Site of 1771 battle between Royal Forces and Regulators; Alamance County

Charles B. Aycock Birthplace — Home of N.C.'s educational governor. During his term of office an average of 1 school per day was built; Wayne County

Historic Bath — N.C.'s oldest town — 1705

Bennett Place — Location of the final surrender to General W.T. Sherman; Durham

Bentonville Battlefield — site of largest Civil War battle fought in N.C.; Johnston County

Brunswick Town — oldest settlement on Cape Fear River; Brunswick

Richard Caswell Memorial and C.S.S. Neuse — Grave of N.C.'s first elected governor and remains of gunboat "Neuse," only Confederate States of America vessel built in N.C.; Kinston

Fort Dobbs — built in 1756 to protect settlers from Indians; Statesville

Duke Homestead — ancestoral home of the Duke family; built near Durham in 1851

Fort Fisher — site of largest land-sea battle of Civil War; near Wilmington

Historic Halifax — birthplace of first state constitution (Halifax Resolves)

House in the Horseshoe — plantation home and scene of Whig-Tory skirmishers; 1780-1781; Moore County

Iredell House — home of James Iredell who served on U.S. Supreme Court; Edenton

Ft. Macon — restored fort garrisoned in 4 wars; Beaufort

N.C. Museum of History — Raleigh

N.C. State Capital — Raleigh

James K. Polk Birthplace — restoration of log house where 11th President of U.S. was born; Mecklenburg County

Reed Goldmine — site of mine where gold was first discovered in N.C.; N.C. was known as leading gold mining state until 1849; Cabarrus County

Tryon Palace — restoration of what was called "the most beautiful building in Colonial America"; New Bern

Zebulon B. Vance Birthplace — reconstruction of log house of N.C.'s Civil War governor; Buncombe County

Thomas Wolfe Memorial — boyhood home of author of "Look Homeward Angel"; Asheville

meats

 THE CAROLINA COLLECTOR'S CONCOCTIONS

. . . Cook Canadian bacon in Coca Cola & serve as a southern dish.

. . . Stuff cored apples with sausage & bake 30 minutes at 350°.

. . . Mix 1 lb. ground beef with 1 chopped onion, 1½ c chili sauce, ½ c pumpkin, 1 t each salt, pepper & pumpkin pie spice & 1 can tomato soup. Simmer 1 hr. & serve on buns.

. . . Make your own shake & bake — ¾ c bread crumbs, ¼ c flour, ½ t garlic powder, salt & pepper. Moisten meat & dip in crumbs.

. . . Stuff tomatoes with corn beef hash, ¼ c dry milk & 1 t prepared mustard. Bake 25 min. at 400°.

. . . A good marinade for roast beef or shish kabobs — purée plums & boil 5 min. with 3 minced garlic cloves, 1 T minced parsley, salt & pepper.

. . . Glaze any meat with 1 c applesauce mixed with ¼ c soy sauce.

. . . Spread baked ham with mixture of rum, pineapple, mustard & brown sugar.

. . . A quick meat loaf sauce — fry onion, green pepper & celery in butter; add tomato soup & ½ c water.

. . . Add crushed oregano to hamburgers & top with mozzarella slices.

. . . A tablespoon or 2 of red wine added to roast beef gravy makes a hot roast beef sandwich.

. . . Use liquid from the chutney bottle to baste ham.

. . . Try a bag of pickling spice added to beef stew while cooking.

. . . Grated carrot adds an unexpected touch to meat loaf.

. . . Sausage simmered in beer gives breakfast a zing.

. . . A great breading mixture is 40 crackers rolled very fine and ¼ c flour added. Press meat into mixture and shake off excess.

. . . Leftover coffee adds richness to beef, ham and pork gravies. Add ½ c coffee to 3-4 cups gravy.

. . . Slip a square of unsweetened chocolate into a brown sauce or gravy to add south-of-the-border richness.

BISHOP'S BARBECUED BEEF

"A favorite from our old cookbook."

2 pounds beef stew
salt
pepper
plain flour
7 tablespoons margarine, divided
2 large onions, sliced
1 green pepper, chopped
4 ounces mushrooms, undrained
2 tablespoons Worcestershire sauce
2 tablespoons molasses
1 cup catsup
2 tablespoons vinegar
1 teaspoon paprika
¼ cup water
rice, cooked

Preheat oven to 300°. Salt and pepper beef; roll in flour. Brown meat thoroughly in 4 tablespoons margarine. Place in casserole. Sauté onion and green pepper in 3 tablespoons margarine. Add to meat along with mushrooms and juice. Combine remaining ingredients; pour over meat. Cover. Bake at least 3 hours. Check after 2 hours to see if water is needed. Serve over rice. Yields: 6 servings.

Wine & tomatoes break down the tough fibers in meat.

Never salt meat until it is cooked as salt draws out the juices.

HOMEMADE BARBECUE

1½ pounds lean beef stew, cubed
½ pound lean pork, cubed
1 cup water
¼ teaspoon salt
1 large onion, chopped
1 small green pepper, chopped
1 cup celery, diced
16 ounces canned tomatoes
5 ounces Heinz barbecue sauce
1 teaspoon sugar
⅓ cup catsup

Place meat, water and salt in large heavy covered saucepan. Boil slowly until meat begins to get tender. Add all other ingredients. Continue to simmer slowly, uncovered, until the meat is tender enough to pull apart and mash with a fork or potato masher. Most of the liquid should be boiled away so that the barbecue is not too thin. Yields: 8-10 sandwiches.

BARBECUED BRISKET

3-4 pound fresh beef brisket
1½ cups catsup or chili sauce
3 tablespoons brown sugar
⅓ cup Worcestershire sauce
1 teaspoon salt
1 teaspoon chili powder
2 dashes Tabasco
1 small onion, chopped
1½ cups water
1-2 tablespoons liquid smoke

Preheat oven to 350°. Cook brisket fat side up 2 hours, uncovered, without liquid. Mix remaining ingredients in a blender, just enough to mix well. Pour over brisket; cook, covered, at 300° for 3-4 hours basting every 30 minutes. Yields: 6 servings.

Curried dishes are better if made a day ahead & reheated.

TEXAS BARBECUED BRISKET

"This makes great sandwiches."

2-3 pound beef brisket
2 ounces liquid smoke
1 onion, thinly sliced
salt
celery salt
garlic powder
Barbecue Sauce

Season meat well. Place in pan with liquid smoke; lay sliced onions on top. Marinate overnight. Preheat oven to 300°. Pour off liquid smoke. Pour Barbecue Sauce over brisket. Bake covered 5-6 hours. Slice to serve. Yields: 4-6 servings.

Barbecue Sauce:
1½ teaspoons salt
¼ cup vinegar
¼-½ cup water
2 tablespoons sugar
1 tablespoon prepared mustard
¼ teaspoon pepper
¼ teaspoon cayenne pepper
1 slice lemon ½ inch thick
1 small onion, diced
4 tablespoons butter
½ cup catsup
4 tablespoons Worcestershire sauce

Combine first 10 ingredients in saucepan; simmer 20 minutes. Remove lemon. Add catsup and Worcestershire sauce; bring to a boil. May be kept in refrigerator.

BOEUF EN VIN ROUGE

4 pound chuck or shoulder roast
1 cup onions, chopped
1 clove garlic, mashed
2 carrots, chopped
6 peppercorns
1 cup Burgundy wine
1 tablespoon maple syrup
10½ ounces canned beef broth
6 ounces tomato paste
1 teaspoon anchovy paste
¼ teaspoon savory leaf
salt
pepper

Brown meat in a little oil in a Dutch oven. Add onions and garlic. Cook 3 minutes. Add all other ingredients. Cover; cook slowly 3 hours. It may also be cooked in a covered pan in a 350° oven. Reserve the juices for gravy. Yields: 6-8 servings.

MARINATED CHUCK ROAST

4-6 pound chuck roast, blade (best) or shoulder
1 tablespoon onion, grated
1 teaspoon dry mustard
1 teaspoon salt
¼ teaspoon pepper
1 teaspoon sugar
⅓ cup soy sauce
⅓ cup oil
3 tablespoons wine vinegar
2 tablespoons chutney
1 clove garlic, minced

Combine all ingredients; marinate roast 3 days in refrigerator. Remove; grill over charcoal until rare or medium rare. May use a meat thermometer. Yields: 8 servings.

GERTRUDE'S CORNED BEEF

1 corned beef brisket
1 whole orange, cut in chunks
1 tablespoon dill weed
4 bay leaves
1 tablespoon rosemary
1 garlic bud, sliced
2 whole peppercorns

Place all ingredients in a large pot of water. Simmer 3-4 hours. Yields: 6-8 servings.

GLORIFIED CORNED BEEF with MUSTARD SAUCE

3-4 pound corned beef round or brisket
4/5 quart white table wine
water
2 cloves garlic, minced
6-9 whole cloves
6 whole peppercorns
2 bay leaves
2 onions, sliced
6 small whole potatoes, pared
6 small carrots
small white onions
6 cabbage wedges

Place beef in a large Dutch oven; barely cover with half wine and half water. Add garlic, seasonings and sliced onions. Cover, simmer about 1 hour per pound of meat or until tender. Remove beef; add potatoes, carrots and whole onions. Cover, bring to a boil; cook about 20 minutes. Add cabbage; cook 20 minutes longer. Replace beef last 10 minutes of cooking time to reheat. Serve with Mustard Sauce.

Mustard Sauce:
1 cup sour cream
2 teaspoons prepared mustard
1 teaspoon horseradish
¼ teaspoon seasoned salt
milk

Combine sour cream with mustard. Add horseradish and seasoned salt. Chill overnight. A little milk may be added if too thick after chilling. Yields: 6-8 servings.

Put flour in a custard cup when roasting meat in the oven. It browns slowly as meat cooks & is ready for a rich brown gravy when meat is done.

THE CAPTAIN'S FLANK STEAK

1½ pounds flank steak
½ cup oil
½ cup soy sauce
½ cup red wine vinegar
juice of one lemon
1 clove garlic, minced
pepper, freshly ground

Combine all ingredients, add flank steak; marinate 6 hours in refrigerator. Remove from refrigerator the last hour. Broil steak until rare (about 5-6 minutes each side). Slice thinly across the grain. Yields: 4-5 servings.

CHILI CON CARNE

1 pound lean beef, ground
1 medium onion, minced
16 ounces stewed tomatoes
6 ounces tomato paste
15½ ounces chili beans
½ cup water or more
2 tablespoons chili powder
dash of red hot pepper
2 tablespoons jalapeno relish (optional — to make it really hot)

Sauté onion and ground beef. Add all other ingredients; simmer about 1 hour. Yields: 4 servings.

PEDERNALES RIVER CHILI

"This may be served on hot dogs too."

4 pounds chuck, coarsely ground or chopped
1 large onion, chopped
2 cloves garlic, crushed
2 tablespoons chili powder
2 teaspoons salt
1 teaspoon oregano, ground
1 teaspoon cumin seed
32 ounces canned tomatoes
2 cups hot water

In a large skillet, cook together meat, onions, and garlic until meat changes color. Add chili powder, salt, oregano, cumin seed, tomatoes, and water; mix well. Simmer about 1 hour, skimming off fat as needed. Yields: 8 servings.

ITALIANO MEAT PIE

1 pound lean beef, ground
⅓ cup green pepper, chopped
¾ cup water
6 ounces canned tomato paste
1½ ounces packaged spaghetti sauce mix
9 inch pie crust
⅓ cup Parmesan cheese, grated
1½ cups mozzarella cheese, grated

Preheat oven to 400°. Brown beef; drain. Add green pepper; cook 2 minutes. Stir in water, tomato paste, and spaghetti mix; cover and simmer 10 minutes. Sprinkle half the Parmesan cheese over bottom of pie shell, add half the meat, then 1 cup mozzarella cheese. Repeat, ending with mozzarella cheese. Bake on a cookie sheet 15-20 minutes, until hot and all cheese melts. Yields: 4-6 servings.

FERRELL ANN'S LASAGNE

2 pounds ground chuck
1 large onion, chopped
4 tablespoons olive oil
2 garlic cloves, minced
1 teaspoon salt
1 teaspoon pepper
6-12 ounces tomato paste
3 cups tomato juice
1 cup water
2 teaspoons basil
8 ounce lasagne noodles
1 pound mozzarella cheese, sliced
2 pounds ricotta cheese
½ cup Parmesan cheese, grated

Sauté onion in olive oil until soft; add minced garlic. In same pan, brown meat. Add salt, pepper, 6 ounces tomato paste, tomato juice, water and basil. Cover and simmer 1½ hours. At the end of this time, if sauce is not thick enough, add 6 ounces tomato paste. Cook noodles by directions on package. In 3 quart casserole layer noodles, sauce, mozzarella cheese and ricotta cheese. Repeat layers. Sprinkle Parmesan cheese on top. The flavor is better if allowed to sit in refrigerator 1-2 days before baking or freezing. Remove and allow to come to room temperature. Bake 20 minutes at 375°. Yields: 8 servings.

Brown meatballs with no fuss in the oven — 25 minutes at 375.°

GOURMET MEAT LOAF

1½ pound beef chuck, ground
¾ cup uncooked regular oats
2 eggs, slightly beaten
2 teaspoons salt
¼ teaspoon pepper
1 teaspoon Worcestershire sauce
⅔ cup milk
Mushroom Filling

Preheat oven to 350°. Combine all ingredients except Mushroom Filling. Place half of meat mixture in a lightly greased 10x6 baking dish or pan. Form into a loaf. Make a shallow well lengthwise in the meat. Spoon mushroom filling into well. Spoon remaining meat mixture over filling, covering all of the filling and shaping into a loaf. Bake about 1 hour. Let stand 5 minutes before cutting. Yields: 6-8 servings.

Mushroom Filling:
1 cup mushrooms, sliced
½ cup onion, chopped
2 tablespoons margarine
⅓ cup sour cream

Sauté mushrooms and onion in margarine until soft. Remove from heat; stir in sour cream. Yields: 1 cup.

SICILIAN MEAT ROLL

2 pounds beef chuck, ground
2 eggs, beaten
¾ cup soft bread crumbs
½ cup tomato juice
2 tablespoons parsley, snipped
½ teaspoon dried oregano
¼ teaspoon salt
¼ teaspoon pepper
small clove garlic, minced
8 slices boiled ham
6 ounces mozzarella cheese, shredded
3 slices mozzarella cheese

Preheat oven to 350°. Combine eggs, bread, tomato juice, parsley, oregano, salt, pepper, and garlic. Stir in ground beef, mixing well. On foil or wax paper, form meat into a 10x12 rectangle. Arrange ham slices on meat, leaving margin around edges. Sprinkle shredded cheese over ham. Starting from short end, roll up meat, using foil to lift. Seal edges and ends. Place seam side down in baking pan. Bake 1 hour and 15 minutes. Place cheese slices over top. Return to oven for 5 minutes until cheese melts. Yields: 8 servings.

Cook meatloaf in muffin tins for a speedy supper.

Lean meat such as veal and lamb may need a covering of bacon, salt pork, or suet to make them self-basting to prevent meat from drying out.

MEAT, TOMATO AND CABBAGE SCALLOP

"You must try this ground beef dish – it's delicious, even if your family doesn't like cabbage."

1 pound beef, ground
2 tablespoons oil
¼ cup onion, chopped
1 cup celery, chopped
20 ounces canned tomato wedges
2 teaspoons salt
pepper to taste
4 cups cabbage, chopped or coarsely shredded
1 cup soft bread crumbs

Preheat oven to 375°. Brown beef in oil; add onion and celery. Cook 5 minutes. Add tomatoes, salt and pepper; bring to a boil. Alternate layers of cabbage and meat mixture in a greased 2½ quart casserole. Top with bread crumbs. Bake 40-45 minutes. Yields: 6-8 servings.

GROUND BEEF GRAND STYLE

1½ pounds beef, ground
1 cup onions, chopped
8 ounces cream cheese, softened
10¾ ounces canned cream of mushroom soup
¼ cup milk
1 teaspoon salt
¼ cup catsup
⅓ cup olives, sliced
10 canned biscuits, split

Preheat oven to 375°. Brown ground beef and onions; drain off fat. Combine softened cream cheese, soup, milk, salt, catsup and olives with beef and onions. Pour into 2 quart casserole. Bake 10 minutes. Place split biscuits around edge of casserole and bake 15-20 minutes or until golden brown. Yields: 4-6 servings.

SATURDAY NIGHT SPECIAL

"When your family wants lasagne and you have no extra time, this is perfect!"

1½ pounds beef, ground
⅓ cup onions, chopped
24 ounces canned tomato sauce
1 teaspoon Worcestershire sauce
1 teaspoon salt
⅛ teaspoon pepper
⅛ teaspoon marjoram
⅛ teaspoon sweet basil
8 ounces cream cheese, softened
1 cup cream style cottage cheese
¼ cup sour cream
½ cup stuffed olives, sliced
8 ounces medium noodles, cooked, drained and rinsed

Preheat oven to 350°. Brown beef and onion; drain. Add tomato sauce and seasonings. Simmer 15-20 minutes. Beat cream cheese until fluffy; add sour cream, cottage cheese and olives; mix. In a greased 3 quart casserole, arrange in layers; ½ noodles, cheese mixture, remaining noodles and tomato mixture. Bake covered 45 minutes. Yields: 8-10 servings.

PIZZA

1 pound mild sausage
1 pound beef, ground
cooking oil
1 large onion, chopped
½ green pepper, chopped
1 clove garlic, minced
1 pound canned tomatoes, chopped
6 ounces tomato paste
1 teaspoon oregano
1 teaspoon salt, or to taste
1 teaspoon chili powder
1 teaspoon sweet basil
4 ounces mushrooms, drained
American cheese, grated
mozzarella cheese, sliced

Cook sausage. Remove from pan; drain. In iron skillet, heat enough oil to saute onion, green pepper and garlic. Cook until tender; add ground beef and brown. Drain off most of liquid. Add tomatoes, tomato paste, spices, mushrooms and sausage. Simmer, uncovered, 1 hour. Refrigerate 24 hours. This makes enough sauce for three 12 inch pizzas or two 14 inch pizzas.

Quick and Easy Pizza Crust:

⅓ cup oil
2 cups plain flour
1 teaspoon baking powder
1 teaspoon salt
⅔ cup buttermilk

Preheat oven to 450°. Add oil to flour, baking powder and salt. Blend until mixture resembles corn meal. Add buttermilk; blend. Roll out to fit 12 inch round pan. Bake until crust turns golden brown. Cover baked crust with sauce; top with cheeses. Bake until cheeses melt.

Yeast Pizza Crust:

1 package active dry yeast
1⅓ cups lukewarm water
4 cups plain flour, sifted
2 tablespoons oil
1 teaspoon salt
olive oil

Sprinkle yeast into warm water. Stir to dissolve. Add to flour, oil and salt. Mix well. Knead on lightly floured surface 10 minutes. Cover with damp cloth; let rise 2 hours. Preheat oven to 400°. Grease two 14 inch pizza pans. Sprinkle with corn meal. Punch dough down; divide in half. Pat and stretch dough into pans. Pinch up a collar around edge to hold filling. Prick dough in about 6 places. Brush dough lightly with olive oil. Spread with meat filling. Bake 25 minutes. Remove; top with cheeses. Return to oven until cheese is melted.

OPEN FACE TACOS

"Children love this."

1½ pounds beef, ground
1 large onion, chopped
2 11½ ounce cans bean and bacon soup
11½ ounces water
8 ounces tomato sauce
2 tablespoons Tabasco
corn chips
lettuce, shredded
tomatoes, chopped
green pepper, chopped
Cheddar cheese, grated

Brown ground beef and chopped onion. Add soup, water tomato sauce and Tabasco; simmer at least 1 hour. Serve over a handful of corn chips on each plate. Top with shredded lettuce, chopped tomatoes, chopped green pepper and grated cheese. Yields: 8 servings.

TACO CASSEROLE

1 pound beef, ground
8 ounces canned refrigerated crescent rolls
1 tablespoon oil
2 tablespoons onions, chopped
2 cups tomatoes, coarsely chopped
⅓ cup green pepper, coarsely chopped
4 ounces canned green chilies
1 teaspoon salt
½ teaspoon leaf oregano
½ teaspoon cumin
⅛ teaspoon pepper
⅛ teaspoon garlic powder
1 teaspoon wine vinegar
lettuce, shredded
Cheddar cheese, grated
avocado slices

Preheat oven to 375°. To prepare crust, seal perforations of crescent rolls; roll out to 12½x8½. Ease into lightly greased 10x6x2 baking dish. Do not stretch dough. Flute edge and prick bottom. Bake 15 minutes. Heat oil in large skillet over medium heat. Add beef and onions; brown. Stir in tomatoes, green pepper, 5 tablespoons green chilies, salt, oregano, cumin, pepper, garlic powder and vinegar. Cook until green pepper is tender crisp. Spoon meat into crust. Top with grated cheese. Arrange shredded lettuce around outsides of dish. Garnish with 4 slices avocado. Spoon some sauce in center and pass the rest. Yields: 6 servings.

Sauce:
8 ounces tomato sauce
1½ teaspoons oil
1½ teaspoons wine vinegar
½ teaspoon leaf oregano
⅛ teaspoon cumin
⅛ teaspoon salt
⅛ teaspoon pepper
⅛ teaspoon garlic powder
⅛ teaspoon onion powder
dash of hot pepper sauce (optional)

Combine all ingredients and heat.

SPAGHETTI WITH MEAT SAUCE

½ pound bacon, chopped
2½ pounds beef, ground
2 cups onion, finely chopped
1 cup green pepper, finely chopped
6 cloves garlic, finely chopped
3 cans Italian tomatoes, 2 pounds 3 ounces each
18 ounces canned tomato paste
1½ cups dry red wine
5 teaspoons oregano
5 teaspoons basil
1½ cups water
½ cup fresh parsley, chopped
2 teaspoons thyme
1 bay leaf, crumbled
2 teaspoons salt
freshly ground pepper

Fry bacon until crisp in a wide 6 quart pot. Remove bacon and all but 2 tablespoons fat. Save both bacon and extra fat. Add ground beef, breaking it up with a spoon; cook until golden brown, stirring occasionally. Stir in onion, green pepper and garlic; cook 10 minutes. Add more bacon fat if needed. Mash tomatoes with a spoon. Stir tomatoes, tomato paste, bacon, 1 cup of wine, 4 teaspoons oregano, 4 teaspoons basil and all remaining ingredients into sauce. Bring to a boil, reduce heat and simmer, uncovered, 3 hours, stirring occasionally. Taste after 1 hour of cooking and correct seasoning. If you make the sauce early, cool and refrigerate until 1-2 hours before dinner. Let it warm to room temperature before you reheat. 10 minutes before serving, blend in 1 teaspoon oregano, 1 teaspoon basil and ½ cup wine. Yields: 12 servings.

PASTITSIO (Greek Pie)

1½ pounds round steak, ground
1 large onion, chopped
2 tablespoons olive oil or butter
¾ teaspoon salt
pepper to taste
¼ teaspoon cinnamon
½ teaspoon oregano
2 cups tomato sauce
2 tablespoons parsley, minced
½ pound small macaroni

Cook onion in butter or oil until soft. Add steak; brown. Season with salt, pepper, cinnamon and oregano. Add tomato sauce and parsley. Simmer 15 minutes. Taste and correct seasonings. Cook macaroni until tender but still slightly firm. Drain. Add a bit of butter or olive oil to keep from sticking. Make topping as follows:

3 tablespoons butter
3 tablespoons plain flour
3½ cups milk
3 egg yolks, beaten
⅛ teaspoon nutmeg
½ cup grated Parmesan cheese

Melt butter; blend in flour. Stir in milk gradually and cook, stirring continuously until thickened. It should be a thin sauce. Gradually add beaten egg yolks. Stir over low heat for a few minutes. Do not let boil. Season with nutmeg only—no salt and pepper are needed. Preheat oven to 350°

To assemble: Grease 3 quart flat casserole. Place a thin layer of macaroni, a layer of meat sauce, a second layer of macaroni, and a second layer of meat sauce. Pour topping over all and jiggle so some of the sauce runs through layers. Sprinkle cheese over all. Bake 35-45 minutes or until sauce is puffed and golden. Remove from oven; let stand 15-20 minutes. Cut into large squares. Yields: 8-10 servings.

"Can be prepared a day ahead and put in refrigerator until ready to bake."

VIRGINIA'S CASSEROLE FOR A CROWD

2½ pounds beef chuck, ground
1 large onion, chopped
3 celery ribs with leaves, chopped
3 large carrots, grated
2 cans Italian style tomatoes, 2 pounds 3 ounces each
2 tablespoons garlic salt
3 teaspoons oregano
1½ pounds macaroni shells (or elbow macaroni or noodles)
20 ounces frozen chopped spinach, thawed
1 cup Parmesan cheese, grated

Preheat oven to 350°. Brown meat; remove from skillet. Sauté onion, celery and carrots in grease 5 minutes. Drain; place meat back in skillet. Stir in tomatoes, garlic salt and oregano. Bring to a boil, lower heat. Simmer 1 hour. Meanwhile, cook macaroni according to package directions; drain and set aside. When sauce is done, stir in spinach and macaroni. Mix thoroughly. Place mixture in two 3 quart casseroles or 1 very large baking dish. Sprinkle cheese on top. Bake 30 minutes. Yields: 12 or more servings. *"Can be prepared several days ahead."*

Fool proof gravy — a pinch of salt added to flour before it is mixed will prevent lumps. 1½-2 T flour & 1 c liquid.

CHINESE PEPPER STEAK

1-1½ pounds sirloin steak, 1 inch thick
¼ cup oil
1 clove garlic, crushed
1 teaspoon salt
½ teaspoon pepper
1 teaspoon ground ginger
3 large green peppers, cut into strips
2 large onions, thinly sliced
½ cup celery, diced
¼ cup soy sauce
½ teaspoon sugar
½ cup beef bouillon
8 ounces water chestnuts, sliced
1 tablespoon cornstarch
¼-½ cup cold water
4 green onions, cut in 1 inch pieces
rice, cooked

Cut steak into slices ⅛ inch thick. Heat oil in skillet; add garlic, salt, pepper and ginger. Sauté until garlic is golden. Add steak slices; brown lightly 2 minutes. Remove meat. Add green peppers, onions and celery. Cook 3 minutes. Return beef to pan; add soy sauce, sugar, bouillon, water chestnuts, cornstarch dissolved in cold water, and green onions. Simmer 10-15 minutes or until sauce thickens. Serve over hot rice. Yields: 6-8 servings.

BEEF JERKY

"Great for taking on camping trips and a real hit as a snack with the younger set."

1½ pounds flank steak
1 teaspoon liquid smoke
⅓ teaspoon garlic powder
⅓ teaspoon black pepper
1 teaspoon Aćcent
1 teaspoon onion powder
¼ cup Worcestershire sauce
¼ cup soy sauce

Semi-freeze meat. Trim off all possible fat. Slice with grain into ⅛ inch slices. Marinate overnight in a shallow glass dish thoroughly covered with sauce made from all other ingredients. Lay strips of marinated meat in single layer on oven racks, place foil underneath to catch drippings. With oven door slightly opened, roast at lowest temperature (about 125° or lower) approximately 4 hours. Taste occasionally. Roast until as chewy as desired. Wrap in paper towel to absorb all grease. Store in jars. Does not need refrigeration.

SUKIYAKI

2 tablespoons butter
1½ pound sirloin or top round, sliced in thin strips
1 cup green onions, sliced
1 cup fresh mushrooms, sliced
1 cup celery, sliced
½ cup green pepper, sliced
8 ounces bamboo shoots, drained
1 cup almonds, chopped
½ cup canned beef stock
¼ cup soy sauce
2 tablespoons sugar

Melt butter in skillet. Sauté strips of steak. Add onions, mushrooms, celery, green pepper, bamboo shoots, and almonds. Sauté lightly. Mix beef stock, soy sauce and sugar; add to meat and vegetables. Simmer about 10 minutes. The vegetables should remain crisp. Serve over cooked rice. Yields: 6 servings.

LONDON BROIL

"Wonderful for those who love rare meat."

2-4 pound London broil
8 ounces Italian salad dressing
5 ounces soy sauce
garlic salt

Place London broil in shallow pan; pour salad dressing and soy sauce over it. Sprinkle generously with garlic salt. Marinate in refrigerator overnight, turning once. Remove from marinade. Grill over charcoal or broil in oven until rare or medium rare. Slice very thin at an angle. Yields: 4-8 servings.

ELEGANT SHORT RIBS OF BEEF

2 pounds beef short ribs
½ cup plain flour
1 teaspoon salt
¼ teaspoon pepper
1 large onion, chopped
1 green pepper, chopped
3 tablespoons margarine, melted
10½ ounces canned beef bouillon
1 cup red wine
¼ teaspoon thyme
4 ounces button mushrooms, drained

Preheat oven to 500°. Dredge short ribs in a mixture of flour, salt and pepper. Place on rack in shallow baking pan; brown 20 minutes. Watch carefully so will not burn. Sauté onion and pepper in margarine; add bouillon, wine, and thyme. Place short ribs in a 3 or 4 quart casserole. Pour bouillon mixture over ribs. Cover; bake at 325° about 2 hours or until meat is tender. About 20 minutes before removing from oven, add mushrooms. Yields: 4-5 servings.

GOURMET BEEF AND MUSHROOMS

"A dinner party special."

4 pounds sirloin steak, cut into strips
plain flour
1 cup margarine
salt to taste
pepper to taste
1 cup onion, chopped
1 bay leaf
1 teaspoon thyme
2 cups Burgundy wine
2 10½ ounce cans beef bouillon
1 pound mushrooms, sliced
rice, cooked

Flour beef strips; brown in skillet in margarine. Salt and pepper to taste. Add onion, bay leaf, thyme, wine and bouillon; simmer about 30 minutes. Add mushrooms the last 15 minutes of cooking. Sauce may need to be thickened with flour or thinned with water. Serve over rice. Yields: 16 servings.

MARINATED RUMP ROAST

4 pound boneless rump roast
2 cups dry red wine
½ cup oil
1 large onion, cut in thin strips
2 teaspoons salt
8 peppercorns, crushed
1 teaspoon thyme
½ teaspoon oregano
1 bay leaf
1 clove garlic, chopped

Place roast in large bowl or non-metallic casserole. Add remaining ingredients. Cover; marinate in refrigerator 8-24 hours, turning once. Remove roast from marinade; wipe with paper towel. Place in shallow roasting pan with a rack. Insert meat thermometer into thickest part of meat. Place in a 450° oven; roast 10 minutes to start the browning. Reduce heat to 275°; continue roasting about 2 hours (30 minutes per pound after browning) or until thermometer reaches 130° for rare or 140° for medium rare. Let stand on heated platter about 15-20 minutes. Slice very thin. Yields: 8 servings.

OVEN BEEF STEW

"This meal-in-a-dish is sure to become one of your family's favorites."

2½ pounds stew beef
28 ounces canned tomatoes, undrained
1 cup celery, chopped
4 medium carrots, sliced
3 potatoes, cubed
3 onions, chopped
3-4 tablespoons tapioca (quick cooking)
2 beef bouillon cubes
1 tablespoon salt
1 tablespoon sugar
pepper to taste
⅛ teaspoon thyme
⅛ teaspoon rosemary leaves
⅛ teaspoon ground marjoram
¼ cup red wine

Preheat oven to 250°. Combine all ingredients in a 5 quart casserole. Cook covered 5 hours. After 3½ hours, stir well. Continue cooking. Yields: 8 servings.

BRAISED SIRLOIN TIPS

3 pounds sirloin steak, cubed
1½ pounds mushrooms, sliced
4 tablespoons butter, divided
1 tablespoon oil
¾ cup beef bouillon, divided
¾ cup red wine
2 tablespoons soy sauce
2 cloves garlic, minced
1 small onion, grated
2 tablespoons cornstarch or plain flour
6 ounces cream of mushroom soup
salt and pepper

Preheat oven to 300°. In fry pan, saute mushrooms in 2 tablespoons butter. Remove to 3 quart casserole. Add remaining butter and oil to fry pan; add meat and brown well. Transfer to casserole. Add ½ cup bouillon, wine, soy sauce, garlic and onion to fry pan. Mix remaining bouillon and cornstarch or flour. Stir into mixture; cook until thick. Pour over mushrooms and meat in casserole. Bake 1 hour. Add mushroom soup and stir, then return to oven for 15 minutes. Serve over almond rice. Yields: 8 servings.

Note: See Index for Almond Rice recipe.

SKEWERED STEAK AND MUSHROOMS

1 pound sirloin steak
½ cup Burgundy (or claret wine)
1 teaspoon Worcestershire sauce
1 clove garlic, peeled
½ cup oil
2 tablespoons catsup
1 teaspoon sugar
½ teaspoon salt
½ teaspoon monosodium glutamate
1 tablespoon vinegar
½ teaspoon marjoram
½ teaspoon rosemary
12 large mushrooms

Mix wine, Worcestershire sauce, garlic, oil, catsup and seasonings. Cut steak into 2 inch squares. Wash mushrooms. Marinate steak squares and mushrooms in wine sauce 2 hours or more — the longer the better. Alternate meat and mushrooms on skewers. Broil, turning sides and basting frequently with remaining marinade. Yields: 4 servings.

Variation: Marinate chuck roast overnight; roast in oven or cook on grill. This is very tender and expensive tasting.

BEEF TENDERLOIN WITH BORDELAISE SAUCE

"Fantastic! We put the best beef recipe last."

6 pound beef tenderloin
Bordelaise Sauce

About 1¼ hours before serving, preheat oven to 450°. Meanwhile, from a 6 pound whole beef tenderloin remove any fat. Place on wire rack in shallow pan, tucking narrow end under to make roast more uniformly thick. Insert meat thermometer into center of thickest part. Roast about 60 minutes or to 140° on meat thermometer. Meat is crusty brown on outside and pink to red on inside. Cut into 1 inch slices. Arrange on a heated platter. Serve with Bordelaise Sauce. Yields: 8-10 servings.

Bordelaise Sauce:

4 tablespoons butter
1 shallot, minced
2 onion slices
½ carrot, sliced
2 sprigs parsley
12 whole black peppercorns
2 whole cloves
1 bay leaf
4 tablespoons plain flour
2 10½ ounce cans beef bouillon
½ teaspoon salt
¼ teaspoon pepper
¼ cup red wine
2 tablespoons snipped parsley

Melt butter in skillet; sauté shallot, onion, carrot, parsley, peppercorns, clove and bay leaf until golden and tender. Add flour; cook over low heat, stirring until flour is lightly browned. Stir in bouillon. Simmer, stirring until thickened and smooth, about 10 minutes. Strain. Add salt, pepper, red wine and snipped parsley.

LIVER DELIGHT

"Even the children enjoy this!"

1 pound calves liver, cut into thin strips
2 tablespoons solid shortening
Bisquick
milk

Melt shortening in a large skillet. Dip strips of liver in Bisquick, then into milk, and then again in Bisquick. Place strips in skillet with hot shortening. Cook about 5 minutes on each side until browned and crisp. Add more shortening if needed. Season to taste. Yields: 4 servings.

Variation: After liver is fried, place sliced onions in hot skillet, cover and steam until soft. Uncover, cook until golden brown.

STUFFED BONED LEG OF LAMB

5½ pound leg of lamb, have butcher bone this and make a pocket
2 cloves garlic, cup up
¾ teaspoon salt
¼ teaspoon pepper
rosemary
3 tablespoons margarine
¼ cup onion, chopped
¼ cup celery, chopped
2 tablespoons green pepper, chopped
¼ cup sliced mushrooms, drained
2 tablespoons pecans, chopped
1½ tablespoons dried parsley
⅛ teaspoon salt
⅛ teaspoon pepper
¾ teaspoon poultry seasoning
2 cups fresh white bread crumbs

Preheat oven to 325°. Using leg of lamb that has been boned and with a pocket, tuck in ends to form a pillow. Wipe lamb with damp cloth. Rub surface with cut clove of garlic; insert 2 or 3 slivers of garlic in lamb. Combine salt, pepper and a generous amount of rosemary; rub over surface of lamb and in pocket. Prepare stuffing. Melt margarine and sauté onion, celery and green pepper until tender, about 5 minutes. Remove from heat. Add remaining ingredients and toss lightly to combine well. Stuff pocket in lamb with dressing. Close with skewers or tie with string. Place roast, fat side up, on rack in shallow roasting pan. Insert meat thermometer, being careful that the tip is in the meat and not the stuffing. Roast about 2¼ hours or until thermometer reads 180° for well done or 175° for medium. Remove to platter. Let stand 20 minutes before carving. Drippings from roast make excellent gravy when thickened. Yields: 8-10 servings.

LAMB CHOPS MADEIRA IN CHOUX PASTE

6 loin lamb chops, 2 inches thick
¾ cup Madeira
salt
pepper
Spice Islands fines herbs (or thyme)
1 cup water
½ teaspoon salt
½ cup butter
1 cup plain flour, unsifted
4 eggs

Preheat oven to broil. Marinate chops in Madeira 30 minutes. Drain; sprinkle lightly with salt, pepper and fines herbs (or thyme). Broil 2 inches from heat until browned on 1 side, approximately 7 minutes. Cool; set aside. Combine water, salt and butter over medium heat. When butter melts and mixture boils, add flour; remove from heat. Stir until smooth. Mixture should come away from sides of pan. Beat in eggs, 1 at a time; paste will be smooth and shiny. Evenly spread ⅓ cup on each chop. Cover; chill 12-24 hours. Preheat oven to 425°. Bake 35 minutes or until brown. Yields: 6 servings.

"*Choux paste can be prepared ahead and refrigerated; allow it to reach room temperature before using.*"

Boneless smoked ham yields 5 servings per lb.

The bone-in ham yields 3 servings per lb.

BAKED COUNTRY HAM

"A Southern specialty!"

10 pound country cured ham
1 cup ginger ale
1 cup brown sugar (or ½ cup molasses)
4 tablespoons plain flour
1 tablespoon dry mustard
2 tablespoons water
whole cloves

Wash ham. Cover with boiling water; boil 10 minutes. Simmer 3 hours. Remove skin; place in roaster, fat side up. Bake at 325° for 1½ hours, basting with a mixture of ginger ale and ham stock. Remove from oven. Cover with paste of brown sugar or molasses, flour, mustard, and water. Dot with cloves. Return to oven in uncovered roaster and bake 30 minutes.

OLD-FASHIONED HOME CORNED HAM

"Wonderful for sandwiches during the holiday season."

12-14 pound fresh ham
1-1½ pounds uniodized salt (amount depends on size of ham)

At both ends of ham, take sharp knife and carve around bone, forming a cavity approximately 6-8 inches deep. Pack cavities with salt. Place ham in roaster skin side down, on a layer of salt. Cover thoroughly with a thick layer of remaining salt. Place lid on roaster and refrigerate 10-14 days. Wash salt off. Boil in clear water until tender.

Note: Pork shoulder does not work. Fresh hams are readily available during the winter holidays.

Try leftover coffee to add richness to beef, ham and pork gravies. Adding ½ c coffee to 3 to 4 c of gravy does the trick.

BRAISED HAM WITH MADEIRA CREAM SAUCE

"A new way to serve ham for a special meal."

4-6 pound precooked ham
3 tablespoons butter
½ cup onions, chopped
½ cup carrots, chopped
¼ cup celery, chopped
½ teaspoon thyme
1 cup dry white wine
24 ounces chicken broth
24 ounces beef broth
1 bouquet garni (4 sprigs parsley, 1 large bay leaf, 3 shallots, tied in cheesecloth)
¼ cup whipping cream
2 tablespoons Madeira wine

Preheat oven to 350°. Melt butter in pot or Dutch oven large enough to hold the ham. Add onions, carrots, celery and thyme; cook over medium heat until they are limp and lightly colored. Place ham fat side up, on vegetable mixture. Pour wine and broths around it. Liquid should reach halfway up ham. If it doesn't, pour in additional broth. Add bouquet garni. Bring liquid to a boil on top of stove. Cover casserole. Put in oven; bake, basting every 15 minutes until it has reached an internal temperature of 130°. When ham is done, remove from braising liquid; keep warm. With a slotted spoon, remove vegetables and place in a blender. Carefully skim fat from liquid; strain 2 cups of liquid into a saucepan. Boil until reduced to 1 cup. Add reduced liquid to vegetables in blender; whirl. Return to saucepan; heat over medium heat. Do not boil. Stir in Madeira and cream; season with salt and pepper. A small amount of arrowroot blended with cold water may be used to make a thicker sauce. Carve ham. Spread each slice with sauce. Yields: 6-8 servings.

HOT HAM MOUSSE

"Perfect for breakfast or brunch."

1 cup ground ham (country ham is the best)
4 tablespoons butter
4 tablespoons plain flour
1 cup milk
½ teaspoon salt
paprika to taste
1 teaspoon lemon juice
3 eggs, separated

Preheat oven to 400°. Make a cream sauce of butter, flour, and milk. Add salt, paprika and lemon juice. Add ham and beaten egg yolks. When cool, add stiffly beaten egg whites. Pour into a buttered casserole. Bake 20-25 minutes. Yields: 4 servings.
"Delicious served with cheese grits and fruit."

Sprinkle an ungreased pan with salt & fry pork chops 10-15 min. on each side with no sticking.

PASTA MELANAISE

"May be served as main dish or side vegetable dish."

2½ cups ham, ground
1½ cups fresh mushrooms, sliced
½ cup butter
2 tablespoons plain flour
1 pint half and half
1 cup milk
¼ cup sherry
1 cup Cheddar cheese, grated
1 clove garlic, minced
1 teaspoon white pepper
salt to taste
1 teaspoon onion juice
1 teaspoon oregano (optional)
12 ounces fine noodles
Parmesan cheese, grated

Sauté mushrooms in butter. Add flour; gradually add half and half and milk to make a cream sauce. Add sherry, Cheddar cheese, ham, garlic, pepper, salt, onion juice and oregano. Cook until smooth. Cook noodles in boiling water until tender; drain. Combine noodles and sauce; place in a 2½ quart casserole. Sprinkle with grated Parmesan cheese. Refrigerate for several hours or overnight. Bring to room temperature. Cook until hot and bubbly in a 350° oven. Yields: 6 servings.
Note: To serve as vegetable dish, decrease ham to 1½ cups.

EASTERN NORTH CAROLINA BARBECUED PORK

pork shoulders and/or pork loins
1 quart vinegar
16 ounces cola carbonated beverage
1 ounce crushed red peppers
¾ ounce ground red peppers
1 ounce black pepper
¼ box salt

Combine vinegar, cola beverage, red peppers, black pepper and salt. Place in refrigerator 24 hours. Insert meat thermometer in thickest part of meat. Place on grill. Turn and baste meat occasionally until done. Remove skin and fat; chop as desired, adding a little chopped fat to insure flavor and moisture. Place chopped meat in large bowl; add salt and sauce to taste. Mix well.

Note: Watch for specials on pork; buy large quantities. Cook at one time, chop and place in freezer.

STUFFED PORK CHOPS GOURMET

4 loin pork chops, 1 inch thick and slit to make a pocket
4 slices Swiss cheese, diced
¼ cup fresh parsley, snipped
½ cup fresh mushrooms, chopped
½ teaspoon salt
1 egg, slightly beaten
dry bread crumbs
3 tablespoons oil
½ cup Chablis

Mix cheese, parsley, mushrooms and salt. Fill pockets in pork chops. Dip each chop in egg and then into bread crumbs. In hot oil in skillet, brown chops well on both sides. Add Chablis; simmer, covered, 45 minutes or until tender. Yields: 4 servings.

INDONESIAN PORK ROAST

5-6 pound pork roast
2 cloves garlic, minced
2 bouillon cubes
2 cups water
½ cup sugar
1 cup soy sauce

Brown pork in its own fat in Dutch oven. Combine remaining ingredients; pour over meat. Cover and simmer 2 hours and 30 minutes, turning 2-3 times. When done, slice and simmer a few minutes in the liquid. Yields: 10 servings.

SWEET AND SOUR PORK

1 pound pork tenderloin, cut in cubes
1 egg yolk
salt
1 teaspoon soy sauce
4 tablespoons cornstarch
½ cup oil
3 tablespoons oil
1 clove garlic, crushed
1 medium onion, quartered
2 small green peppers, cut in 1 inch pieces
5 tablespoons sugar
5 tablespoons catsup
5 tablespoons vinegar
2 teaspoons cornstarch
½ cup water
2 slices pineapple, cut into 6 pieces

Boil pork 2 minutes in water, remove and pat dry. Combine 1 egg yolk, 1 teaspoon soy sauce and salt to taste. Mix well. Mix meat with this marinade; let stand 15 minutes. Coat pork with the cornstarch, and deep fry in ½ cup heated oil in a wok until brown. Remove meat; drain. Remove remaining oil from wok. Heat 3 tablespoons of oil on medium; stir-fry garlic, onion, and green pepper. Add sugar, catsup and vinegar and bring to a boil. Combine cornstarch and water; add to wok mixture. Stir until thick; add meat and pineapple. Cook 2-3 minutes. Yields: 2-3 servings.

MONGOLIAN BARBECUE

"Those who enjoy a fondue-type meal will surely love this."

2 pound pork roast
2 pounds top round beef
2 pounds boned chicken
1 cup onion, chopped
1 cup carrot, thinly sliced
1 cup cabbage, shredded
1 cup green pepper, chopped
1½ tablespoons ginger root, grated
½ cup soy sauce
¼ cup sesame oil
¼ cup peanut oil
⅓ cup sherry
hefty dash grated garlic
½ teaspoon salt
½ teaspoon onion salt
1 teaspoon sugar in ¼ cup water
¼ teaspoon pepper
½ teaspoon monosodium glutamate

Slice the meats paper thin; place in a bowl. Place vegetables in another bowl. Mix other ingredients in another bowl. Place 1 tablespoon of liquid in wok or fry pan and add a handful of meat mixture and a handful of vegetable mixture. Stir fry. (If feasible, cook over charcoal. If cooking indoors on the stove, add charcoal seasoning to taste.) Any vegetable may be added as long as it can be stir-fried quickly. Yields: 10 servings.

LAZY MAN'S LUAU

3-4 pound pork shoulder roast
20 ounces frozen spinach
1 tablespoon salt
2 tablespoons liquid smoke
4-6 medium sweet potatoes
4-6 bananas
brown sugar
juice of 1 lemon
cinnamon
butter
2 tablespoons rum

Preheat oven to 325°. Line a 9x13 pan with heavy duty foil. Lay frozen spinach on bottom. Top with pork shoulder. Sprinkle meat with salt, and liquid smoke. Cover with foil; seal tightly. Bake at least 5 hours. Add sweet potatoes and continue to bake 1 hour. Lay peeled bananas side by side in baking pan. Sprinkle with brown sugar, lemon juice and cinnamon. Dot butter on bananas; sprinkle with rum. Return to oven. Continue to bake 1 hour or until potatoes and bananas are tender. Yields: 4-6 servings.

PORK LOAF

2 pounds pork, ground
1 pound cooked ham, ground
1 egg, beaten
1 cup bread crumbs
½ cup milk
3 tablespoons canned tomato soup, undiluted
½ teaspoon paprika
¼ teaspoon salt
1 medium onion, sliced
Mustard Sauce

Preheat oven to 350°. Combine all ingredients except onion and Mustard Sauce. Shape into a loaf in a 10x6x1¾ baking dish; arrange onion slices over top. Bake 1½ hours. Baste occasionally with a few drops of hot water. Serve with Mustard Sauce. Yields: 8 servings.

Mustard Sauce:
10¾ ounces canned tomato soup (minus 3 tablespoons)
½ cup prepared mustard
½ cup butter
½ cup vinegar
½ cup sugar
3 egg yolks, beaten

Combine all ingredients. Cook over low heat, stirring constantly, until thickened. Serve hot.
"This may be kept indefinitely in refrigerator."

CHINESE PORK STRIPS

1 pound lean pork, cut in 3x½x1 strips
2 tablespoons cornstarch
pinch salt
2 eggs
4 tablespoons plain flour
oil
2 tablespoons dry sherry
2 tablespoons soy sauce
2 teaspoons salt
¾ cup sugar
4 tablespoons vinegar
2 tablespoons cornstarch
2 cups water
cherry tomatoes (optional) for garnish

Coat pork strips with cornstarch and salt mixture. Blend eggs and flour with beater. Heat oil to medium in a wok. Dip pork strips in the egg and flour mixture and fry in wok; drain. Combine the dry sherry, soy sauce, salt, sugar, vinegar, cornstarch and water in a saucepan. Stir until thick over low heat. Add fried pork; stir. Remove to serving plate. Decorate with cherry tomatoes. Yields: 2-3 servings.
"Serve over hot rice."

Do not thaw meat in water unless it is to be cooked in water.

COLD PORK LOIN

5-6 pound pork loin, boned and tied (or boston butt)
dry mustard
thyme
¾ cup dry sherry
½ cup soy sauce
3 cloves garlic, chopped
2 tablespoons fresh ginger, grated
16 ounces currant jelly
2 tablespoons soy sauce
4 tablespoons dry sherry
parsley for garnish
cherry tomatoes for garnish

Day before — rub roast with dry mustard and thyme. Prepare marinade of sherry, ½ cup soy sauce, garlic and ginger. Pour over roast; marinate 2 hours at room temperature, turning frequently. Refrigerate. Next day, remove from marinade. Roast, uncovered, 30 minutes per pound at 325°. Baste every 20 minutes with marinade. Remove from oven when meat reaches a temperature of 170° on meat thermometer. Melt jelly in a heavy pan. When bubbly, add 2 tablespoons soy sauce and 2 tablespoons sherry. Cook 2 minutes; spoon over pork. Cool in a chilly room. Do not refrigerate unless the day is very hot. Garnish with parsley and cherry tomatoes. Serve with sauce. Yields: 8-10 servings.

SAUSAGE CASSEROLE

"A great smörgasbord dish. Goes well with ham or chicken."

1½ pounds lean pork sausage
2 envelopes chicken noodle soup mix
4 or 5 spring onions and tops, chopped
1 large green pepper, chopped
4 ribs of celery, chopped
3 tablespoons margarine
1 cup uncooked rice
8½ ounces water chestnuts, drained and sliced
salt and pepper to taste
¼ cup slivered almonds

Preheat oven to 350°. Cook 2 envelopes of soup in 4½ cups of boiling water 7 minutes. Cook sausage until fat is rendered. Sauté onions, green pepper and celery in margarine. Add soup, rice and water chestnuts; mix well, add salt and pepper to taste. Bake, covered, in a greased 3 quart casserole 1½-2 hours. Remove cover. Sprinkle with almonds the last 30 minutes. Yields: 6 servings.

Vinegar tenderizes meat.

Thaw meats in refrigerator to keep in juices.

BARBECUED SPARERIBS

"An excellent barbecue sauce.
Would also be good for barbecued chicken."

5-7 pounds spareribs
1 teaspoon paprika
½ teaspoon cayenne pepper
2 tablespoons sugar
2 teaspoons salt
1 teaspoon pepper
½ cup vinegar
1½ cups water
1 teaspoon prepared mustard
1 teaspoon Worcestershire sauce
1 teaspoon Tabasco sauce
2 tablespoons chili sauce
½ lemon (juice and rind)
1 medium onion, grated
½-1 cup butter
2 tablespoons catsup
1 teaspoon liquid smoke

Combine all ingredients except spareribs and liquid smoke. Simmer 30 minutes. Then add 1 teaspoon liquid smoke. Pour sauce over spareribs and charcoal. (Can bake in a 325° oven 1½ hours). Yields: 5-7 servings.

CUMBERLAND CASSEROLE GRANDE

"Good served with tomato soup instead of a sandwich."

½ pound bulk sausage
½ cup corn meal
½ teaspoon salt
¼ teaspoon soda
½ cup milk
1 egg, beaten
1 cup cooked rice
8 ounces cream style corn
¼ cup onion, chopped
¼ cup green chillies, chopped
2 tablespoons pimento, chopped
1 cup Cheddar cheese, grated

Preheat oven to 375°. Cook sausage until done, stirring often to crumble. Drain off all but 2 tablespoons of drippings. Set aside. Sift dry ingredients into a mixing bowl. Add remaining ingredients and sausage, stirring only to blend well. Pour into a 10 inch oven proof skillet or a greased square cake pan. Bake 40-45 minutes. Yields: 6-8 servings.

SPAGHETTI BOLOGNESE

"This is a spaghetti sauce you'll prepare often. It is so good."

½ pound Italian sausage (casings removed)
½ pound bulk pork sausage
¼ pound mushrooms, sliced
1 carrot, sliced
1 clove garlic, crushed
½ cup onion, chopped
½ cup celery, chopped
½ cup green pepper, chopped
2 tablespoons oil
30 ounces canned tomato sauce
½ cup water
¼ cup dry red wine
1 teaspoon sugar
¼ teaspoon Italian herb seasoning

Sauté mushrooms, carrot, garlic, onion, celery, and green pepper in oil. Add sausages; cook until it looses its redness. Drain fat; add remaining ingredients. Simmer, uncovered, 40 minutes, stirring occasionally. Serve over hot cooked spaghetti. Yields: 4-6 servings.

THIN VEAL FONESTIER

1½ pounds veal cutlets
1 clove garlic
plain flour
4 tablespoons butter
½ pound fresh mushrooms, sliced thin
salt to taste
pepper to taste
⅓ cup dry vermouth
1 teaspoon lemon juice
fresh snipped parsley

Pound veal until very thin. Rub all sides with cut garlic clove. Dredge veal in flour to coat all sides thoroughly. Heat butter in a skillet. Brown veal well on both sides. Heap mushrooms on top of veal. Sprinkle with salt, pepper, and vermouth. Cover; cook on low heat 20 minutes or until fork tender. Add a few teaspoons of vermouth if veal seems to be drying out. Remove from heat; sprinkle with lemon juice and parsley. Yields: 4 servings.

VEAL PARMIGIANA

1 pound veal cutlets, pounded thin and cut into small pieces
4 tablespoons butter
½ cup bread crumbs, toasted
½ Parmesan cheese, grated
½ teaspoon salt
dash pepper
1 egg, slightly beaten and diluted with small amount of water
8 ounces canned tomato sauce
½ teaspoon oregano
½ teaspoon sugar
dash onion salt
½ pound mozzarella cheese

Preheat oven to 375°. Melt butter in baking dish. Combine next 4 ingredients in another dish. Dip veal into dry mixture, egg mixture and dry mixture again. Place veal in 1½ quart casserole. Bake about 20 minutes. Turn veal over; bake 10-15 minutes more. Combine tomato sauce, oregano, sugar and onion salt. Pour over meat. Place cheese on top. Bake 3-4 minutes longer. Yields: 4 servings.

CHINESE VEAL CASSEROLE

1½ pounds veal round steak, cut into bite-size pieces
1½ cups onions, chopped
1½ cups green peppers, chopped
1 cup celery, chopped
10¾ ounces canned cream of mushroom soup
10¾ ounces water
½ cup raw rice
3 tablespoons pimento, chopped
3 tablespoons soy sauce
1 cup peas
salt and pepper to taste
3 ounces chow mein noodles

Preheat oven to 325°. Brown veal and add onions, green pepper and celery; cook until tender. Add soup, water, rice, pimento, soy sauce, peas, salt and pepper. Put in 2 quart casserole. Bake, uncovered, 1½ hours or until rice is done. Five minutes before finished, top with chow mein noodles. Yields: 4-6 servings.

COLLECTION OF NATIONAL HISTORIC SITES

Carl Sandburg's Home — "Connemara" — home of famed poet; Flatrock

Fort Raleigh — Location of the first English colony in North America; Roanoke Island

Guilford Courthouse National Military Park — Site of decisive Revolutionary War Battle (March 15, 1781); Greensboro

Moores Creek National Military Park — Site of important early Revolutionary War Battle (February 27, 1776); Pender County

Wright Brothers National Memorial — Site of world's first powered aircraft flight on December 17, 1903; Kitty Hawk

COLLECTION OF NATIONAL PARKS AND FORESTS

Great Smoky Mountains National Park — most popular national park in U.S.

Blue Ridge Parkway — called America's most scenic highway

Cape Hatteras National Seashore Park — first designated seashore park in U.S.; 70 miles of open beach

Cape Lookout National Seashore Park — When completed it will include 58 miles of open beach

Pisgah National Forest — includes Cradle of Forestry in America (first school for foresters), Linville Gorge Wilderness Area and Shining Rock Wilderness Area

Nantahala National Forest — Joyce Kilmer Forest, author of poem "Trees"

Croatan National Forest — only national forest in eastern N.C.; 155,000 acres

Uwharrie National Forest — contains oldest mountain range in Central N.C.

pickles
and
preserves

BREAD AND BUTTER PICKLES

6 quarts cucumbers, very thinly sliced
8 onions, very thinly sliced
½ cup salt
5 cups vinegar
5 cups sugar
2 tablespoons mustard seed
½ teaspoon turmeric

Place sliced cucumbers and onions in large container. Sprinkle with salt; cover with water. Let stand 2-3 hours or overnight. Bring remaining ingredients to a rolling boil. Drain cucumbers and onions and add to syrup. Cook only until cucumbers are hot. Pack in warm, sterilized jars. Yields: 8 pints.

Liquid & powdered pectin can't be used interchangeably. The powdered must be added before the sugar & the liquid added after the sugar.

KOSHER DILL PICKLES

16 grape leaves (from cultivated or wild vines)
16-18 pounds medium size cucumbers

Line the warm sterilized jars with 1 or 2 grape leaves. Wash, slice and pack cucumbers into jars. To each jar add:

1 clove garlic
1 small piece hot pepper
pinch of alum
1 whole clove
1 teaspoon dill seed
¼ teaspoon dill weed

Bring the following to a boil:

1 quart vinegar
3 quarts water
1 cup, less 2 tablespoons, kosher salt
2 tablespoons sugar

Pour hot mixture into packed jars. Seal. Beginning on the second day, turn upside down for several days to mix the spices. Yields: 8 quarts.

MARY'S CUCUMBER PICKLES

6 pounds cucumbers
1 cup uniodized salt
9 cups water
7 teaspoons alum
2 quarts vinegar
4-5 pounds sugar
2 ounces pickling spices

Wash cucumbers. Combine salt and water in uncovered crock jar. Add whole cucumbers to brine. Weight down with a plate to keep cucumbers submerged. Soak 2 weeks. Pour off brine; soak cucumbers in fresh water overnight. Pour off; cut cucumbers into slices. Soak in alum water — 7 teaspoons alum to enough water to cover cucumbers — 6 hours. Remove; rinse in fresh water. Drain. Heat enough vinegar to cover cucumbers to boiling point; pour over cucumbers. Weight down again. Let stand 24 hours. Drain and discard vinegar. Take out cucumbers. Pack in crock in layers of sugar and pickling spices. Let stand 3 days. Pack in jars. It is not necessary to seal these pickles. They will keep indefinitely. Yields: 3 quarts.

Variation: For Sweet Dill Pickles – substitute dill weed for pickling spices and cut cucumbers in strips.

Add a small piece of butter when cooking fruit for jam or jelly to prevent foam on top.

SWEET CRISP PICKLES

7 pounds medium size cucumbers
2 cups lime
2 gallons water
2 quarts vinegar
4½ pounds sugar
1 tablespoon salt
1 teaspoon mixed pickling spices
1 teaspoon whole cloves
1 teaspoon celery seed

Slice cucumbers in ½ inch slices. Place cucumbers in an enameled pan or crock. Cover with solution of lime and water. Soak 24 hours. Rinse pickles through several changes of cold water. Cover with fresh water; soak 3 hours. Drain. Combine remaining ingredients. Add cucumbers; let stand overnight. The next day, boil 40 minutes, pack into hot, sterilized jars, and seal. Yields: 8 pints.

"This recipe may also be used for sliced green tomato or watermelon rind."

CARROT PICKLES

"A ready to serve hors d'oeuvre when chilled."

3 pounds carrots
1 pint distilled vinegar (colorless)
½ tablespoon whole cloves
½ tablespoon whole allspice
½ tablespoon mace
2 cups sugar
½ stick cinnamon

Peel carrots; cut in strips, desired size and length. Boil in water until just heated through. Pack hot carrots lengthwise in hot sterilized jars. Pour boiling syrup made of vinegar, sugar and spices, tied in a bag, over carrots. Seal; process 10 minutes in hot water bath. Yields: 3-4 pints.

GARLIC OKRA PICKLES

3 pounds fresh okra, uncut
3 cups water
1 cup white vinegar
¼ cup pickling salt
2 cloves garlic, crushed

Wash okra well. Drain; pack into hot clean pint jars. In saucepan, combine remaining ingredients. Bring to a boil; pour into jars to within ½ inch of tops. Adjust lids. Process in boiling water bath 5 minutes. Yields: 4 pints.

PEACH PICKLES

"A great way to preserve North Carolina peaches."

3 cups vinegar
3 cups water
3 pounds sugar
10 two inch pieces cinnamon stick
1 teaspoon whole cloves
6 pounds peaches, clingstone preferred

Combine vinegar, water, sugar and spices in a kettle. Heat until sugar is dissolved. Peel peaches; add to hot syrup. Simmer fruit in syrup until tender, about 5 minutes. Remove from heat; let stand overnight. In the morning, drain off syrup and boil until thick. Pack fruit in sterilized jars. Fill each jar with hot syrup. Seal. Yields: 3 quarts.

"Tie spices in a cheesecloth bag or stick a clove in each peach before simmering."

SQUASH PICKLES

"A favorite from our old cookbook."

4 quarts yellow summer squash, thinly sliced
4 small onions, thinly sliced
½ cup salt
4 cups vinegar
1 teaspoon turmeric
3 cups sugar
2 cups brown sugar
2 tablespoons mustard seed
1 teaspoon celery seed

Place layers of squash and onions in a deep pan; cover with salt. Cover this with ice. Repeat. Cover with lid. Put in refrigerator for at least 3 hours. Drain, do not wash. Make a syrup of remaining ingredients. Bring to a rolling boil. Add squash and onions. Heat 5 minutes. Put in hot, sterilized jars. Seal at once. Be sure vegetables are covered with syrup. Yields: 12 pints.

Never use iodized salt as it causes pickles to turn dark.

SLICED GREEN TOMATO PICKLES

"This pickle is always a best seller at our Holly-Day Event."

7 pounds small green tomatoes
8/10 ounces calcium hydroxide (or 2 cups lime)
5 pounds sugar
3 pints white vinegar
1 pint water
1 teaspoon whole cloves
1 teaspoon ginger
1 teaspoon allspice
1 teaspoon mace
1 stick cinnamon

Wash green tomatoes; slice very thin. Soak overnight in 2 gallons water mixed with calcium hydroxide or lime. Drain the following morning; cover with cold water. Soak 4 hours, changing the water every hour. Mix the sugar, vinegar, and water. Tie the spices in a bag; add to the syrup mixture. Bring syrup to a boil; pour over tomatoes. Let stand overnight. On the third day, bring the pickles and syrup to a boil. Boil 1 hour or until tomatoes are clear. Seal in jars while hot. Yields: 10 pints.

"If recipe is doubled, you need to more than double the syrup in order to have enough to cover tomatoes when packed in jars. Calcium hydroxide is found in the pharmacy."

WATERMELON RIND PICKLES

"A favorite in the melon growing area."

7 pounds watermelon rind, peeled
3 tablespoons slack lime
1½ pints vinegar
5 pounds sugar
1 pint water
½ teaspoon oil of cinnamon (found in pharmacy)
½ teaspoon oil of cloves
3 lemons, thinly sliced

Trim green from rind. A slight rim of pink may be left on rind. Cut rind into cubes, strips or any desired shape. For a crisp pickle, soak rind in 3 quarts of water with 3 tablespoons slack lime 3 hours. Drain. Cover with cold water; cook about 20 minutes at a fast boil. If rind is thick, it may take a little longer. The rind should stick tender. Make a syrup of vinegar, sugar, water, spices and lemon slices. Heat. Drain rind thoroughly; pour syrup over it. Let stand overnight. Next morning, drain off syrup. Heat to boiling point. Pour over rind. Repeat this procedure 2 more mornings. On the fifth day, heat syrup and rind. Pack into hot, sterilized jars. Process to seal. Yields: 7 pints.

When canning be sure that you do not use copper, brass or zinc utensils. Glass, pottery or unchipped enamel is preferred.

END-OF-THE-GARDEN RELISH

"Beautiful and delicious."

1 cup green tomatoes, chopped
1 cup green pepper, chopped
1 cup red pepper, chopped
1 cup onion, chopped
1 cup cucumber, pared and chopped
1 cup cauliflower, cut in small florets
2 tablespoons salt
1 cup carrots, chopped
1 cup green beans, cut in ½ inch slices
1 cup celery, chopped
2 cups vinegar
2 cups sugar
1 tablespoon mustard seed
1 teaspoon celery seed

In a large bowl, combine tomatoes, peppers, onions, cucumbers, cauliflower, salt and 3 cups water. Let stand overnight. Next day, in medium saucepan, cook carrots, green beans and celery in salted water 10 minutes or until tender. Drain. Drain tomato mixture; discard liquid. Mix vinegar, sugar, mustard and celery seed. Bring to a boil, stirring until sugar dissolves. Add vegetables, reduce heat; simmer 10 minutes, uncovered. Pack in hot, sterilized jars; process 10 minutes. Yields: 6, ½ pts.

CHOW-CHOW RELISH

"A nice addition for buffet or family meals."

salt
2 quarts green tomatoes, shredded
2 quarts cabbage, shredded
1 quart onions, shredded
1 pint green peppers, shredded
1 pint sweet red peppers, shredded
2 hot peppers, diced
1 tablespoon turmeric powder
2 tablespoons celery seed
2 tablespoons whole mustard seed
1 quart apple cider vinegar
3⅓ cups sugar

Mix vegetables and a liberal amount of salt. Mix spices with vinegar; bring this mixture to a boil. Add vegetables to boiling mixture; scald well. Taste test for flavor. Add more salt if needed. Pack in hot sterilized jars. Yields: 8 pints.

GREEN TOMATO PICKLE RELISH

"This is an old favorite of League members."

1 peck green tomatoes, sliced
1 gallon cabbage, shredded
8 green peppers, sliced
24 medium onions, sliced
1 cup salt
2 quarts vinegar
3 pounds brown sugar
2 tablespoons celery seed
4 tablespoons mustard seed
2 tablespoons mace
2 tablespoons ground cloves
2 tablespoons cinnamon
2 tablespoons turmeric (optional)

Slice all vegetables thinly; sprinkle with salt. Leave at room temperature overnight. Drain. Combine remaining ingredients; bring to a boil. Add vegetables; cook until tender, which will be about 1½ hours after they come to a boil. Pack in hot sterilized jars. Seal. Yields: 15-18 pints.

APRICOT CONSERVE

16 ounces dried apricots, chopped
20 ounces canned crushed pineapple
1 cup water
5½ cups sugar

Combine first 3 ingredients; let stand overnight. Add sugar; cook over low heat, stirring often, until thick. Seal in jelly glasses. Yields: 8 half pints.

BLUEBERRY MARMALADE

1 orange
1 lemon
1 cup water
3 cups blueberries, crushed
5 cups sugar
3 ounces Certo
paraffin, melted

Peel orange and lemon very carefully, excluding the white membrane. Chop finely the transparent bits of orange and lemon peel. Cover with water; simmer 10 minutes. Remove any white left on orange and lemon. Chop pulp finely. Add this to cooked peel. Also add crushed blueberries. Simmer 10 minutes. Add sugar, bring to a boil; boil 1 minute. Remove from heat; stir in Certo. Alternately stir and skim foam off top for 7 minutes. Pour into hot, sterilized jars. Seal with ¼ inch melted paraffin. Yields: 6 cups.

Before pouring paraffin in jelly or preserve glasses, place string across top — this will make the paraffin easier to remove.

PEACH CONSERVE

"Delicious!"

1 orange
7 cups peaches, peeled and chopped
5 cups sugar
½ teaspoon ground ginger
2 tablespoons lemon juice
¾ cup chopped blanched almonds
paraffin, melted

Peel orange; chop peeling very fine. Chop orange sections. Combine fruit and orange peel in a large saucepan. Place over medium heat; simmer 30 minutes. Add sugar, ginger and lemon juice; stir until sugar dissolves. Continue to simmer over low heat until thick. Add almonds; cook an additional 5 minutes. Remove from heat. Ladle quickly into sterilized jelly glasses. Seal at once with ⅛ inch layer of hot paraffin. Yields: 8 half pints.

"This can also be used as a topping over fruit-filled crepes, ice cream or on waffles."

PEPPER JELLY

"With this on your shelf, you have an hors d'oeuvre on hand or a welcome gift for someone special."

⅓ cup red or green hot pepper, diced
1 cup bell pepper, diced
2 cups vinegar
6½ cups sugar
6 ounces Certo
paraffin

Combine diced hot pepper, bell pepper, 1 cup vinegar and 1 cup sugar in blender container; blend well. Mix remaining vinegar and sugar in a large pot; add mixture from blender container. Bring to a boil. Boil 5 minutes at a high roll. Add Certo; boil 1 minute. Remove from heat, let stand 5 minutes and skim foam from top surface. Pour into warm, sterilized jars. Seal with paraffin. Yields: 7-8 half pint jars.
"Serve with pork or poultry. Also great with cream cheese on crackers. Green or red food coloring may be added."

SPARKLING BURGUNDY JELLY

2 cups Burgundy
3 cups sugar
6 ounces Certo
4 ounces block paraffin, melted

Combine wine and sugar in top of double boiler over rapidly boiling water. Stir until sugar is dissolved, usually 2-10 minutes. Do not allow this mixture to boil. Stir in Certo at once. Pour into sterilized jelly jars. Seal with melted paraffin. Yields: five 8-ounce jars.

LUSCIOUS STRAWBERRY PRESERVES

"The whole strawberries make this a beautiful preserve."

4 cups whole strawberries
5 cups sugar
3 tablespoons lemon juice (or ¼ teaspoon cream of tartar)
paraffin, melted

In a large pot, alternate layers of berries and sugar. Slowly bring to a boil. After the entire mixture is boiling, cook 9 minutes. Remove from heat; add lemon juice or cream of tartar. Pour into a bowl; let stand overnight. The second day, boil 9 minutes again, allow to cool slightly. Pour into sterilized jelly glasses. Seal with melted paraffin. Yields: 6 jelly jars.

COLLECTION OF NORTH CAROLINA GARDENS

Arlie Gardens — 155 acres of live oaks, magnolias, azaleas; Wilmington

Greenfield Gardens — One of nations most beautiful municipal gardens; Wilmington

Orton Plantation — Ante-bellum rice plantation with formal gardens; Wilmington

Tryon Palace and Gardens — Formal 18th Century gardens; New Bern

Bonner House Garden — 19th Century "meditation garden"; Bath

Elizabethan Garden — Formal 16th Century gardens; Manteo

Coker Arboretun — 350 species of woody plants; Chapel Hill

Carolina Botanical Garden — Collection of native plants, Chapel Hill

Sarah P. Duke Gardens — One of the nation's most impressive displays of chrysanthemums — Duke University Campus; Durham

Martha Franck Fragrance Garden (for the blind) — Butner

Clarendon Gardens — Nation's largest holly show — over 200 varieties; Pinehurst

Reynolda Gardens — 110 acres of the R. S. Reynolds estate; Winston-Salem

Iron Gate Gardens — Intricate iron works, outstanding collection of day lilies; Cherryville

Roan Mountain — 100s of acres of rhododendron; near Asheville

Biltmore Gardens — Formal gardens, largest and most complete collection of native American azaleas; Asheville

Daniel Boone Native Gardens — Informal collection of native plants; Boone

Craggy Gardens — 600 acres of rhododendron; near Asheville

Freedlander Dahlia Gardens — One of the nation's largest staked dahlia displays; Waynesville

pies

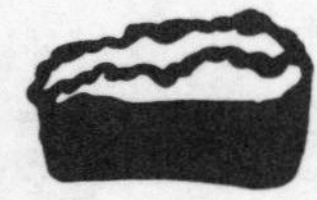

THE CAROLINA COLLECTOR'S CONCOCTIONS

. . . Press slivered almonds in pie crust before baking.

. . . Add a few crushed mint leaves to a fresh berry pie.

. . . For an unusual apple pie crust add ½ t cinnamon to flour & salt mixture; for mincemeat crust use allspice; for raisin or other fruit pie, use nutmeg.

. . . Line pie plate with ginger snaps, top with sliced bananas & fill with a cream filling.

. . . Spread coffee ice cream over graham cracker pie shell; spread fudge frosting on top & garnish with pecans. Freeze.

. . . Whole-wheat pie crust is 1 c plus 2 T whole-wheat flour, 1 T sugar, ⅛ t salt, 7 T oil & 2 T cold water.

. . . Spread pie crust with jam before adding filling & meringue.

. . . Make a pie cobbler with apple pie filling, shredded cheese, cinnamon sugar & top with 1 can refrigerated biscuits dipped in melted butter.

. . . A custard made with sour cream to which chopped prunes have been added & baked makes a good & different pie.

. . . Add a bit of lemon rind to meringue of lemon meringue pie before baking.

. . . Spread 1 c coconut over apples before adding top crust on apple pie.

. . . Top a fruit pie with sauce made with 3 oz. cream cheese, 1 T sugar & frozen orange juice concentrate.

. . . Lemon pie — mix 1 large can frozen lemonade, 1 can condensed milk, 1 large carton Cool Whip. Pour into graham cracker crust & chill or freeze.

. . . For a good quick pie, melt 1 large chocolate almond bar & fold into large carton Cool Whip. Pour into baked pie shell & chill.

ANGEL PIE

2 egg whites
½ cup sugar
½ cup pecans, chopped
5-6 milk chocolate bars, 1.05 ounces each
3 tablespoons water
1 teaspoon vanilla extract
1 cup whipping cream, whipped

Preheat oven to 300°. Beat egg whites until they form peaks. Add sugar gradually and beat until stiff. Fold in pecans and gently spread into *well greased* 9 inch pie pan. Bake 55 minutes. Cool.

Melt chocolate bars in water. Cool; add vanilla. Whip cream; fold chocolate mixture into cream. Pour into cooled pie shell. Refrigerate for several hours before serving.

Place pie shells, which need more intense heat from underneath in order to bake through properly, on the lowest rack.

ANGEL PECAN PIE

18 single saltine crackers
1 cup pecans, finely chopped
3 egg whites
½ teaspoon cream of tartar
1 cup plus 1 tablespoon sugar (used separately)
1 teaspoon vanilla extract
½ pint whipping cream, whipped
2 tablespoons commercial pineapple topping
½ cup angel flake coconut, toasted

Preheat oven to 325°. Roll saltine crackers until fine between waxed paper. Beat egg whites with cream of tartar until stiff. Gradually add 1 cup of sugar, continue beating until whites are stiff and shiny. Combine cracker crumbs and nuts; fold into beaten egg whites. Stir in vanilla. Grease a 9 or 10 inch pie plate with oil. Spoon the egg white mixture into pie plate; bake *exactly* 15 minutes. Turn off oven; leave pie shell inside for *exactly* 10 minutes. (It will not be quite golden.) Cool. Whip cream with 1 tablespoon sugar. Fold pineapple topping into whipped cream. Spread this mixture on prepared shell; sprinkle with coconut. Chill thoroughly.

BLUE RIDGE APPLE CHEESE PIE

5-6 cups tart apples, sliced
½ cup sugar, brown or white
1 teaspoon cinnamon
¼ teaspoon salt
½ cup brown sugar
½ cup plain flour, sifted
5½ tablespoons butter
1 cup sharp Cheddar cheese, grated
9 inch pie shell, unbaked

Preheat oven to 400°. Combine apples, sugar, cinnamon and salt. Toss to cover apples completely. If apples lack tartness, add a little lemon juice. Set mixture aside. Blend brown sugar and flour. Cut butter in with fork or pastry blender. Place apple mixture in unbaked pie shell. Sprinkle cheese over apples; sprinkle sugar-flour mixture on top of cheese. Bake 30-40 minutes.

Note: This recipe can be prepared without the pie shell. It is equally as good prepared in heavily greased baking dish.

For a fresh fruit pie, toss fruit with cornstarch instead of flour. 1 T cornstarch=2 T flour.

APPLE PIE with CHEESE PASTRY

4 cups tart apples, pared and sliced
1 cup sugar
2 tablespoons plain flour
⅛ teaspoon salt
1 teaspoon cinnamon
¼ teaspoon nutmeg
2 tablespoons butter
Cheese Pastry

Preheat oven to 450°. Pare apples; slice thin. Add sugar mixed with flour, salt and spices. Fill 9 inch pie pan lined with cheese pastry. Dot with butter. Adjust top crust. Bake 10 minutes; reduce heat to 350° and bake 40 minutes.

Cheese Pastry:
2 cups plain flour
½ teaspoon salt
½ cup sharp Cheddar cheese, grated
⅔ cup butter, cold
4-5 tablespoons ice water

Sift together flour and salt. Stir in cheese; cut in butter. Add ice water slowly; mix lightly with fork. On floured board, roll out slightly thinner than plain pastry.

FROZEN BLUEBERRY ALASKA PIE

2 tablespoons butter, softened
1½ cups coconut, flaked
1 quart lemon custard ice cream
2 egg whites
¾ cup sugar

Preheat oven to 300°. Spread a 9 inch pie pan heavily with softened butter. Press coconut into pie pan. Bake 15-20 minutes or until light brown. Cool completely. Fill coconut pie shell with lemon ice cream. Cover with foil; freeze. At serving time, beat egg whites until stiff, gradually adding ¾ cup sugar. Spread egg whites over ice cream, sealing edges; brown under broiler 1-2 minutes.

Sauce:
1 cup fresh blueberries (or canned blueberries in syrup)
½ cup sugar
1 tablespoon cornstarch

Combine fresh blueberries with ½ cup sugar (if using canned, omit sugar) and cornstarch. Cook over medium heat until thick. Remove and keep warm. To serve, pass hot blueberry sauce to dribble over each slice of pie.

To prevent meringue from weeping, cool it to room temperature before refrigerating.

WHITE LAKE BLUEBERRY PIE

"Ideal for spring garden club luncheon."

3 ounces cream cheese, softened
9 inch pie shell, baked
1 quart fresh blueberries, divided
1 cup sugar
3 tablespoons cornstarch
½ teaspoon lemon juice
whipping cream, whipped and sweetened

Spread softened cream cheese on bottom of cooled baked pie shell. Place 1 cup blueberries over cream cheese. Mash 2 cups blueberries; place in saucepan. Bring to a boil over medium heat. Mix sugar, cornstarch and lemon juice; add to blueberries. Cook until slightly thickened. Cool. Pour over blueberries in pie shell; chill until firm. Top with sweetened whipped cream and remaining blueberries.

CHERRY CRISP PIE with LEMON PASTRY

42 ounces cherry pie filling
1-2 teaspoons allspice
1 teaspoon almond extract
1½ tablespoons lemon juice
1 tablespoon lemon peel, grated
Lemon Pastry
whipped topping

Preheat oven to 425°. In saucepan, combine pie filling, allspice, almond, lemon juice and lemon peel. Cook over medium heat 5 minutes. Pour in 10 inch pie plate lined with Lemon Pastry. Bake 25 minutes or until crust is golden brown. Serve warm or cold with dollops of whipped topping.

Lemon Pastry:
2 cups plain flour
½ teaspoon salt
¾ cup shortening
1 tablespoon lemon peel, grated
2 egg yolks
1 tablespoon lemon juice
4-5 tablespoons cold water

Sift together flour and salt. Using pastry blender cut shortening into flour until mixture resembles coarse cornmeal. Mix in lemon peel. Beat egg yolks slightly with lemon juice and water. Add to dry ingredients. Mix until ball is formed. Knead 5 times. Refrigerate 15 minutes. Roll ¾ of dough to fit 10 inch pie plate. Use remainder of dough to cut out decorative cherries with stems and leaves.

CHOCOLATE FUDGE PIE

½ cup butter
3 ounces unsweetened chocolate
4 eggs, well beaten
3 tablespoons white corn syrup
1½ cups sugar
¼ teaspoon salt
¼ cup milk
1 teaspoon vanilla extract
10 inch pie shell, unbaked
ice cream (optional)
whipping cream, whipped (optional)

Preheat oven to 350°. Melt butter and chocolate in top of double boiler; set aside to cool. Beat eggs until light and thick; add other ingredients; add chocolate and butter mixture. Mix well; pour into pie shell. Bake 30-35 minutes or until top is crusty and filling is set. Do not over bake.
"This pie does not need meringue; it may be served with ice cream or whipped cream. The recipe is easily doubled so you can freeze a pie for later use."

SUPREME COCONUT PIE

3 eggs, beaten
1½ cups sugar
½ cup butter
4 teaspoons lemon juice
1 teaspoon vanilla extract
1½ cups coconut, flaked
9 inch pie shell, unbaked

Preheat oven to 350°. Thoroughly combine eggs, sugar, butter, lemon juice and vanilla. Stir in coconut. Pour filling into unbaked pie shell. Bake 40-45 minutes. (A knife inserted half way between the center and edge should come out clean.) Cool before serving.
"This is delicious served with whipped cream and toasted coconut."

Substitute light cream or sour cream for water called for in pie crust for a rich pastry.

APRICOT CREAM CHEESE PIE

8 ounces cream cheese softened
1 can condensed milk
⅓ cup lemon juice
1 can apricot halves
1 graham cracker crust
¼ cup sugar
1½ tablespoon cornstarch
dash of salt
½ cup apricot syrup
½ cup strained orange juice

Beat cream cheese until fluffy. Gradually add milk beating until well blended. Beat in lemon juice. Pour into baked crust and chill for 3 hours. Arrange apricots on top of pie. In a small pan, mix sugar, cornstarch and salt. Stir in apricot syrup and orange juice. Mix until smooth. Cook stirring until thick and clear. Pour over pie. Chill for 2 hours.

EGGNOG PIE

"A perfect dessert for a Christmas dinner."

9 inch graham cracker crust (or chocolate wafer crust)
1 envelope unflavored gelatin
¼ cup cold water
⅓ cup sugar
2 tablespoons cornstarch
⅛ teaspoon salt
2 cups commercial eggnog
1½ ounces unsweetened chocolate, melted
1½ teaspoons vanilla extract
2 tablespoons rum
2 cups whipping cream, whipped and divided
¼ cup confectioners' sugar
¼ cup rum
chocolate curls

Sprinkle gelatin over water to soften. Mix sugar, cornstarch and salt. Gradually stir in eggnog. Cook in top of double boiler, stirring constantly, until thickened. Remove from heat; stir in softened gelatin until dissolved. Divide filling in half; add chocolate and vanilla to ½ of mixture; set aside. Allow remaining ½ to cool; add 2 tablespoons rum and 1 cup whipping cream, whipped. Pour rum flavored mixture into pie shell; pour chocolate mixture on top. Set aside. Beat 1 cup cream, sugar and ¼ cup rum lightly. Spread on pie. Sprinkle with chocolate curls. Chill several hours before serving.

GRASSHOPPER PIE

"A grand finale to a dinner party."

24 marshmallows
4 tablespoons milk
¼ cup crème de menthe, or to taste
1 cup whipping cream, whipped
8 inch chocolate wafer pie shell
pecans, crushed (optional)
milk chocolate, slivered (optional)

In top of double boiler, combine marshmallows and milk. Heat until marshmallows are completely melted. Remove from heat and cool. Add crème de menthe to marshmallow mixture; mix until well blended. Gently fold whipped cream into marshmallow mixture; mound into pie shell. Sprinkle with crushed pecans and slivered milk chocolate. Chill several hours or overnight. Serve cold.

Chocolate Wafer Pie Shell:
18 Famous Chocolate Wafers, crushed
¼ cup margarine or butter, melted

Combine crushed chocolate wafers and butter. Mix thoroughly. Press mixture into bottom and sides of 8 inch pie plate. Chill.

KEY LIME PIE

"This is a beautiful and delicious summer dessert!"

1 envelope unflavored gelatin
½ cup sugar
¼ teaspoon salt
4 eggs, separated
½ cup fresh lime juice, reserve rind
¼ cup water
1 teaspoon lime rind, grated
green food coloring
½ cup sugar
1 cup whipping cream, whipped
9 inch baked pie shell (or graham cracker shell)

Mix gelatin, ½ cup sugar, and salt in saucepan. Beat egg yolks well; add lime juice and water. Stir into gelatin mixture. Cook over low heat, stirring constantly, just until mixture comes to a boil. Remove from heat, stir in grated rind and a few drops of food coloring. Chill, stirring occasionally, until mixture mounds slightly when dropped from spoon. Beat egg whites until soft peaks form. Gradually add ½ cup sugar, beating until stiff. Fold into chilled gelatin mixture. Fold in whipped cream, reserving some cream for topping. Mound filling into baked pie shell or graham cracker shell. Top with cream; sprinkle with grated lime rind. Chill until firm.
Note: Use key limes when available.

To keep custard pie crust from getting soggy, brush an egg white on uncooked pie shell; bake 8 min. at 425° & then fill.

LUSCIOUS LEMON PIE

"This is a 'must' for lemon pie lovers."

1 cup sugar
3 tablespoons cornstarch
1 tablespoon lemon rind, grated
4 tablespoons butter
¼ cup fresh lemon juice
1 cup milk
3 egg yolks, slightly beaten
1 cup sour cream
9 inch pie shell, baked
whipping cream, whipped (optional)
grated lemon rind (optional)

Combine sugar, cornstarch, lemon rind, butter, lemon juice, milk and egg yolks in heavy saucepan. Cook over medium heat until smooth and very thick, stirring constantly; cover and cool. Fold sour cream into filling; pour into baked pie shell. Chill at least 2 hours before serving. Top with whipped cream and grated lemon rind.

MANDARIN DREAM PIE

5½ tablespoons butter
¾ cup plain flour
¼ cup brown sugar, firmly packed
⅛ teaspoon ground ginger
½ cup nuts, finely chopped
1 cup sour cream
¾ cup milk
⅓ cup instant vanilla pudding
1 tablespoon orange peel, grated
1 cup mandarin orange slices, drained (reserve syrup)
1 tablespoon mandarin orange syrup
½ cup orange marmalade

In a heavy fry pan, melt butter. Stir in flour, brown sugar, ginger and nuts. Blend well. Cook over low heat, stirring constantly, until crumb mixture is toasted and brown. Cool. Press crumb mixture into bottom and sides of 8 inch pie plate. In small bowl of electric mixer, combine sour cream, milk, orange peel and pudding. Mix at low speed to blend. Beat at high speed about 30 seconds or until thickened. Do not over beat. Pour pudding into pie shell and refrigerate until set, about 1 hour. Arrange orange slices on top of chilled pie. Combine marmalade and syrup in small saucepan; cook over low heat, stirring constantly, until marmalade melts. Spoon over oranges to cover. Refrigerate pie until served.

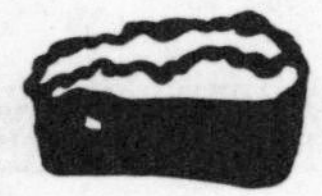

To darken light molasses, add 1 t melted chocolate per cup of molasses.

MOLASSES CUSTARD PIE

3 eggs, slightly beaten
¾ cup dark corn syrup (or molasses)
½ cup sugar
1 tablespoon corn meal
½ teaspoon cinnamon
½ teaspoon ground ginger
dash salt
¼ cup water
3 tablespoons butter, melted
1 tablespoon white vinegar
½ teaspoon lemon extract
9 inch pie shell, unbaked

Preheat oven to 450°. Combine eggs, syrup or molasses, sugar, corn meal, spices, salt, water, butter, vinegar and lemon extract. Blend all ingredients thoroughly and pour into pie shell. Bake 10 minutes; reduce heat to 325° and bake 20-25 minutes more or until crust is brown and filling nearly set. If crust browns too quickly, cover with a tent of foil toward end of baking time.

SANDHILLS PEACHES AND CREAM PIE

9 inch deep dish pie shell, unbaked
3-4 large fresh ripe peaches, pared, halved and drained
⅔ cup sugar
4 tablespoons plain flour
½ teaspoon cinnamon
1 cup whipping cream
vanilla ice cream or whipped cream (optional)

Preheat oven to 375°. Arrange 7-8 peach halves, cut side down, in pie shell. Combine sugar, flour, cinnamon and cream, beating gently with a fork until smooth and slightly thickened. Pour over peach halves. Bake 35 minutes or until custard is set and pie is golden. Serve warm with ice cream or dollops of whipped cream.

To keep pie crust from getting soggy, brush sides and bottom with beaten egg white and place in hot oven about four minutes.

For an extra flakey upper crust, brush lightly with cold water or milk.

RUM PECAN PIE

½ cup butter, softened
½ cup sugar
¾ cup light corn syrup
¼ cup maple flavored syrup
3 eggs, slightly beaten
2 tablespoons rum
¾ cup pecans, coarsely chopped
Brandied Butter Pastry
¾ cup pecan halves

Preheat oven to 350°. Cream butter and sugar until light and fluffy. Add corn syrup, maple syrup, eggs and rum; beat well. Stir in chopped pecans. Set aside.

Brandied Butter Pastry:
1 cup plain flour
¼ teaspoon salt
6 tablespoons cold butter
2-3 tablespoons cold brandy

Combine flour and salt; cut in butter until mixture resembles coarse meal. Sprinkle brandy over mixture; stir until particles cling together when pressed gently. Shape dough into ball; chill 10 minutes before rolling on floured board. Line a 9 inch pie pan with Brandied Butter Pastry. Pour pecan filling into pastry and top with pecan halves. Bake 55 minutes.

PRALINE PUMPKIN PIE

"This is an unusual pumpkin pie. A delight for the holiday season."

⅓ cup pecans, finely chopped
⅓ cup light brown sugar
2 tablespoons butter, softened
9 inch pie shell, unbaked and chilled

Blend pecans with sugar and butter. Press gently with the back of spoon into bottom of pie shell.

3 whole eggs
2 eggs, separated
8 ounces canned pumpkin
½ cup light brown sugar
1½ cups whipping cream
¼ cup dark rum
½ teaspoon salt
1 teaspoon cinnamon
¼ teaspoon ground cloves
¼ teaspoon ground ginger
¼ teaspoon mace (optional)
2 tablespoons granulated sugar

Preheat oven to 400°. Blend all ingredients except egg whites and granulated sugar. Pour into pie shell. Bake about 50 minutes. Make a meringue by beating egg whites until stiff, adding the reserved 2 tablespoons of sugar while beating. After 50 minutes remove pie from oven, cover with meringue and return to 425° oven just to brown meringue.

PEPPERMINT PERFECTION PIE

"The rich flavor of chocolate and mint in a light dessert."

1 envelope unflavored gelatin
½ cup water
3 egg whites
½ cup sugar
½ cup peppermint candy canes, crushed
1-2 drops red food coloring (optional)
¼ cup nuts, finely chopped (optional)
1 cup whipping cream, whipped
9 inch chocolate wafer pie shell (see Index for recipe)
chocolate curls

Sprinkle gelatin over water in cup to soften. Transfer cup to pan of hot water to dissolve gelatin. Set aside. Beat egg whites until light; gradually add sugar and continue to beat until stiff. Gently fold gelatin into egg whites, then peppermint candy and nuts. Whip cream and gently fold into peppermint filling. Mound filling high into pie shell. Sprinkle with chocolate curls. Refrigerate several hours, preferably overnight. Serve cold.

RUM PIE

"This is an elegant company dessert."

1¼ cups graham cracker crumbs
4 tablespoons butter, softened
2 tablespoons sugar
1½ teaspoons unflavored gelatin
2 tablespoons water
2 egg yolks
½ cup evaporated milk
¼ cup sugar
¼ teaspoon salt
2 egg whites
⅓ cup light corn syrup
4 tablespoons dark rum, divided
1 cup whipping cream, whipped
2-3 tablespoons confectioners' sugar, sifted

Preheat oven to 375°. In bowl combine graham cracker crumbs, butter and 2 tablespoons sugar. Mix thoroughly. Press this mixture (reserving 1 tablespoon) into bottom and sides of 8 inch pie pan. Bake 8 minutes. Cool. Sprinkle gelatin over water to soften. Let stand 10 minutes. In saucepan combine egg yolks, evaporated milk, ¼ cup sugar and salt. Cook over moderately low heat, stirring constantly, until mixture is thick enough to coat a spoon, but do not let it boil. Remove from heat; stir in softened gelatin. Let cool, but not set. In bowl of electric mixer, beat egg whites until they hold stiff peaks; add corn syrup in a stream, beating, and continue to beat mixture 10 minutes. Beat in 2 tablespoons rum and fold in custard. Transfer just enough filling to shell to fill; chill pie 20 minutes. Transfer remaining filling to shell, mounding it; chill 20 minutes more, or until the filling is set. Whip cream with confectioners' sugar and 2 tablespoons rum. Spread cream over pie, mounding it; reserve about ½ cup. Transfer reserved cream to pastry bag fitted with a decorative tip; pipe around edge of pie. Sprinkle center with reserved crumb mixture. Chill 3 hours. Let pie stand at room temperature for at least 30 minutes before serving.

BASIC PIE PASTRY

3 cups plain flour
1 teaspoon salt
1¼ cups shortening
1 egg, beaten
1 teaspoon vinegar
5-7 tablespoons water

Preheat oven to 425°. Mix flour and salt. Cut in shortening with pastry blender. In a measuring cup, beat egg; add vinegar and fill with water to make ⅔ cup. Sprinkle egg mixture over flour, a little at a time, until entire mixture becomes moistened. Press into ball; handle as little as possible. Chill at least 10 minutes before rolling pastry on floured board. Bake 10-12 minutes. Yields: Four 9 inch pie shells.

"This pastry keeps well in the refrigerator up to 3 weeks."

COLLECTION OF HISTORICAL OUTDOOR DRAMAS

"The Lost Colony" — Story of the first English settlement in America; Manteo

"Unto These Hills" — Story of the tragic saga of the Cherokees removal from N.C.; Cherokee

"Horn in the West" — Story of Daniel Boone and the mountain people during the American Revolution; Boone

"From This Day Forward" — Story of the struggle for survival of the Waldenses settlers in America; Valdese

"Strike at the Wind" — Story of Henry Lowrie and the Lumbee Indians; Pembroke

"The Sword of Peace" — Story of N.C. Quakers caught between their religious convictions and the birth of patriotism; Snow Camp

"Revolution" — Story of "how reasonable men are driven to the extreme act of violent revolt"; Southport

"House in the Horseshoe" — Story of the recreation of a revolutionary battle in this area in 1781; Glendon

"Liberty Cart" — Story of Dublin County from pre-revolution era through the Civil War and Reconstruction; Kenansville

"Blackbeard — Knight of the Black Flag" — Story of the life and death of the infamous pirate Edward Teach; Bath

poultry and game

THE CAROLINA COLLECTOR'S CONCOCTIONS

. . . For German chicken add onion, salt & pepper to chicken pieces in a baking pan; add beer, garlic salt & caraway seeds.

. . . For Greek chicken add tomato juice & lemon juice, oregano, garlic salt, cinnamon & nutmeg.

. . . Serve chicken a la king in pastry cups made of rice cereal & butter browned in oven.

. . . Bake chicken with ¼ c rum, garlic salt, paprika; add a bay leaf and pinch of saffron.

. . . Stir fry chicken strips, pea pods, green onion, ginger & soy sauce.

. . . Marinate chicken breasts in ½ c orange juice & ½ t each of marjoram, basil, garlic salt & pepper. Bake 1 hr. at 350°.

. . . Coat chicken in peanut butter, honey & milk mixture before coating with cornmeal, flour, MSG mixture & frying.

. . . Fill green peppers with chicken salad & slice crosswise ½″ thick. Serve on lettuce.

. . . For Chicken Wellington, stuff breasts with wild rice and wrap in crescent dinner rolls.

. . . Brown boned breasts in butter; add sliced pimento, olives & white wine.

. . . Make a cranberry barbecue sauce with 1 can jellied sauce, ½ c mustard, 1 t Worcestershire sauce, ⅛ t garlic powder & 2 T vinegar; baste chicken.

. . . Layer rice, chicken pieces, dry onion soup mix & enough water to coat rice. Cover & cook until done.

Boil 2 frying chickens with 2 c barbecue sauce, 16 oz. Coca Cola & 1 onion for 1 hr. Serve with sauce thickened with cornstarch.

. . . Cook a frozen turkey breast in a brown paper bag; split the bottom & tuck bag tightly around turkey; roast in pan 1 hr. per lb. at 350°.

. . . Mix 1 can chicken with 1 can macaroni and cheese, 1 T sherry, mushrooms & mushroom soup poured over all. Top with crumbs & Parmesan cheese; bake until hot.

. . . Blend 1 can peaches & juice, 2 T wine vinegar & 4 T soy sauce in blender. Pour over chicken pieces & bake 1 hr. at 375°.

. . . For a special brunch, have a stack of pancakes filled with minced chicken laced with sour cream & mushroom sauce.

CAROLINA CHICKEN BOG

"Pepper is the secret to this simple and delicious recipe."

5-6 pound hen
½ pound bacon
1 small onion, chopped
1 small green pepper, chopped
1 tablespoon salt (or to taste)
1 tablespoon pepper (or to taste)
4 cups raw rice
½ cup butter
6 hard cooked eggs, chopped

Boil hen in heavy Dutch oven with enough water so there will be at least 6 cups of broth. When tender, remove meat from bones; set meat aside. Fry bacon until crisp; crumble coarsely and set aside. Sauté onion and green pepper in small amount of bacon grease until soft. In Dutch oven, combine 6 cups chicken broth, salt, pepper, onion and green pepper. Bring to a boil; add chicken, rice and butter. Mix well; reduce heat to low. Cook approximately 1 hour, stirring infrequently (too much stirring will make it sticky). Thoroughly blend in bacon and eggs. Yields: 10 servings.

Protect exposed bones of drumsticks with little foil caps to prevent charring during cooking.

CHICKEN WITH CHEESE AND MUSHROOMS

4 chicken breast halves, boned
plain flour
2-3 tablespoons butter
salt and pepper
6 or more mushrooms, sliced and sautéed
4 slices mozzarella (or Munster) cheese
½ cup dry white wine
½ cup chicken broth
1 tablespoon butter

Place breasts between pieces of waxed paper; pound until thin. Dredge chicken in flour. In large frying pan, melt butter. Sauté chicken until tender, about 4-5 minutes per side. Transfer chicken to broiler pan. Sprinkle with salt and pepper. Arrange a few mushrooms on each breast; cover with a slice of cheese. To juices remaining in frying pan, add wine and broth. Boil until slightly reduced and thickened. Add salt and pepper if necessary and swirl in 1 tablespoon butter. Do not stir — just lift pan and swirl. Place chicken under broiler and broil until cheese melts. Serve sauce separately. Yields: 2-4 servings.

Variation: Thin slices of country ham, regular ham or prosciutto may be added by arranging on top of mushrooms before adding cheese.

CHICKEN DIVAN

8 chicken breast halves, cooked and boned
30 ounces frozen broccoli
3 10½ ounce cans cream of chicken soup
1½ cups salad dressing (or mayonnaise)
1½ tablespoons lemon juice
1-1½ teaspoons curry powder
1 cup sharp cheese, shredded
1½ cups Pepperidge Farm Stuffing Mix
3 tablespoons butter, melted
pimento strips (optional)

Preheat oven to 350°. Cook and drain broccoli. Place in greased 3 quart baking dish. Place chicken on top of broccoli. Combine soup, salad dressing, lemon juice and curry powder; spread on top. Sprinkle with cheese. Combine stuffing mix and butter. Sprinkle on top. Bake 30 minutes. Garnish with pimento before serving. Yields: 8 servings.
Variation: Asparagus spears may be substituted for broccoli.

APRICOT GLAZED CHICKEN

"Quick, easy and so very, very good.

4 chicken breast halves, boned
4 ounces Russian dressing
6 ounces apricot preserves
1 package Lipton dry onion soup mix

Preheat oven to 325°. Mix Russian dressing, preserves and dry onion soup. Place chicken in shallow 1½ quart casserole. Cover with sauce. Cover. Bake 1 hour and 15 minutes. Remove cover after 40 minutes so chicken will brown. Yields: 4 servings.

CHEESY CHICKEN CASSEROLE

"Relatively simple to prepare and yet a delicious result."

4 pounds chicken (or 6 chicken breasts)
20 ounces frozen broccoli spears
16 ounces cream cheese, softened
2 cups milk
1 teaspoon salt
¾-1 teaspoon garlic salt
1½ cups Parmesan cheese, grated and divided

Simmer chicken 1-1½ hours or until tender. Remove meat from bone. Preheat oven to 350°. Cook broccoli, salting to taste. Drain. Arrange broccoli in 2 quart greased casserole. Add chicken. Blend cream cheese, milk and seasonings in heavy saucepan; cook over medium heat until smooth. Stir in 1¼ cups Parmesan cheese. Pour over chicken. Sprinkle with ¼ cup Parmesan cheese. Bake, uncovered, 25-30 minutes. Yields: 6 servings.

CHEESE STUFFED CHICKEN BREASTS

12 chicken breast halves, boned and pounded lightly
6 tablespoons blue cheese, crumbled
12 squares Swiss cheese, 1½x1½
plain flour
salt and pepper to taste
1 egg
½ cup milk
1 cup dry bread crumbs
butter or margarine

Place about ½ teaspoon blue cheese and 1 square Swiss cheese on each breast. Roll each breast and fasten with 3 toothpicks. Roll in flour seasoned with salt and pepper. Dip breasts into egg and milk mixture; roll well in fine, dry bread crumbs. Let this set at least 30 minutes. Preheat oven to 325°. In skillet, brown chicken rolls on all sides in butter. Place in 3 quart casserole, cover and bake 45 minutes. Yields: 12 servings.

Note: Chicken may be prepared to baking point in advance and baked just before serving.

Add preserves to chicken bouillon for a fruity chicken gravy.

CRESCENT CHICKEN SQUARES

2 cups chicken, cooked and cubed
3 ounces cream cheese, softened
2 tablespoons margarine, melted
2 ounces sliced mushrooms, drained
¼ teaspoon salt
⅛ teaspoon pepper
2 tablespoons milk
1 tablespoon chives or onion, chopped
1 tablespoon pimento, chopped
8 ounces canned crescent dinner rolls
1 tablespoon margarine, melted
¾ cup seasoned croutons, crushed

Preheat oven to 350°. Blend cream cheese and margarine until smooth. Add chicken, mushrooms, salt, pepper, milk, chives and pimento. Mix well. Separate crescent rolls into 4 rectangles; seal perforations. Spoon ½ cup chicken mixture onto center of each rectangle; pull 4 corners of dough to center of mixture and seal. Brush tops with melted margarine. Dip in crushed croutons. Bake on ungreased cookie sheet 20-25 minutes until golden brown. Refrigerate any leftovers. Yields: 4 sandwiches.

STUFFED CHICKEN CRAB ROLLS

8 chicken breast halves, boned and skinned
3 slices bread, toasted
⅓ cup mayonnaise
1 tablespoon lemon juice
½ cup chicken bouillon
dash hot sauce
⅔ cup celery, finely chopped
⅔ cup green onion, finely chopped
¾ cup butter, melted and divided
¼ teaspoon basil
¼ teaspoon marjoram
¼ teaspoon thyme
1 teaspoon sage
¼ teaspoon pepper
½ teaspoon seasoned salt
1 cup fresh crab meat, flaked
⅓ cup Swiss cheese, shredded
2 tablespoons parsley, minced
⅓ cup plain flour
paprika
fresh parsley for garnish

Preheat oven to 350°. Pound chicken breasts between sheets of waxed paper until ¼ inch thick. Tear bread into small pieces. Combine mayonnaise, lemon juice, bouillon and hot sauce; pour over bread. Sauté celery and onion in ½ cup butter; add to bread mixture. Stir in seasonings, crabmeat, cheese and parsley; mix well. Place an equal amount of stuffing mixture on each breast. Fold long sides of chicken over stuffing; roll up, and secure with toothpick. Dredge each roll in flour; dip in remaining ¼ cup butter. Place in 10x6 baking dish. Sprinkle with paprika. Bake 45-60 minutes. Garnish with fresh parsley. Yields: 8 servings.

CRUNCHY CHICKEN

4-4½ pounds chicken, cut up
2 cups Ritz cracker crumbs
¾ cup Parmesan cheese, grated
¼ cup parsley, chopped
⅛ teaspoon pepper
2 teaspoons salt
⅛ teaspoon garlic powder
1 cup butter, melted

Preheat oven to 350°. Blend together Ritz cracker crumbs, Parmesan cheese, parsley and seasonings. Dip each piece of chicken in melted butter and then in crumb mixture. Arrange in shallow pan or casserole. Pour remaining butter over chicken. Bake 1 hour. Do not turn chicken. Yields: 8 servings.

TACO CHICKEN WINGS

3 pounds chicken wings, disjointed
½ cup plain flour
1-1¼ ounces Taco seasoning mix
6 tablespoons margarine or butter
1 cup corn chips, crushed

Preheat oven to 350°. Combine flour and Taco mix in plastic bag. Add 2-3 pieces chicken at a time; shake to coat. Melt margarine or butter; dip chicken in to coat; roll in corn chips. Place on broiler pan. Bake 40-45 minutes. Yields: 4-6 servings.

CURRIED CHICKEN AND RICE CASSEROLE

3-4 cups chicken, cooked and diced
2 cups cooked rice
8½ ounces water chestnuts, drained and sliced
¼ cup mayonnaise
2 10¾-ounce cans cream of chicken soup
6 tablespoons milk
1-2 teaspoons curry powder
3 ounces canned french fried onion rings
¾ cup raisins, rinsed in hot water
6-8 slices bacon, cooked and crumbled

Preheat oven to 350°. Combine all but last three ingredients; blend well. In a 2½ quart flat casserole, place ⅓ of chicken mixture, ⅓ onion rings, raisins and bacon; repeat twice. Bake 30-40 minutes. Yields: 6 servings.

EIGHT BOY CHICKEN CURRY

5-6 pound stewing hen, cut up
6 cups water
3 medium onions, chopped
2 apples, minced
8 stalks celery, minced
¼ cup olive oil
¼ cup curry powder (may alter to taste)
¼ teaspoon pepper
½ teaspoon ginger
½ teaspoon Tabasco
¼ cup plain flour
2 cups whipping cream
3 egg yolks, slightly beaten
½ cup sherry
salt to taste
6 cups hot cooked rice

Simmer chicken in water, covered until tender. Reserve broth. Cook onions, apples and celery in olive oil until browned, stirring frequently. Add curry powder; simmer 5 minutes. Add 4 cups of broth from chicken. Simmer 20 minutes. Blend in flour smoothly; cook until it thickens, stirring constantly. Bone and dice chicken. Add to sauce; let stand at least 3 hours. When ready to serve, add cream, egg yolks, sherry and salt to taste. Heat thoroughly. Serve over hot rice. Yields: 6-8 servings.

Serve with the following, each in separate dish:

4 hard-cooked eggs, chopped
2 cups chutney
1 fresh coconut, grated
2 green peppers, chopped
½ pound bacon, fried and chopped
½ cup currant jelly
½ cup pickles, chopped
½ pound salted peanuts, chopped

FRUIT AND CHICKEN KABOBS

4 chicken breast halves, skinned, boned and cut into 1½ inch pieces
¼ cup oil
2 tablespoons lemon juice
½ teaspoon salt
⅛ teaspoon pepper
1 teaspoon Accent
1 large green pepper, cut in chunks
8 ounces pineapple chunks, drained
1 orange, cut in eighths (optional)
¼ cup commercial barbecue sauce
12 ounces pineapple preserves

Combine oil and lemon juice; add chicken and marinate at least 1 hour in refrigerator. Drain reserving marinade. Sprinkle meat with salt, pepper and Accent. Alternate pieces of chicken, green pepper, pineapple and orange on skewers. Combine reserved marinade, barbecue sauce and pineapple preserves in saucepan; heat thoroughly, stirring constantly. Baste kabobs with sauce. Grill kabobs 20 to 25 minutes over medium heat, basting with sauce and turning occasionally. Yields: 4 servings.

Rub the insides of chicken and other fowl with lemon juice. This tenderizes as well as sweetens.

SWEET 'N SOUR CHICKEN

2 pounds chicken breasts, boned and cut in slivers
2 tablespoons butter
½ cup chicken bouillon
2 large carrots, sliced
8 ounces canned pineapple chunks, drained, reserving juice
¼ cup brown sugar, firmly packed
2 tablespoons constarch
¼ cup vinegar
2 tablespoons soy sauce (or more depending on taste)
1 medium onion, thinly sliced
½ green pepper, cut in strips
8 ounces canned water chestnuts, drained and thinly sliced
cooked rice

Sauté chicken in butter until no longer pink. Add bouillon and carrots. Cover; cook until carrots are tender. Combine pineapple juice, brown sugar, cornstarch, vinegar and soy sauce. Add to chicken; cook until mixture thickens. Just before serving, add pineapple chunks, onion, green pepper and water chestnuts. Cook 3-5 minutes. Serve over hot rice. Yields: 4-6 servings.

Note: This does not *freeze.*

CHICKEN PACIFIC

6 chicken breast halves
2 cups sour cream, at room temperature
1 teaspoon tarragon
1 teaspoon thyme
½ teaspoon garlic powder
1 teaspoon paprika
1 teaspoon salt
1½ cups cornflake crumbs
¼ cup butter, melted
1 cup shrimp, cooked and cleaned
¼ cup ripe olives, chopped

Preheat oven to 350°. Mix sour cream with tarragon, thyme, garlic powder, paprika and salt. Dip chicken into sour cream mixture; coat with cornflake crumbs. Arrange in a greased, shallow casserole. Drizzle butter over chicken. Bake 45 minutes, turn and bake 20 minutes. To remaining sour cream mixture add shrimp and olives. Spoon over chicken and bake 10 minutes. Yields: 6 servings.

CHICKEN POJARSKI

4 pounds chicken breast, boned and ground
½ pound very lean pork, ground
5 slices white bread, crusts removed
2 cups chicken broth
½ cup butter, melted
4 eggs, beaten
salt and pepper to taste
2 tablespoons dill weed
½ cup plain flour
5 tablespoons butter
1½ tablespoons olive oil (or vegetable oil)

Preheat oven to 300°. Break bread; soak in chicken broth. Stir in melted butter. Using fork, stir in chicken, pork, eggs, salt, pepper and dill weed; blend well. Make plump oblong patties (not flat) about 2x3. Dredge with flour. Heat 5 tablespoons butter and oil in frying pan; brown patties on both sides. Place 1 layer deep in 3 quart flat casserole. Bake 45 minutes, uncovered. Pour hot Mushroom Sauce over patties and serve. Yields: 10-12 servings.

Mushroom Sauce:
½ cup butter
1 medium onion, chopped
4 ounces sliced mushrooms, drained
3 tablespoons tomato paste
2 tablespoons plain flour
2 tablespoons dill weed
2 cups chicken broth
2 cups sour cream
salt and pepper to taste

Sauté onion and mushrooms in butter; add tomato paste, flour and dill weed; blend well. Slowly stir in broth. Bring to a boil, stirring constantly. Reduce heat and simmer 20 minutes. Add sour cream immediately before serving. If too thick, thin with additional broth.

CHICKEN AND SAUSAGE CASSEROLE

"Wonderful combination – your family will love it."

1½-2 pounds chicken, cooked and broth reserved
6 ounces long grain and wild rice with herbs
1 pound country sausage
8 ounces mushrooms, drained
10¾ ounces canned cream of mushroom soup
1 cup chicken broth
salt and pepper to taste
8 ounces herb seasoned stuffing
½ cup margarine, melted
fresh parsley for garnish

Preheat oven to 350°. Bone cooked chicken; place in shallow 2 quart casserole. Prepare rice according to package directions. Brown sausage; drain and crumble. Combine sausage, mushrooms, mushroom soup, broth, salt, pepper and cooked rice; mix well. Pour over chicken. Sprinkle stuffing generously on top and drizzle with margarine. Bake 25 minutes. Garnish with fresh parsley. Yields: 8 generous servings.

CHICKEN BREASTS IN SOUR CREAM

"Quick, easy and delicious."

8 chicken breast halves
10¾ ounces canned cream of mushroom soup
½ cup sherry
1 cup sour cream
3 ounces sliced mushrooms, drained
paprika
fresh parsley for garnish

Preheat oven to 350°. Arrange chicken in 3 quart casserole. Mix soup, sherry and sour cream. Pour over chicken. Arrange mushrooms over chicken; sprinkle with paprika. Cover. Bake 1 hour and 15 minutes; uncover, bake 15 minutes. Garnish with fresh parsley. Yields: 8 servings.

MARINATED DRUMSTICKS

12 chicken drumsticks
¼ cup catsup
2-3 tablespoons lemon juice
2 tablespoons soy sauce
¼ cup oil
¼ teaspoon monosodium glutamate

Combine all ingredients except chicken; blend well. Add drumsticks; turn to coat. Refrigerate overnight, spooning marinade over occasionally. Place in wire broiler basket. Broil over medium coals about 1 hour or until tender, turning occasionally. Baste with marinade occasionally. Yields: 4-6 servings.

CHICKEN AND SEAFOOD CASSEROLE

"Outstanding blending of ingredients. A very good recipe."

2½-3 pound chicken (or 8 chicken breast halves)
½ cup plain flour
4 tablespoons butter, melted
1 onion, diced
1 clove garlic, minced
8 ounces canned tomato sauce
1 teaspoon salt
½ teaspoon pepper
1 teaspoon basil
2 teaspoons fresh parsley, chopped
1 teaspoon paprika
7½ ounces minced clams, undrained
8 ounces mushrooms, sliced and drained
¼ cup sherry
½ pound shrimp, cooked and cleaned

Preheat oven to 350°. Dredge chicken in flour. Brown in butter. Place in casserole. Using same pan, sauté onion and garlic until golden. Add tomato sauce, salt, pepper, basil, parsley, paprika, clams and liquid, mushrooms and sherry. Simmer 10 minutes. Pour sauce over chicken. Bake, covered, 1 hour. Uncover; add shrimp. Spoon sauce over shrimp. Bake 10 minutes. Yields: 4 servings.

CHICKEN TETRAZZINI PUFF

1 cup chicken, cooked and chopped
6 tablespoons Parmesan cheese, grated and divided
3 ounces sliced mushrooms, drained
4 tablespoons butter, melted
¼ cup plain flour
1 cup half and half
1 cup chicken broth
½ teaspoon salt
¼ teaspoon pepper
½ cup Swiss cheese, shredded
5 eggs, separated
1 cup cooked spaghetti

Preheat oven to 250°. Grease a 2 quart soufflé dish; dust with 2 tablespoons Parmesan cheese. Sauté mushrooms in melted butter; add flour and cook until bubbly, stirring frequently. Remove from heat. Gradually stir in half and half and chicken broth; stir until smooth. Add salt and pepper to taste. Cook over medium heat, stirring constantly, until sauce is thickened; remove from heat. Add Swiss cheese and 4 tablespoons Parmesan cheese; stir until cheese melts. Cool 10 minutes. Beat egg yolks; slowly add to sauce stirring briskly with a wire whisk. Add spaghetti and chicken. Beat egg whites until stiff; fold into chicken mixture. Pour into prepared dish. Baked 50-60 minutes. Yields: 6 servings.

CHICKEN-WILD RICE SUPREME

"Such a good company dish to fix ahead."

4-5 pound hen
1 cup water
1 cup dry sherry
1½ teaspoons salt
½ teaspoon curry powder
1 medium onion, sliced
½ cup celery, sliced
1 pound fresh mushrooms, sliced
4 tablespoons butter or margarine
12 ounces wild and long grain rice mixture
1 cup sour cream
10¾ ounces canned cream of mushroom soup
¾ cup slivered almonds

Simmer chicken plus the next six ingredients for approximately 1 hour, covered tightly. Strain and reserve broth. When chicken is cool, remove meat from bones, skin and cut in bite-size pieces. Set aside. Preheat oven to 350°. Sauté mushrooms in butter or margarine, drain and set aside. Measure chicken broth and use as part of liquid for cooking rice firm, following directions on box. Combine chicken, rice and sautéed mushrooms in 3 quart casserole. Blend sour cream and soup together and add to chicken mixture. Sprinkle almonds on top and bake 1 hour. Yields: 8-10 servings.

Variations: Almonds could be added to body of recipe and buttered crumbs placed on tops. Also sliced water chestnuts could replace the almonds in body of recipe.

"This freezes beautifully."

Chickens will keep satisfactorily frozen for up to 12 months; turkey, ducks, geese — 6 months.

CHICKEN AND YELLOW RICE

"This is a one dish meal."

2-3 pound frying chicken
½ scant cup Spanish olive oil
1 medium onion, chopped
⅛ teaspoon garlic powder
1 medium green pepper, chopped
½ cup canned tomatoes, mashed
3 cups water
2 cubes chicken bouillon, crushed
1 tablespoon salt
pinch Spanish saffron
1 bay leaf, crushed
3 drops yellow food coloring (optional)
1½ cups raw rice
½ cup small peas for garnish
½ cup Spanish pimento for garnish
¼ cup parsley, chopped for garnish
1 hard cooked egg, sliced for garnish
asparagus tips for garnish

Preheat oven to 350°. Cut chicken into quarters; brown in olive oil in 3 quart baking dish on top of stove. Remove chicken and drain on paper towel, reserving olive oil. Combine onion, garlic, green pepper and tomatoes in same olive oil, cook until tender. Place chicken on top of vegetables. Add bouillon and water; bring to boil. As casserole begins to boil, add salt, saffron, bay leaf, food coloring and rice; bring to second boil. Remove from heat, cover, and bake for 20 minutes. Garnish with small peas, pimento, parsley, egg and asparagus. Yields: 4 generous servings.
Note: Sangria is a delightful addition.

Rub chicken inside & out with lemon juice to tenderize.

A 4 lb. stewing chicken yields 4 c cut up meat.

CHICKEN BREASTS WELLINGTON

"An eye-opener and taste pleaser."

12 chicken breast halves, boned
seasoned salt
seasoned pepper
6 ounces long grain and wild rice mix
¼ cup orange peel, grated
2 eggs, separated
3 8-ounce cans refrigerated crescent dinner rolls
1 tablespoon water
20 ounces red currant jelly
1 tablespoon prepared mustard
3 tablespoons port wine
¼ cup lemon juice

Preheat oven to 375°. Pound chicken breasts with mallet; sprinkle with seasoned salt and pepper. Cook rice according to package directions for drier rice; add orange peel. Cool. Beat egg whites until soft peaks form; fold into rice mixture. On floured surface, roll 2 triangular pieces of dinner roll dough into a circle. Repeat with remaining rolls until you have 12 circles. Place a chicken breast in center of each circle. Spoon about ¼ cup rice mixture over chicken; roll chicken jelly roll fashion. Bring dough up over stuffed breast. Moisten edge of dough with water, and press together to seal. Place seam side down on baking sheet. Slightly beat egg yolks with water; brush over dough. Bake, uncovered, 45-50 minutes or until breasts are tender. If dough browns too quickly, cover loosely with foil. Heat currant jelly in saucepan; gradually stir in mustard, wine and lemon juice. Serve warm with chicken. Yields: 12 servings.

WESTERN PARTY CHICKEN

3 cups chicken, cooked and chopped
2 cups chicken stock
8 ounces whipping cream
6 tablespoons plain flour
1½ cups canned crushed pineapple, drained
¼ cup pineapple juice
1 cup slivered almonds
1¼ cups cooked rice, seasoned to taste
8 patty shells

Combine stock, cream and flour, blending thoroughly. Cook over medium heat, stirring constantly, until thickened. Add remaining ingredients and heat through. Place in individual patty shells. Yields: 8 servings.

CHICKEN LIVERS GOURMET

"Lovers of chicken livers will adore this one."

1 pound chicken livers
6 slices bacon, cooked and coarsely crumbled
6 tablespoons butter, divided
½ medium green pepper, cut in thin julienne strips
1 medium onion, thinly sliced
½ pound fresh mushrooms
2½ tablespoons plain flour
salt and pepper to taste
1½ cups chicken broth
¼ cup sherry
1 tablespoon fresh parsley, minced
cooked rice (or toast points)

Dry livers, cut in half; sauté in 3 tablespoons butter until browned on all sides. Remove from pan, add remaining butter and sauté green pepper, onion and mushrooms. Blend in flour, salt and pepper. Slowly add chicken broth, stirring constantly until thickened. Stir in sherry, parsley, chicken livers and bacon; simmer over low heat, covered, 15 minutes. Serve on rice or toast points. Yields: 4 servings.

OLD-FASHIONED TURKEY PIE

2 cups cooked turkey, cut up (or chicken)
4 tablespoons butter or margarine
5 tablespoons plain flour
2 cups turkey broth (or 2 cups hot water plus 6 chicken bouillon cubes)
1 cup milk
6 small white onions, cooked
1 cup cooked potatoes, diced
10 ounces frozen peas and carrots, cooked
salt
pepper

Melt butter in saucepan. Add flour and stir until smooth. Gradually add broth and milk, stirring constantly. Continue to cook, stirring until thickened. Add turkey, vegetables, salt and pepper. Turn into greased casserole. Cover with biscuit dough. Preheat oven to 450°.

Biscuit Dough:

1½ cups plain flour, sifted
1½ teaspoons baking powder
½ teaspoon salt
5 tablespoons shortening
½ cup milk

Mix flour, baking powder and salt together. Cut in shortening. Gradually add milk, stirring until soft dough is formed. Turn onto lightly floured board; knead 30 seconds. Roll out and place on top of casserole. Cut several slits in top to permit steam to escape. Bake 25 minutes or until brown. Yields: 6 servings.

Close the vent of poultry with crushed foil instead of skewering or sewing. It keeps the stuffing in, is easier to remove.

TURKEY-CRANBERRY SQUARES

"A marvelous way to use leftover Thanksgiving or Christmas turkey."

1½ pounds turkey, cooked and ground
2 tablespoons butter
½ cup sugar
1 teaspoon orange rind, grated
2 cups fresh cranberries, chopped
1 cup turkey broth (or chicken broth)
1 cup milk
1 teaspoon salt
¼ teaspoon pepper
2 tablespoons onion, finely chopped
2 cups soft bread crumbs (or leftover stuffing)
2 eggs, slightly beaten

Preheat oven to 400°. Melt butter in 8x8 baking pan; blend in sugar and orange peel. Cover with cranberries. Combine remaining ingredients, mixing thoroughly. Pack over cranberries. Bake 45 minutes. Turn out, upside down, onto serving platter; cut into squares. Yields: 8 servings.

VENISON ROAST

venison roast
2 cups vinegar
2 stalks celery, chopped
2 carrots, chopped
1 cup onion, chopped
2 bay leaves
5 whole cloves
salt pork

Mix vinegar, celery, carrots, onion, bay leaves and cloves together. Bring to a boil. Simmer 15 minutes. Cool; pour over venison in a glass dish. Marinate 12-24 hours. (Marinating tenderizes the meat and takes away some of the wild flavor.) Preheat oven to 350°. Remove venison from marinate and lard well with strips of salt pork. Roast 30 minutes per pound. Cool.

Sauce:
drippings from roasting pan
1 tablespoon plain flour
½ package dry onion soup mix
1 onion, finely chopped
½ cup dry red wine
1 cup water
pepper
garlic salt
parsley, minced

Into drippings, stir flour, onion soup mix, onion and wine. Add water; cook over medium heat, stirring constantly, until thickened. Preheat oven to 350°. Slice entire venison roast thinly. In a 3 quart casserole layer roast slices, lightly sprinkle with pepper and garlic salt and drizzle with sauce. Repeat until casserole is filled. Bake until thoroughly hot. Before serving, sprinkle with chopped parsley. Yields: 10-12 servings.
Note: This may be made ahead and heated, covered, just before serving. This may be frozen and re-heated.

SAUCY DOVE

12-15 medium dove, cleaned
1 cup plain flour
1¼ teaspoons salt
¼ teaspoon pepper
½ teaspoon poultry seasoning
½ cup margarine, melted
8 ounces tomato sauce
4 ounces mushrooms, drained
1 large onion, diced
⅓ cup milk

Combine flour, salt, pepper and poultry seasoning in a bag; add dove and shake to coat birds well. Brown dove in butter in large skillet. Add tomato sauce, mushrooms and onions. Cover and cook over low heat until tender, about 20 minutes. Remove dove and keep warm. Add milk to pan drippings, scraping sides and bottom of skillet. Heat, stirring constantly, to make a sauce. Spoon over dove. Yields: 6 servings.

MAXINE'S DELICIOUS WILD DUCK

1 duck
salt and pepper to taste
1 cup red wine
3 green onions, chopped
1 tablespoon soy sauce
cooking oil
apple, halved
rib of celery

Clean and prepare duck; salt and pepper to taste. Place in marinade container or tightly covered pot; cover with red wine, onions and soy sauce. Marinate for 24 hours, turning container frequently (or basting occasionally if placed in pot). Preheat oven to 250°. Remove duck and fry in small amount of oil to remove as much fat as possible from duck. Drain well. Salt and pepper cavity and place apple and celery inside. Place in Dutch oven, cover with marinade and cook approximatley 4-5 hours or until tender. Serve with wild rice. Yields: 2 servings.

Rub quail with a cut lemon before cooking. This tenderizes it and brings out the flavor. Use currant jelly as a condiment.

To remove "gamey" taste from venison, marinate overnight in a cheap white wine.

QUAIL IN WINE

8 quail
2 tablespoons butter
¼ pound salt pork, diced
2 tablespoons flour
1 cup chicken broth
1 cup dry white wine
½ teaspoon salt
¼ teaspoon pepper
4 ounces whole mushrooms, drained
8 ounces small whole onions, drained
croutons, for garnish
parsley, for garnish

Brown quail in butter; remove. Brown salt pork in same pan; stir in flour. Add broth, wine, salt and pepper; stir until sauce is smooth. Add quail; simmer for 30 minutes. Add mushrooms and onions; simmer for 15 minutes longer. Garnish with croutons and parsley. Serve with wild rice. Yields: 4 servings.

COLLECTION OF MAJOR NORTH CAROLINA COLLEGES & UNIVERSITIES

Nowhere in the United States is there a better collection of colleges and universities recognized throughout the nation as examples of academic excellence. There are more than 100 institutions of higher learning in N.C., including the following:

The Greater University of N.C. (oldest state chartered university in U.S. — 1789)

- UNC — Chapel Hill
- NCSU — Raleigh
- A&T University — Greensboro
- Appalachian State University — Boone
- UNC-A — Asheville
- UNC-C — Charlotte
- East Carolina University — Greenville
- Elizabeth City State University — Elizabeth City
- Fayetteville State University — Fayetteville
- UNC-G — Greensboro
- N.C. Central University — Durham
- Pembroke State University — Pembroke
- Western Carolina University — Cullowhee
- UNC-W — Wilmington
- Winston-Salem State University — Winston-Salem
- N.C. School of Arts — Winston-Salem

Duke University — Durham

Wake Forest University — Winston-Salem

Davidson College — Davidson

Salem College — Winston-Salem

Meredith College — Raleigh

St. Mary's College — Raleigh

Peace College — Raleigh

Methodist College — Fayetteville

Queens College — Charlotte

Artichoke Bottoms w/ Parmesan Cheese

The tinier the better for these. They make a luxurious addition to any buffet party.

12 cooked, small artichoke bottoms
2 T. olive oil
2 T. soft sweet butter
2/3 c. Parmesan cheese, freshly grated
1 T. chopped fresh parsley

Preheat oven to 450°

In shallow baking dish, combine olive oil and 1 T. butter.
Arrange artichoke bottoms in a single layer, cut side up. Dot w/ remaining butter
Sprinkle w/ cheese
Bake for 12 min until cheese turns golden brown.
Place on paper towel for 1 min. to drain.
Sprinkle with parsley. Serve hot.

Panzanella Salad
(Tuscan bread salad)

½ loaf stale crusty sourdough bread sliced into 1" pieces
4 anchovies
¼ c. milk
3 large tomatoes, peeled and coarsely chopped
3 stalks celery, chopped
2 egg, hard-boiled & chopped
1 med red onion thinly sliced
1 can tuna (optional)
½ c. peeled chopped cucumber
½ c. basil leaves
2 T. capers, drained and chopped
2 cloves garlic, minced
½ c. extra virgin olive oil
¼ c. red wine vinegar

½ t. salt
½ t. finely ground black pepper

Soak the anchovies in milk for 15 min. Drain and chop finely.
Place bread in large bowl and cover w/ cold water; let soak for 10 min. With your hands gently squeeze out as much water as possible. Tear bread into bite-size pieces.

Combine to line. Combine (whisk together) remaining ingred. Pour over salad. Toss gently to coat. Refrig at least 2 hrs or up to 8 hrs. before serving.

If making in winter us hothouse tomatoes.

salads
salads
salads
salads

THE CAROLINA COLLECTOR'S CONCOCTIONS

. . . For a zesty chicken salad, add soy sauce and curry powder to mayonnaise; sprinkle with oregano.

. . . Add shredded cabbage, diced apple and 1 T horseradish to lemon gelatin.

. . . Add shredded carrots, celery and sliced olives to lime gelatin.

. . . Add 1 c grated Cheddar cheese, celery and tomato juice to orange gelatin for a barbecue salad treat.

. . . Stuff pear halves with diced crystallized ginger, pecans, cream cheese; put 2 halves together with sprigs of mint in the end and serve on lettuce.

. . . A good salad to have on hand is made with 1 can each of artichoke hearts, bean sprouts, green beans and sliced water chestnuts all marinated in garlic dressing.

. . . Add spiced meat balls to your green salad along with olives, mushrooms and mozzarella cheese.

. . . Toasted sesame seeds give a zip to wilted lettuce.

. . . Make a cheese to serve with fruits with 1 lb. cottage cheese, ¼ c sugar and ¼ c white wine.

. . . To a can of pork and beans add chopped tomato, onion, cucumber & 1 T mayonnaise.

. . . Chop zucchini, carrots, celery, onion and a dash of dill leaves and add 2 cans pork and beans.

. . . Potato salad takes on new life with chopped pears and Parmesan cheese.

. . . Salt and pepper tomato slices and marinate in Italian dressing.

. . . Sprinkle fresh chopped mint on chicken or shrimp salad.

. . . Add orange juice and orange rind to sour cream for a zesty fruit salad.

. . . For a zippy cole slaw, add a little finely grated fresh ginger.

. . . Chicken salad has an unusual flavor by adding chopped ripe olives.

. . . A little paprika, a touch of Tabasco, a tiny bit of cayenne pepper or a spoonful of grated fresh horseradish can turn a bland mayonnaise into something special.

. . . Add peas, celery and unpeeled apple to store-bought slaw.

. . . Alternate orange and beet slices on greens and pour Italian dressing over all.

APRICOT-CHEESE LAYERED SALAD

16 ounces apricot halves
3 ounces lime flavored gelatin
¾ cup boiling water
¾ cup apricot syrup
1 cup green grapes, halved
1 envelope unflavored gelatin
½ cup water
2 cups cottage cheese
⅓ cup blue cheese, crumbled
½ cup sour cream
¾ cup celery, chopped
crisp greens, for garnish
small bunches of grapes, for garnish

Drain apricots, reserving ¾ cup of syrup. Dissolve lime gelatin in boiling water; add syrup. Chill until partially set. Add apricots and grapes; turn into a 7 cup salad mold. Chill until set. In saucepan, sprinkle unflavored gelatin on water to soften. Heat over low heat until dissolved, stirring occasionally. Cool slightly. Beat cheeses together until smooth. Add sour cream, celery and gelatin. Spread on top of lime layer. Chill until firm. Yields: 8-10 servings.

1 lb. head lettuce yields 10-12 leaves.

1 lb. potatoes yields ⅔ c diced potatoes.

1 lb. cheese yields ⅔ c cubed or finely cut.

CHERRY SALAD SUPREME

3 ounces raspberry flavored gelatin
1 cup boiling water
21 ounces cherry pie filling
3 ounces lemon flavored gelatin
1 cup boiling water
3 ounces cream cheese, softened
⅓ cup mayonnaise
8¾ ounces crushed pineapple, undrained
½ cup whipping cream
1½ cups miniature marshmallows
3 tablespoons pecans, chopped

Dissolve raspberry gelatin in 1 cup boiling water; stir in pie filling. Put into a 9x9 baking dish; chill until set. Dissolve lemon gelatin in 1 cup boiling water. Beat together cream cheese and mayonnaise. Gradually add lemon gelatin, blending well. Stir in undrained pineapple. Whip cream; fold into lemon mixture with marshmallows. Spread on top of congealed cherry layer. Sprinkle nuts on top. Chill until set. Yields: 10 servings.

CRANBERRY SALAD

8 ounces whole fresh cranberries
1 orange
½ cup crushed pineapple, drained, juice reserved
½ cup pecans, chopped
1 tablespoon lemon juice
2½ cups boiling water
6 ounces cherry flavored gelatin
½ cup sugar
1 tablespoon plain flour
½ cup sugar
juice from drained pineapple
2 eggs, slightly beaten
dash of salt
mayonnaise

Grind whole cranberries and orange in food grinder. Place in bowl with pineapple, pecans and lemon juice. Dissolve gelatin in boiling water; add ½ cup sugar; combine with pineapple mixture. Chill until partially set; put into a 9x9 pan. Chill until set. Mix flour and ½ cup sugar in saucepan; add juice, eggs and salt. Cook over medium heat, stirring constantly, until thick. Cool; mix with desired amount of mayonnaise (2 tablespoons mayonnaise to ½ cup sauce suggested) for salad topping. Yields: 12 servings.

CRAN-RASPBERRY RING

3 ounces raspberry flavored gelatin
3 ounces lemon flavored gelatin
1½ cups water, boiling
10 ounces frozen raspberries
14 ounces cranberry-orange relish
7 ounces lemon-lime carbonated beverage

Dissolve gelatins in boiling water. Stir in frozen raspberries, breaking up large pieces with a fork. Add cranberry-orange relish. Chill until cold, but not set. Carefully pour in lemon-lime carbonated beverage; stir gently. Put into a 6½ cup mold; chill until set. Yields: 8-10 servings.

CRÈME DE MENTHE SALAD

"So good for ladies' luncheons."

2 envelopes unflavored gelatin
8½ ounces crushed pineapple, drained, reserve juice
14 ounces pears, diced, drained, reserve juice
2 tablespoons sugar
⅛ teaspoon salt
¼ cup lemon juice
½ cup creme de menthe
1 cup sour cream

Soften gelatin in pineapple juice. Heat pear juice; add pineapple juice — gelatin mixture, stirring until dissolved. Add sugar, salt and lemon juice. Cool; add crème de menthe. Mix in sour cream with wire whisk until smooth. Chill until thickened; add pears and pineapple. Place in 4 cup mold; refrigerate until firm. Yields: 6-8 servings.

FROZEN FRUIT SALAD

"An expensive salad but well worth it. A hit with everyone – truly delicious!"

8 ounces cream cheese, softened
¾ cup mayonnaise
1 pint whipping cream, whipped (or 2 cups dairy topping)
½ cup maraschino cherries, diced
20 ounces frozen strawberries, thawed, undrained
1 cup mandarin oranges, drained (optional)
34 ounces fruit cocktail, drained
20 ounces crushed pineapple, drained
3 bananas, sliced
1½ cups miniature marshmallows
¾ cup pecans, chopped (optional)
lettuce leaves

With electric mixer, beat cream cheese and mayonnaise until smooth. By hand, fold in whipped cream or dairy topping. Add remaining ingredients. Pour into a 3 quart rectangular pan. Place in freezer. Remove approximately 15-20 minutes before serving. Cut in squares; serve on lettuce leaves. Yields: 16 servings.

PINK CHRISTMAS FROZEN FRUIT SALAD

8 ounces cream cheese, softened
2 tablespoons salad dressing
2 tablespoons sugar
8¼ ounces crushed pineapple, undrained
8 ounces jellied cranberry sauce
½ cup pecans, chopped
1 cup refrigerated whipped topping

Blend softened cream cheese with salad dressing, sugar, pineapple, cranberry sauce and nuts. Mix well. Fold in whipped topping. Place paper cups in muffin tins; fill with salad mixture. Freeze. Yields: 12 servings.

Note: When frozen, remove from muffin tins. Place in plastic bag in freezer. They will keep for 2 months.

MAKE-AHEAD FRUIT SALAD

⅓ cup salad dressing
½ cup whipping cream, whipped
1 tablespoon lemon juice
2 cups peach slices, drained
1 cup miniature marshmallows
½ cup maraschino cherries, halved
1 banana, sliced
¼ cup nuts, chopped

Combine salad dressing, whipped cream and lemon juice. Fold in remaining ingredients. Chill. Yields: 8 servings.

Note: This is a good, quick salad that can be made hours ahead of serving.

FRUIT WINE JELLY

2 envelopes unflavored gelatin
1 cup cold water, divided
1 cup orange juice, strained
1 cup sugar
juice of 2 lemons
1½ cups port wine, sherry or Madeira
8 ounces crushed pineapple, undrained
16 ounces pitted bing cherries, drained
½ cup almonds, blanched

Soften gelatin in ½ cup cold water. Add remaining ½ cup water to orange juice; heat to boiling. Add sugar; stir well. Pour over softened gelatin. Stir until gelatin and sugar are dissolved. Cool thoroughly; add lemon juice and wine. When mixture begins to thicken, add fruits and nuts. Pour into a 6 cup mold or individual molds. Refrigerate until firm. Yields: 6-8 servings.

Note: If you omit last 3 ingredients, you will have a perfectly delightful wine jelly to use for a holiday dessert served with whipped cream.

GRAPEFRUIT SOUFFLÉ SALAD

3 ounces lime flavored gelatin
1 cup boiling water
½ cup grapefruit juice
1 tablespoon vinegar
½ cup mayonnaise
1 large grapefruit, peeled and diced (1 cup)
½ cup celery, chopped
pecans, chopped (optional, but delicious)

Dissolve gelatin in boiling water. Add grapefruit juice, vinegar and mayonnaise. With an electric mixer, beat until well blended. Pour into a 4 cup refrigerator tray. Chill until partially set. Return to bowl; beat until fluffy. Fold in grapefruit, celery and nuts. Return to tray. Chill until firm. Yields: 5 servings.

MACÉDOINE OF FRESH FRUIT

"Also great for a dessert."

Fruits:

melon balls from watermelon
2 cups fresh strawberries, halved
2 cups fresh peaches, sliced
2 cups seedless green grapes, halved
1 cup fresh blueberries
2 oranges, sectioned
1 fresh pineapple, cut in chunks

Combine all fruits in large bowl or scooped out watermelon half. Pour syrup over. Cover. Refrigerate at least 8 hours or overnight. Yields: 8-10 servings.

Sugar Syrup:

1 cup sugar
¾ cup water
6 tablespoons fruit flavored brandy (or liqueur)
fresh orange juice to taste (optional)

Bring sugar and water to a slow boil; boil 5 minutes. Cool; add brandy or liqueur. If desired, add orange juice. Mix well. For a mint flavored syrup, pour hot mixture over mint leaves and let sit until cooled. Strain mixture and proceed with remaining directions. Garnish fruit with fresh mint leaves.

PINEAPPLE-ORANGE DELIGHT

6 ounces orange flavored gelatin
2½ cups boiling water
20 ounces crushed pineapple, undrained
1 cup orange slices, diced
6 ounces canned frozen orange juice concentrate, thawed
1 cup cold milk
3¾ ounces lemon instant pudding mix
1 cup whipping cream, whipped
2 bananas, sliced
11 ounces mandarin oranges, drained, for garnish

Dissolve gelatin in boiling water; stir in pineapple, oranges and orange juice. Pour mixture into a 13x9x2 pan; chill until firm. Combine milk and pudding mix; beat at low speed of electric mixer 1-2 minutes. Fold in whipped cream and sliced bananas. Spoon over firm gelatin mixture; garnish with orange slices. Cover and chill. Yields: 10-12 servings.

PEACH CHEESE SURPRISE

29 ounces sliced peaches, drained, reserve juice
15½ ounces crushed pineapple, drained, reserve juice
3 ounces lemon flavored gelatin
3 ounces orange flavored gelatin
2 cups boiling water
2 cups of combined fruit juices, divided
¾ cup pecans, chopped
½ cup sugar
3 tablespoons plain flour
1 egg, slightly beaten
2 teaspoons lemon juice
2 teaspoons butter, softened
1 cup whipping cream, whipped
¾ cup Cheddar cheese, shredded

Drain peaches and pineapple, reserving juices. Combine juices, adding water if necessary to make 2 cups liquid. Dissolve gelatin in boiling water; add 1 cup fruit juice, stirring well. Chill until slightly thickened. Fold in fruits and pecans; spoon into 9 inch pan. Refrigerate until firm. Meanwhile, combine sugar and flour; blend in egg. Stir in 1 cup remaining fruit juices and lemon juice. Cook over low heat, stirring constantly, until thickened. Remove from heat; stir in butter and cool. Fold in whipped cream; spread on salad. Sprinkle with cheese. Yields: 8-10 servings.

Rub a fruit salad mold with crushed fresh mint before pouring in hot gelatin.

SANGRIA SALAD

3 envelopes unflavored gelatin
1 cup orange juice
½ cup sugar
¼ cup lemon juice
2½ cups red wine or rosé
¾ cup club soda
2 oranges, peeled and sliced crosswise
2 bananas, sliced
2 peaches, peeled and chopped
1 cup strawberries, halved

Soften gelatin in orange juice; place over low heat, stirring until gelatin dissolves; add sugar, stirring until dissolved. Remove from heat; cool. Add lemon juice, wine and club soda. Chill until consistency of unbeaten egg white. Fold fruit into thickened gelatin; spoon into an 8 cup mold. Refrigerate until firm. Yields: 12-14 servings.

BOURBON STREET SALAD

"Unique and delightful salad."

6 ounces strawberry flavored gelatin
1½ cups strawberry soda, hot
½ cup sugar
½ cup bourbon whiskey
3 tablespoons lime juice
½ cup celery, finely chopped
1 cup strawberries, halved
½ cup walnuts, chopped
1 cup seedless grapes, halved

Dissolve gelatin in hot strawberry soda. Add sugar; stir well. Add remaining ingredients. Chill in a 4 cup mold until firm. Yields: 4-6 servings.

To easily peel tomatoes and peaches, place in boiling water for 10 seconds; remove and plunge in cold water.

STRAWBERRY ROSÉ MOLD

"A special company salad."

2 envelopes unflavored gelatin
1¾ cups cold water, divided
½ cup sugar
1 tablespoon orange rind, grated
1¾ cups rosé wine
1 cup fresh strawberries, sliced
¾ cup honeydew melon balls
additional strawberries and melon balls for garnish

Sprinkle gelatin over ½ cup water to soften. Bring remaining 1¼ cups water and sugar to a boil. Remove from heat; add gelatin and orange rind. Stir until gelatin is dissolved. When cool, add wine. Pour ½ cup gelatin mixture into a 5 cup ring mold; chill until set, but not firm. Cool remaining gelatin. Arrange sliced strawberries in a flower design on set gelatin. Cover carefully with a few spoonfuls of cooled gelatin to anchor design; chill until set, but not firm. Combine remaining cooled gelatin and melon balls. Gently put into mold. Chill until firm. Unmold on serving plate, fill center with cheese dressing. Garnish with strawberries and melon balls. Yields: 4 servings.

Cheese Dressing:

3 ounces cream cheese, softened
½ cup ricotta cheese
¼ cup whipping cream
1 tablespoon sugar
¼ teaspoon vanilla extract

Whip all ingredients together until smooth. Yields: 1 cup.

RASPBERRY WINE SALAD

"A delicious, refreshing salad."

9 ounces raspberry flavored gelatin
2½ cups boiling water
20 ounces frozen raspberries, thawed and undrained
20 ounces crushed pineapple, undrained
1 cup pecans, chopped
3 bananas, diced
1 cup fresh orange sections
½ cup orange juice
¾ cup red wine

Dissolve gelatin in boiling water, stirring well. Add remaining ingredients. Mix well. Refrigerate until firm. Yields: 12-14 servings.

RED RASPBERRY RING

8 ounces sour cream
¾ cup pecans, chopped
1 envelope unflavored gelatin
½ teaspoon salt
10 ounces frozen raspberries, thawed, reserve juice
6 ounces raspberry flavored gelatin
1½ cups boiling water
1 pint vanilla ice cream, softened
6 ounces frozen pink lemonade concentrate

Thoroughly mix together sour cream, pecans, gelatin and salt. Spread evenly in bottom of 6 cup, lightly greased, mold. Chill. Drain raspberries, reserving juice. Dissolve gelatin in boiling water; add ice cream, by spoonfuls, stirring until melted. Stir in lemonade and reserved juice. Chill until partially set. Fold in raspberries. Spoon on top of sour cream mixture. Refrigerate until firm. Yields: 8 servings.

TANGY AVOCADO ASPIC

6 ounces raspberry flavored gelatin
4 cups cocktail vegetable juice, hot
2 tablespoons prepared horseradish
1 cup celery, finely diced
2 small avocados, peeled and sliced

Dissolve raspberry gelatin in hot cocktail vegetable juice. Add horseradish; mix well. Pour ½ of gelatin mixture in bottom of 4 cup mold; add ½ cup of diced celery. Refrigerate until sticky firm. Cover with avocado slices; top with remaining gelatin and celery. Refrigerate until completely firm. Yields: 6-8 servings.

RUBY RED AVOCADO SALAD

"A real guest pleaser."

20 ounces pineapple tidbits, drained and juice reserved
2 cups cranberry juice cocktail
6 ounces raspberry flavored gelatin
1 avocado, peeled and sliced
1 cup apples, diced and peeled
½ cup celery, finely chopped
½ cup port wine

Drain pineapple; heat pineapple and cranberry juices to boiling. Dissolve gelatin in hot liquids. Add wine. Use enough of this mixture to cover pineapple tidbits and sliced avocado arranged on the bottom of a 2 quart rectanglar dish. Chill until almost set. Place apples and celery on top of this, cover with remaining gelatin mixture. Refrigerate until set. Yields: 8 servings.

AVOCADO DELIGHT

3 ounces lime flavored gelatin
1 cup boiling water
½ cup sour cream
½ cup mayonnaise
2 medium ripe avocados
1 teaspoon lemon juice
1 cup pecans, chopped
½ cup green pepper, chopped
1 teaspoon onion, grated
2 teaspoons celery, minced
½ teaspoon salt

Dissolve gelatin in boiling water; chill until thickened. Whip gelatin until foamy; add sour cream and mayonnaise, beating until thoroughly blended. Peel avocados and mash with lemon juice until smooth. Add remaining ingredients, mixing well. Fold avocado mixture into gelatin. Pour into 1 quart mold. Chill until firm. Yields: 6-8 servings.

EMERALD CUCUMBER MOLD

3 ounces lime flavored gelatin
¾ cup hot water
1 cup cucumber, unpeeled, shredded, and seeded
2 tablespoons onion, grated
1 tablespoon horseradish
1 cup cream style cottage cheese
1 cup mayonnaise
⅓ cup slivered almonds, blanched
parsley for garnish

Dissolve gelatin in hot water. Chill until slightly thick. Combine cucumber, onion and horseradish, draining off excess liquid. Add cottage cheese, mayonnaise and almonds. Fold into gelatin mixture. Pour in 8 inch square dish; chill until firm. To serve, cut into squares and garnish with parsley. Yields: 6 servings.

CUCUMBER MOUSSE

2 cucumbers
1 envelope unflavored gelatin
½ cup cold water
3 ounces lime flavored gelatin
1½ cups boiling water
½ cup lemon juice
2 teaspoons onion juice
¾ teaspoon salt
⅛ teaspoon cayenne pepper
½ cup celery, finely chopped
¼ cup parsley, minced
½ pint whipping cream, whipped

Peel cucumbers; remove and discard seeds. Coarsely grate cucumber; drain on paper towel. Soften unflavored gelatin in cold water. Dissolve lime gelatin in boiling water; stir in unflavored gelatin, lemon juice, onion juice, salt and cayenne pepper; chill until consistency of unbeaten egg white. Fold cucumber, celery, parsley and whipped cream into thickened gelatin. Pour into 4 cup mold. Chill until firm. Yields: 6-8 servings.

PICKLED BEET SALAD

3 ounces strawberry flavored gelatin
3 ounces raspberry flavored gelatin
3 ounces cherry flavored gelatin
4 cups boiling water
20 ounces French cut beets, drained and juice reserved
20 ounces crushed pineapple, drained and juice reserved
½ cup sweet pickle juice

Dissolve gelatins in boiling water. Drain liquid from cans (about 1½ cups); add with pickle juice to gelatin mixture. Chill until syrupy. Stir in beets and pineapple. Chill in 3 quart mold until firm. Serve with following dressing. Yields: 8-10 servings.

Dressing:
1 cup mayonnaise
1 tablespoon green onions and tops, chopped
1 tablespoon celery, diced
1 tablespoon green pepper, chopped

PARMESAN POTATO SALAD

4 cups cooked potatoes, diced
4 hard-cooked eggs, chopped
½ cup celery, chopped
¼ cup onion, chopped
¼ cup green pepper, chopped
salt to taste
8 slices bacon, fried and crumbled
¾-1 cup Parmesan cheese, grated
mayonnaise to moisten

Combine ingredients; mix lightly. Chill. Sprinkle with additional cheese, if desired. Yields: 6-8 servings.

HOT POTATO SALAD

2 pounds small white potatoes, unpeeled
1 teaspoon salt
½ cup bacon, diced
½ cup onion, minced
1½ teaspoons plain flour
4 teaspoons sugar
1 teaspoon salt
¼ teaspoon pepper
¼-⅓ cup vinegar
½ cup water
¼ cup onion, minced
2 tablespoons parsley, minced
1 teaspoon celery seed
½ cup sliced radishes (optional)
celery leaves, for garnish

About 1 hour before serving, cook potatoes in boiling water with 1 teaspoon salt in covered saucepan until fork tender — about 35 minutes. Peel; cut in ¼ inch slices. In small skillet, fry bacon until crisp. Add minced onion; sauté until tender, not brown. In bowl, mix flour, sugar, 1 teaspoon salt and ¼ teaspoon pepper; stir in vinegar (amount depends on tartness desired) and water until smooth. Add to bacon. Simmer, stirring until slightly thickened. Pour hot dressing over potatoes. Add ½ cup minced onions, parsley, celery seeds and radishes. Serve lightly tossed and garnished with celery leaves. Yields: 6-8 servings.

Grated lemon peel sprinkled over a salad perks up the flavor.

PETITE POIS SALAD

20 ounces frozen tiny green peas (or 17 ounces canned peas, drained)
head of lettuce
1 medium onion, thinly sliced (red onions are prettier)
3 tablespoons mayonnaise (or enough to hold salad together)
10 slices bacon, cooked and crumbled
¾ cup Swiss cheese, grated
½ cup Parmesan cheese, grated
1 teaspoon salt

Cook peas in boiling water about 3 minutes; cool. Shred lettuce; combine with peas, onion, mayonnaise, bacon, Swiss cheese, Parmesan cheese and salt. Toss until ingredients are mixed well. Chill overnight. Yields: 8 servings.

Variation: ½ head cauliflower bits may be substituted for peas.

SUPER RICE SALAD

"A fantastic salad – a refreshing change from potato salad."

1 cup long grain rice
3 tablespoons spring onions, chopped
3 tablespoons green pepper, chopped
3 tablespoons celery, chopped
3 tablespoons cucumber, seeded and chopped
3 tablespoons kosher dill tomatoes, chopped
3 tablespoons olives, chopped
1 tablespoon capers
sunflower seeds or chives (optional)

Cook rice according to package directions; when it has cooled to room temperature, add above ingredients and toss lightly. Add the following dressing. Sprinkle top with chives and/or sunflower seeds, if desired.

Dressing:
⅓ cup fresh olive oil
3 tablespoons garlic flavored wine vinegar
2 teaspoons fresh parsley, minced
1 teaspoon seasoning-blend

Blend all ingredients well and pour over rice salad. Stir to moisten. Refrigerate at least 4 hours. Before serving, toss with your favorite Italian dressing. Yields: 6 servings.

HARVEST SPINACH SALAD

"A real favorite – really hard to choose between these two completely different spinach salads."

2 pounds fresh spinach, washed and trimmed
10 medium fresh mushrooms, sliced
½ pound bacon, cooked, drained and crumbled
3 hard cooked eggs, chopped
½ cup slivered almonds, blanched
4 medium green onions, sliced
croutons (optional)

Tear thoroughly washed and drained spinach into bite size pieces. Combine with remaining ingredients, except croutons, and place in large salad bowl. Use your favorite dressing on salad just before serving. Caesar bottled, commercial dressing is perfect, or use the following delicious dressing. Yields: 6-8 servings.

Dressing:

½ cup salad oil
¼ cup bacon drippings
¼ cup garlic flavored wine vinegar
2 tablespoons white wine
2 tablespoons soy sauce
1 teaspoon sugar
1 teaspoon dry mustard
½ teaspoon curry powder
½ teaspoon salt
½ teaspoon seasoned pepper

Combine all ingredients in a jar with lid. Shake thoroughly. Refrigerate until ready to use. Shake before pouring over salad.

MARY'S SPINACH SALAD

"So excellent – one of our favorite recipes."

1 pound fresh spinach
11 ounces mandarin orange slices, drained
2 ripe avocados, sliced
½ cup slivered almonds

Carefully and thoroughly wash and dry spinach. Tear into bite sized pieces. Add other ingredients, making sure that spinach predominates. Mix gently, being careful with avocado. Immediately before serving add dressing. Serve on chilled plates. Yields: 6-8 servings.

Dressing:

1 cup salad oil
¼ cup fresh orange juice
2½ tablespoons lemon juice
¼ cup sugar
1 tablespoon vinegar
1 teaspoon salt
1 teaspoon paprika
1 teaspoon onion, grated

Combine ingredients in a jar. Cover; shake vigorously. Yields: Approximately 1¾ cups.

14 DAY SLAW

1 medium head cabbage (2 pounds), shredded
1 medium onion, thinly sliced
1 medium green pepper, finely chopped
1 cup garlic flavored wine vinegar
¾ cup salad oil
1 cup sugar
1 teaspoon dry mustard
1 teaspoon celery seed
1 tablespoon salt

Mix all vegetables together. Put remaining ingredients in a saucepan; bring to a boil. Cool; pour over vegetables. Cover tightly, shake well, and refrigerate. Yields: 12-14 servings.
"This will keep 2 weeks in refrigerator."

COLE SLAW SOUFFLÉ

"This is an elegant party salad."

8 ounces crushed pineapple
3 ounces orange flavored gelatin
¾ cup boiling water
¾ cup mayonnaise
1 cup cabbage, finely shredded
1 cup carrots, shredded
½ cup raisins
½ cup walnuts, chopped
3 egg whites, stiffly beaten

Drain pineapple; save juice. Dissolve gelatin in boiling water. Add pineapple juice. Beat in mayonnaise. Freeze in loaf pan until firm 1 inch from edge, but soft in center. This takes about 20 minutes. Put in large bowl; beat until fluffy. Fold in pineapple, cabbage, carrots, raisins, nuts and egg whites. Pour into a 1 quart soufflé dish (firmly tape a 22 inch piece of aluminum foil, folded lengthwise, around the edge of dish to provide a high stand to the soufflé). Chill until set. Remove foil before serving. Yields: 6 servings.

CAULIFLOWER SLAW

2 pound head cabbage, finely shredded
1½ cups cauliflower, thinly sliced
¼ cup green onions, finely chopped
¼ cup radishes, sliced
¼ cup green pepper, chopped

Combine vegetables and toss with the following dressing until well coated. Chill 1-2 hours before serving.

Garlic Cheese Dressing:

1 cup mayonnaise
1 cup sour cream
1 package garlic cheese dressing
1 tablespoon vegetable oil
1 tablespoon lemon juice
4 teaspoons caraway seeds
½ teaspoon salt

Mix all ingredients together until well blended. Use with slaw. Yields: 6 servings.

SAUERKRAUT SLAW

27 ounces sauerkraut, drained
¾ cup green pepper, chopped
¾ cup celery, chopped
½ cup green onions, chopped
4 tablespoons carrot, finely grated
½ cup tarragon vinegar
½ cup oil
1¼ cups sugar
½ teaspoon salt
pepper to taste
¼ cup pimento, chopped (optional)

Drain sauerkraut; do not rinse. Combine vegetable ingredients; mix. Boil vinegar, oil, sugar and salt together. When cool, pour over vegetables. Chill several hours. Yields: 8-10 servings.
Note: This will keep indefinitely in the refrigerator.

TOMATO DILL AND ARTICHOKE ASPIC

3 envelopes unflavored gelatin
5½ cups cocktail vegetable juice
⅓ cup lemon juice
1 tablespoon onion, grated
1 clove garlic, crushed
2 teaspoons dried dill weed
2 teaspoons salt
1 teaspoon basil
1 teaspoon oregano
1 bay leaf, crushed
14½ ounces artichoke hearts

Soften gelatin in ½ cup cocktail vegetable juice. Combine remaining vegetable juice with lemon juice, onion, garlic and seasonings. Simmer 10 minutes stirring occasionally. Remove from heat; strain. Add softened gelatin; stir until dissolved. Cool. Drain artichokes; arrange in bottom of 2 quart ring mold. Pour in approximately ¼ of the tomato mixture. Chill until firm. Add remaining mixture and chill again until firm. Serve with Caviar Mayonnaise. Yields: 6-8 servings.

Caviar Mayonnaise:
1 cup mayonnaise
1 cup sour cream
1 tablespoon lemon juice
2 teaspoons prepared mustard
2 ounces black caviar

Blend together first 4 ingredients. Fold in caviar. Chill.

TOMATO ASPIC

16 ounces tomatoes, undrained and mashed
½ cup sugar
½ cup vinegar
1 small onion, finely chopped
1½ envelopes unflavored gelatin
⅓ cup cold water
salt and pepper, to taste
1 cup celery, finely chopped
1 cup nuts, finely chopped
¼ cup green pepper, finely chopped
1 teaspoon pickle relish

Cook tomatoes, sugar, vinegar and onion over medium heat until onion is tender. Dissolve gelatin in cold water; add to hot tomato mixture. Season with salt and pepper. Let cool; add celery, nuts, green pepper and relish. Put into a 9x9 pan. Chill until firm. Yields: 9 servings.
Variation: Worcestershire sauce, lemon juice and garlic salt may be added according to taste, if a tangier flavor is desired.

GARDEN MEDLEY VEGETABLE MOLD

2 medium tomatoes, finely chopped
2 cucumbers, peeled, seeds removed, finely chopped
1 cup celery, finely chopped
¼ cup onion, finely chopped
1 green pepper, finely chopped
1½ cups carrots, finely grated
1 envelope unflavored gelatin
¼ cup cold water
¼ cup boiling water
1 teaspoon salt
3 tablespoons mayonnaise
2 tablespoons lemon juice
16 ounces cream cheese, softened
4-5 tablespoons crisply cooked bacon, crumbled

Drain chopped vegetables on paper towels. Soften gelatin in cold water; add boiling water; stir until gelatin is dissolved. Add salt, mayonnaise, lemon juice and gelatin to softened cream cheese. Mix well. Blend in vegetables. Place in lightly greased 1½ quart mold. Chill until firm. Unmold, place on greens, and sprinkle with crumbled bacon. Yields: 8-10 servings.

Note: All vegetables can be chopped in blender, except tomatoes. Drain well. This recipe is also good for sandwich filling. To make sandwiches, chill mixture for several hours. Spread filling on white bread and cover with dark bread. The bacon crumbs should be stirred into filling just before preparing sandwiches.

ITALIAN SALAD

1 head romaine lettuce, washed, drained and chilled
½ cup garbanzo beans, rinsed in cold water
½ cup pimento, diced
½ cup salami, cut in narrow strips
¼ cup onion, diced
2 tomatoes, diced
½ cup Parmesan cheese, freshly grated

Tear the romaine in pieces and place in salad bowl. Add beans, pimento, salami, onion and tomatoes. Toss together. Add dressing and toss. Sprinkle cheese over salad. Toss once more. Yields: 6 servings.

Dressing:
⅓ cup mayonnaise
2 teaspoons catsup
¼ teaspoon monosodium glutamate
¼ teaspoon garlic powder
1 teaspoon red wine vinegar
2 teaspoons lemon juice
3 tablespoons cold water

Mix all ingredients together with a wire whisk. Chill.

ORIENTAL SALAD

"Great for outdoor barbecue party."

1 cup sugar
1 cup wine vinegar
½ cup oil
1 teaspoon salt
dash of pepper
16 ounces French style green beans, drained
16 ounces small garden peas, drained
8 ounces water chestnuts, drained and sliced
8 ounces fresh mushrooms, washed, uncooked and diced
16 ounces bean sprouts, drained
2 ounces pimento, diced
1 medium onion, finely chopped
1 cup celery, chopped
1 medium green pepper, chopped

Make a dressing of sugar, wine vinegar, oil, salt and pepper. Toss remaining ingredients together. Pour dressing over them. Refrigerate overnight. Drain before serving. Yields: 12 servings.

Serve salad dressing in a cut & scooped out lemon half. Notch edges for a pretty effect.

DELICIOUS PERFECTION SALAD

2 envelopes unflavored gelatin
¼ cup cold water
1½ cups boiling water
⅓ cup sugar
½ cup cider vinegar
2 teaspoons salt
1 teaspoon curry powder
dash of cayenne pepper
2 green onions, finely chopped
1½ cups cabbage, finely shredded
1¼ cups celery, finely chopped
½ cup carrot, grated
½ cup green pepper, finely chopped
½ cup green olives, sliced
¼ cup radishes, sliced
mayonnaise (or favorite dressing) for garnish

Sprinkle gelatin in cold water; add boiling water, stirring until gelatin dissolves. Add sugar, vinegar, salt, curry and cayenne pepper. Chill until slightly thickened. Stir vegetables into thickened gelatin mixture. Pour into 8 cup mold; chill until firm. Serve with mayonnaise. Yields: 8-10 servings.

SEAFOOD SALAD SUPREME

"Marvelous recipe; well worth the expense."

1 cup cooked crab meat, diced
1 cup cooked lobster, diced
1 cup cooked white fish, diced
½ pound cooked shrimp, diced
2 tomatoes, diced
6 ripe olives, halved
mixed greens (romaine, spinach, escarole, watercress, scallion tops, celery tops, lettuce)
Hot Spice Dressing (recipe below)

Combine all ingredients in large salad bowl. Toss with Hot Spice Dressing. Yields: 6 servings.

Hot Spice Dressing:
¾ cup tarragon vinegar
1¾ cups oil
¼ cup onion, grated
3 bay leaves, crumbled
1 teaspoon chili powder
½ teaspoon cayenne pepper
1 teaspoon salt
ground pepper

Combine all ingredients; mix well.

AVOCADO PONCHARTRAIN WITH SHRIMP REMOULADE

4 medium avocados, halved and pitted
2 pounds shrimp
1 bay leaf
1 rib celery with leaves
2 sprigs parsley
12 peppercorns
1 tablespoon salt

Peel and clean shrimp. Place next 5 ingredients in 2 quarts water. Bring to a boil. Boil 5 minutes. Add shrimp; simmer 5 minutes. Drain and cool.

Sauce:
¼ cup mustard
¼ cup tarragon vinegar
¾ cup olive oil (or vegetable oil)
¼ teaspoon fresh ground pepper
¼ teaspoon dried tarragon
2 tablespoons parsley, minced
1 clove garlic, finely minced
1 scallion, including green part, chopped
½ cup celery, chopped
2 tablespoons green pepper, chopped
3 tablespoons horseradish
1 tablespoon capers, chopped

Combine all ingredients. Mix well; pour over shrimp. Cover; refrigerate 24 hours. Drain and serve in avocado halves. Yields: 8 small servings.

SHRIMP 'N RICE ELEGANTÉ

"An absolutely delicious salad, perfect for luncheon or outdoor summer party."

1½ pounds shrimp, cleaned and cooked
4 cups rice, cooked and cooled
½ cup celery, chopped
½ cup green pepper, chopped
½ cup green olives, sliced
2 tablespoons chives
2 tablespoons pimento
2 tablespoons onion, grated (optional)
½ pound mushrooms, fresh, sautéed and drained
¾ cup slivered almonds, toasted
lettuce, for garnish
parsley (optional), for garnish

Mix all ingredients together, except almonds. Add the following dressing:

Dressing:
1 cup mayonnaise
2 tablespoons garlic flavored wine vinegar
2 tablespoons olive oil
1 teaspoon Worcestershire sauce
2 dashes Tabasco
1 teaspoon Dijon mustard
1 teaspoon lemon juice
1 teaspoon horseradish (or more, if desired)
½ teaspoon paprika
salt to taste
pepper to taste

Thoroughly blend ingredients together. Mix dressing with shrimp and rice mixture. Chill; serve on lettuce beds, with a sprinkle of almonds on top. Yields: 8 servings.

TUNA MOUSSE

1½ envelopes unflavored gelatin
½ cup cold water
¼ cup lemon juice
1 cup mayonnaise
13 ounces tuna fish, drained
½ cup cucumber, peeled, seeded and chopped
½ cup celery, minced
½ cup olives, sliced
2 teaspoons onion juice
1½ teaspoons horseradish
¼ teaspoon salt
¼ teaspoon paprika
1 cup whipping cream, whipped

Soften gelatin in water; add lemon juice. Stir over medium heat until dissolved. Cool; add mayonnaise, drained and flaked tuna, cucumber, celery, olives, onion juice, horseradish, salt and paprika. Fold in whipped cream. Pour into lightly greased 1½ quart mold. Chill until firm. Yields: 8-10 servings.

CORN BEEF SALAD MOLD

"This makes a nice summer luncheon dish."

3 ounces lemon flavored gelatin
1½ cups boiling water
1 cup celery, finely chopped
2 tablespoons onion, finely chopped
2 green peppers, finely chopped
3 hard-cooked eggs, finely chopped
1 cup salad dressing
12 ounces canned corn beef, shredded
½ teaspoon salt

Dissolve gelatin in boiling water. Add remaining ingredients; mix well. Put into a 9x9 pan. Chill until firm. Yields: 8 servings.

EXOTIC TURKEY FRUIT SALAD

1 cup mayonnaise
½ cup sour cream
2 tablespoons lemon juice
1 teaspoon curry powder
½ teaspoon salt
15¼ ounces pineapple chunks, drained
1½ cups orange sections, diced and drained
1 cup apple, diced
1 cup white grapes, sliced
½ cup celery, diced
4 cups cooked turkey, diced
1 cup pecans, chopped

Combine mayonnaise, sour cream, lemon juice, curry and salt; blend well. Add remaining ingredients; toss. Chill 2-3 hours. Yields: 10 servings.

Note: This is delicious and so attractive when served over cantaloupe slices on lettuce cups.

ORIENTAL LUNCHEON SALAD

"This is excellent – a real treat."

32 ounces whole green beans, drained
4 green onions, sliced
2 medium firm tomatoes, chopped
½ cup oil
¼ cup fresh lemon juice
2½ tablespoons soy sauce
½ teaspoon sugar
½ teaspoon ground ginger
⅛ teaspoon garlic powder
dash salt
dash pepper
4 tablespoons mayonnaise
2 teaspoons soy sauce
3-4 cups cooked chicken, cut into thin strips
4 cups assorted salad greens, torn into bite size pieces
17 ounces bean sprouts, drained
6-8 radishes, thinly sliced
½ cup toasted almonds, sliced

Combine green beans, onions and tomatoes in a medium bowl. Mix vegetable oil, lemon juice, soy sauce, sugar, ginger, garlic powder, salt and pepper; pour over green bean mixture. Refrigerate at least 1 hour, stirring occasionally. Blend mayonnaise and soy sauce together in another bowl; mix well with chicken. Refrigerate. Just before serving, combine in a large salad bowl, the salad greens, bean sprouts, radishes, almonds, chicken and marinated green bean mixture. Toss to mix well. Yields: 8 servings.

SWISS AND HAM SALAD

½ cup mayonnaise
1 teaspoon seasoned salt
dash of pepper
2 teaspoons onion, grated
½ pound cooked ham in julienne strips
8 ounces sliced Swiss cheese in thin strips
¼ cup sweet pickle relish
2 cups cooked rice
1 cup cooked peas
½ cup celery, diced
¼ cup oil and ¼ cup vinegar
dash of Worcestershire sauce
lettuce, for garnish
2 tomatoes, cut in wedges, for garnish

At least 2 hours before serving, in a large bowl, mix mayonnaise, salt, pepper, and onion. Add ham, cheese, relish, rice, peas, celery, oil and vinegar, and Worcestershire sauce. Toss gently. Cover and refrigerate. At serving time, arrange on lettuce and garnish with tomato wedge. Yields: 4 servings.

TACO SALAD

1½ pounds ground beef
1½ cups onion, chopped
1 cup celery, chopped
1 cup green pepper, chopped
1½ teaspoons chili powder (or more to taste)
3 cloves garlic, minced
1 teaspoon ground cumin
salt to taste
pepper to taste
1 pound Velveeta cheese
10 ounces canned tomatoes with hot peppers (or Ro-tel tomatoes), undrained and chopped
1 head lettuce, torn into bite size pieces
3 large tomatoes, chopped
6 ounces corn chips, crushed (or taco chips)

Sauté ground beef, onion, celery, and green pepper until beef is browned. Stir in seasonings; simmer 15 minutes. Combine cheese and tomatoes with hot peppers in top of double boiler; cook until cheese melts, stirring constantly. Toss together meat mixture, cheese mixture, lettuce, tomatoes, and corn chips. Serve immediately. Yields: 8 servings.

AVOCADO SALAD DRESSING

2 avocados
juice of 2 lemons
2 cups sour cream
2 cups mayonnaise
½ onion, minced
2 tablespoons honey
2 tablespoons Worcestershire sauce
1 clove garlic, minced
½ teaspoon salt
few drops hot pepper sauce
pinch cayenne pepper

Peel avocados, remove seeds; mash with lemon juice. Add remaining ingredients; blend very thoroughly. Allow to mellow, refrigerated at least 1 day. Yields: 5 cups.

Variation: Instead of avocado, use 16 ounces canned asparagus, drained and finely chopped.

FRENCH DRESSING

1½ cups salad oil (or olive oil)
½ cup wine flavored vinegar
1 teaspoon Worcestershire sauce
1 clove garlic, crushed
2 teaspoons sugar
1 teaspoon salt
1 teaspoon paprika
½ teaspoon dry mustard (or Dijon mustard)
¼ teaspoon pepper
½ teaspoon thyme
1 teaspoon onion, grated

Combine all ingredients in screw top jar. Shake well. Refrigerate. Shake thoroughly before serving. Yields: 2 cups.

ROQUEFORT DRESSING

"Thick, creamy and outstanding."

1 cup sour cream
8 ounces Roquefort cheese, crumbled
2 cups mayonnaise
3 tablespoons lemon juice
½ cup fresh parsley, minced
3 green onions, finely chopped
1 tablespoon salt
1 teaspoon white pepper
1 garlic clove, crushed
2 tablespoons wine vinegar
dash or 2 of Tabasco

Combine all ingredients, beating thoroughly after each addition. Chill, preferably overnight. This dressing keeps well. Yields: approximately 1 quart.

SUMMER FRUIT SALAD DRESSING

1 cup mayonnaise
½ cup sour cream
¼ cup confectioners' sugar
2 fresh mint leaves
½ cup fresh strawberries, sliced

Combine all ingredients in blender. Blend until smooth. Yields: 2 cups. *"Serve over any combination of fresh fruits or melons, or over avocado and grapefruit salad."*

GREEN GODDESS SALAD DRESSING

"Such a wonderful blend of ingredients."

1 cup mayonnaise
½ cup sour cream
3 tablespoons white wine tarragon vinegar
1 tablespoon lemon juice
⅓ cup fresh parsley, minced
3 tablespoons onion, minced
3 tablespoons mashed anchovy filets (or 1 tablespoon anchovy paste)
1 tablespoon chives, chopped
2 teaspoons capers, chopped
1 small clove garlic, minced
⅛ teaspoon salt
⅛ teaspoon pepper
drop of green food coloring (optional)

Combine all ingredients in pint screw-top jar. Cover jar tightly. Shake until well blended. Chill 3-4 hours. Shake well before using. Yields: 1 pint.

CAESAR-SEASONED CROUTONS

Method I:
10 slices firm textured white bread
¼ cup olive oil (or cooking oil)
½ teaspoon garlic salt
¼ cup Parmesan cheese, grated

Preheat oven to 300°. Brush both sides of bread with oil; sprinkle with garlic salt and Parmesan cheese. Cut into ½ inch cubes. Place in 15x10x1 baking pan. Bake 30 minutes, stirring once. Store in air-tight container. Yields: 4 cups.

Method II:
3 slices white bread
¼ cup salad oil
1 small garlic clove

Trim crusts from bread; cut slices into ½ inch cubes. In 10 inch skillet, over medium heat, heat oil and add garlic clove. Cook until golden — about 2 minutes. Discard garlic. Add bread cubes; cook, stirring frequently, until cubes are golden. Drain on paper towels.

Variation: Bread cubes may also be deep fried until golden brown and sprinkled with Parmesan cheese while hot. Any type bread may be used.

COLLECTION OF ANNUAL EVENTS

January — Old Christmas celebration; Rodanthe
January — Field Trials; Pinehurst
February — Snow Carnival; Boone
March — Fox Hunt; Nags Head
March — Greater Greensboro Open; Greensboro
March or April — Moravian Easter Service; Old Salem
April — Azalea Festival; Wilmington
April — North-South Invitation Golf Championship; Pinehurst
April — Stoneybrook Steeple Chase; Southern Pines
April — Sports Car Climb; Chimney Rock
April — Old Time Fiddlers Convention; Union Grove
May — Strawberry Festival; Chadbourn
June - August — Summer Festival of Music; Brevard
June — Singing on the Mountain; Grandfather Mountain
June — Rhododendron Festival; Roan Mountain
July — Craftsman's Fair; Asheville
July — Highland Games & Gathering of the Scottish Clans; Grandfather Mountain
August — Mountain Dance & Folk Festival; Asheville
August — Mineral & Gem Festival; Spruce Pine
August — National Hollering Contest; Spivey's Corner
August — N.C. Apple Festival; Hendersonville
September — International Cup Regatta; Elizabeth City
September — State Championship Horse Show; Raleigh
September — Mule Day's Celebration; Benson
September — Gourd Festival; Cary
October — State Fair; Raleigh
October — Mullet Festival; Swansboro
October — National 500 Auto Race; Charlotte
October — Surf Fishing Tournament; Nags Head
November — Carolina's Carrousel; Charlotte
November — Formal Fox Hunt Meets; statewide
December — Moravian Love Feast; Old Salem

seafood
Janet Parks

THE CAROLINA COLLECTOR'S CONCOCTIONS

. . . Add tuna to potato pancake batter, fry until crispy & serve with sour cream.

. . . Dip fish sticks in bread crumbs, then egg, then chopped peanuts & fry.

. . . Layer sliced onion & salmon in casserole & top with cream soup. Bake 35 min. at 400°.

. . . An easy shrimp bisque — 1 can cream of shrimp soup & 1 can tomato soup, 2 c milk & dash curry powder. Serve hot or cold.

. . . Top seafood casseroles with crushed cereals.

. . . Serve poached salmon steaks with mayonnaise and minced dill added.

. . . Add a lemon wedge dipped in chopped parsley, paprika, mint or nutmeg to garnish your fish steaks.

. . . Sprinkle fish sticks with chili powder or an herb blend before cooking.

. . . Add herbed mayonnaise to broiled fish filets.

. . . Roll up fish filets with seasoned stuffing & baste with lemon butter.

. . . Stuff a whole fish with chopped celery, onions, & tarragon. Bake in white wine.

. . . Dip fish in Caesar salad dressing, sprinkle with crushed potato chips & grated cheese & bake 20 min. at 500°.

. . . Coat fish with sesame seeds & sauté.

. . . Make tuna patties with tuna, stuffing mix, ½ can cream of chicken soup & 2 eggs. Brown patties in butter.

. . . Make chow mein using tuna, shrimp or crabmeat instead of chicken.

. . . Stuff potato shells with mashed potatoes mixed with shrimp, crabmeat & sprinkled with grated cheese. Bake.

CLAMBAKE

"A great beach dinner!"

2½ pounds shrimp, shelled
24 fresh clams in shells
3 cups butter or margarine, divided
2 pounds chicken pieces
20 small new potatoes, halved
8 onions, quartered
12 ears of shucked corn, cut in half
salt
pepper

A large work area is needed. Using double thickness of heavy duty aluminum foil, connect two long pieces of foil with a double fold to make a large square. Coat the foil with 1 cup butter (use your hands) being careful not to puncture the foil. Place chicken, potatoes, onions, corn, shrimp, 2 cups butter cut up and lots of salt and pepper in center of foil square in the order given. Place clams on top and carefully wrap foil around all ingredients. Seal with double fold to make it air tight. Carefully place on charcoal grill for 1 hour and 45 minutes. This can also be baked in the oven in a large covered cooker at 350°. Use clam shells to scoop up juice to pour over vegetables. Yields: 12 servings.

CRAB AND ARTICHOKE DELUXE

"A very special company dish."

2 pounds fresh crab meat
3 tablespoons spring onions, chopped
¾ pound fresh mushrooms, sliced
4 tablespoons margarine
3 tablespoons butter
3 tablespoons plain flour
1 pint half and half
8 ounces artichokes, drained and chopped
5 tablespoons sherry
1 tablespoon lemon juice
1 tablespoon Worcestershire sauce
½ teaspoon paprika
salt and pepper to taste
1 cup sharp cheese, grated

Preheat oven to 350°. Sauté onions and mushrooms in margarine. Make white sauce with butter, flour and cream. Add onion-mushroom mixture to white sauce and all remaining ingredients except cheese. Mix well and place in greased 3 quart casserole. Top with grated cheese. Bake 20-25 minutes. Yields: 10 servings.

Variation: For a delicious shrimp casserole, substitute 2 pounds shrimp, cleaned and cooked, and 10¾ ounces canned cream of shrimp soup for the white sauce.

BAKED DEVILED CRAB MEAT

1 pound crab meat
¼ cup celery, minced
¼ cup green onions, minced
¼ cup green pepper, minced
2 tablespoons pimento, chopped
3 tablespoons butter or margarine
2 tablespoons plain flour
1 cup half and half
½ cup bread crumbs
½ teaspoon celery salt
1 teaspoon Worcestershire sauce
1 teaspoon dry mustard
1 tablespoon fresh parsley, chopped
1 tablespoon lemon juice
1 tablespoon dry sherry
1 teaspoon Tabasco, or to taste
salt and pepper to taste
paprika
1 cup buttered bread crumbs

Preheat oven to 350°. Sauté celery, onions, green pepper and pimento in butter. Add flour all at once, stirring constantly. Add half and half slowly, stirring until thickened. Add ½ cup bread crumbs and all seasonings, except paprika, and crab meat. Blend well and turn into a buttered 1½ quart casserole. Sprinkle with paprika and buttered bread crumbs. Bake approximately 20 minutes. Yields: 4 servings.

CRAB WITH RICE PILAF

14 ounces frozen king crab, defrosted
½ cup shrimp, cooked and cleaned
3 tablespoons butter
¼ cup onion, chopped
1 cup raw rice
2½ cups chicken broth
1 teaspoon lemon juice
½ cup canned sliced mushrooms
½ teaspoon seasoned salt
⅛ teaspoon pepper
8 ounces tiny peas, drained
2 tablespoons butter
2 tablespoons plain flour
1 cup half and half
⅓ cup dry sherry
1 tablespoon lemon juice
3 tablespoons Cheddar spread
½ teaspoon onion salt
⅛ teaspoon pepper

Over medium heat, heat 3 tablespoons butter in pan; stir in onion. Add raw rice and cook until golden brown. Stir in chicken broth, lemon juice, mushrooms, seasoned salt and pepper. Cover and simmer 30 minutes until rice is done. Last, gently mix in the peas. Firmly pack into a 2 quart, well buttered ring mold. Turn out immediately. Make a sauce of 2 tablespoons butter in a saucepan over low heat, stirring in flour. Slowly pour in half and half, dry sherry and lemon juice. Stir in Cheddar spread. Season with onion salt and pepper. Add shrimp and crab. Stir mixture to a quick boil, and then pour into the unmolded rice ring. Let set and serve. Yields: 6 servings.

BAKED RED SNAPPER

"Very, very different and tasty."

1 large (5-7 pound) red snapper, cut in steaks
salt and pepper to taste
4 tablespoons lemon juice
4 tablespoons butter
½ cup celery, chopped
½ cup onion, chopped
¼ cup green pepper, chopped
2 cloves garlic, minced
2 tablespoons parsley, minced
¼ teaspoon thyme
¼ teaspoon oregano
10 ounces cocktail vegetable juice
½ cup dry white wine
bacon strips to cover

Preheat oven to 350°. Place fish steaks in large, greased baking pan. Season lightly with salt and pepper, half of the lemon juice and dot with half of the butter. Bake for 15 minutes. Simmer celery, onion, green pepper, garlic, parsley, thyme and oregano in vegetable juice and wine, uncovered for 10 minutes. Remove fish from oven, dash with more salt and pepper, sprinkle with remaining lemon juice, and pour simmered vegetables over fish. Place bacon strips on top of fish and dot with remaining butter. Bake 20 to 40 minutes or until flakes easily, basting occasionally. Garnish with lemon slices and parsley. Yields: 8 servings.

Note: Mackerel, or any other large fish, is equally as good with this recipe. Baking time will vary, depending on thickness of steak.

FLOUNDER BAKED IN SOUR CREAM

"Garnished with fresh parsley and sautéed mushroom caps, this dish makes a delicious company treat."

2-3 pounds flounder fillets
4 tablespoons butter, divided
1 teaspoon salt
¼ teaspoon white pepper
½ teaspoon hot pepper sauce
1 tablespoon paprika
1 tablespoon fresh parsley, chopped
1 tablespoon chives, chopped
3 tablespoons dry sherry (optional)
½ cup Parmesan cheese, grated
1 cup sour cream

Preheat oven to 350°. Grease a flat 2 quart casserole with 1 tablespoon butter. Arrange flounder in casserole. Mix remaining ingredients together with the sour cream and spread over fish. Dot with remaining butter. Bake uncovered for 30 minutes. Yields: 4-6 servings.

TROUT MARGUERY

1 pound frozen trout fillets, thawed
1 cup shrimp, cooked and cleaned
6 ounces frozen crab meat, thawed
3 tablespoons olive oil
salt and pepper to taste
2 egg yolks, beaten
½ cup butter, melted and cooled
1 tablespoon plain flour
¼ cup dry white wine
1 tablespoon lemon juice
4 ounces sliced mushrooms, drained
¼ teaspoon paprika
salt and pepper to taste

Preheat oven to 375°. Place fillets in shallow 2 quart baking dish and drizzle with olive oil. Sprinkle with salt and pepper. Bake for 20 minutes or until fish flakes easily when tested with a fork. Place egg yolks in top of a double boiler; add melted butter and blend well. Cook, stirring constantly, until mixture thickens. Stir in flour, blending well. Add wine, lemon juice, shrimp, crab meat, mushrooms, paprika, salt and pepper. Cook, stirring constantly, 15 minutes. Place fish on platter and cover with sauce. Yields: 4 servings.

To enhance the flavor of tuna for salad etc., add 1 apple grated on the small grater for each can of tuna. An alternative is to add the juice of 2 lemons.

PIQUANT FISH

"Delicious and simple!"

2 pounds fillet of flounder
Ritz cracker crumbs
salt to taste
pepper to taste
½ cup butter or margarine
2 teaspoons lemon juice
2 teaspoons vinegar
4 teaspoons hot sauce
½ teaspoon dry mustard
½ teaspoon paprika
⅛ teaspoon garlic powder
1 teaspoon parsley, minced

Preheat oven to 450°. Coat fish in cracker crumbs; salt and pepper to taste. Place in greased 2 quart casserole with skin side down. Melt butter and add remaining ingredients. Pour over fish and bake 20 minutes. Yields: 3-4 servings.

OLD-FASHIONED OYSTER AND CREAM PIE

1 pint oysters, well drained
8 ounces minced clams, undrained
1 cup carrots, thinly sliced
1 cup celery, chopped
1 cup onion, chopped
1 cup raw potatoes, diced
1 tablespoon dried parsley
¼ cup water
2 tablespoons butter or margarine
1 teaspoon salt
½ cup whipping cream or evaporated milk
2 egg yolks
1-3 tablespoons plain flour
¼ teaspoon nutmeg
½ package of pie crust mix, enough for 1 top crust

Preheat oven to 350°. Combine carrots, celery, onions, potatoes, parsley, water, butter or margarine and ½ teaspoon salt. Bring to simmering point; cover. Cook until vegetables are tender, about 15 minutes. Add oysters and undrained clams and heat until edges of oysters curl. Combine cream, egg yolks, flour, nutmeg and remaining ½ teaspoon salt. Beat until free of lumps and pour over seafood. Cook gently until sauce thickens, stirring carefully. Spoon into a deep dish 9 inch pie plate. Top with pastry made from pie crust mix. Bake until crust is brown and filling is hot and bubbling, about 30 minutes. Yields: 6 servings.

FANCY SCALLOPED OYSTERS

"So perfect for your Thanksgiving or Christmas meal."

1½ pints oysters, drained with liquor reserved
6 slices bacon, cooked and crumbled
8 ounces fresh mushrooms, sliced, sautéed and drained
2½ cups soda cracker crumbs
½ cup butter, melted
1 cup half and half
¼ cup oyster liquor
1 tablespoon fresh parsley, minced
1 teaspoon Worcestershire sauce
2 teaspoons grated onion (optional)
2 tablespoons dry sherry (optional)
salt and pepper to taste

Preheat oven to 350°. Combine cracker crumbs and butter. Place approximately ⅓ of the crumbs in a greased 1½ quart flat casserole. Cover with half of oysters. Sprinkle half of bacon and half of mushrooms on top. Cover with another ⅓ of crumbs and repeat for a second layer. Combine remaining ingredients; pour evenly over casserole. Top with remaining ⅓ of the crumbs. Bake 30 minutes. Yields: 4 servings.

DEVILED OYSTERS

"Also a great party hors d'oeuvre when served in chafing dish and spread on crackers."

3 pints oysters
1 large onion, finely chopped
1 small bell pepper, finely chopped
3 cloves garlic, minced
1 rib celery, finely chopped
½ cup butter
1 teaspoon salt
½ teaspoon mustard
½ teaspoon red pepper
½ teaspoon black pepper
juice of 1 lemon
½ loaf French bread, cut in ½ inch slices
2 eggs
½ cup milk
½ cup fresh parsley, chopped
½ cup green onion tops, chopped
bread crumbs

Preheat oven to 375° or 400°. Sauté onion, bell pepper, garlic and celery in butter in a large skillet. Grind oysters on large blade of meat grinder and add to mixture in skillet. (A blender may be used.) Add seasonings and bring to a boil. Remove from heat; cool. Toast French bread and roll into crumbs. Add to oyster mixture. Beat eggs and milk. Add to oysters. Mix in parsley and onion tops. If serving as individual entrée, place in ramekins and top with bread crumbs. Bake at 400° for 20 minutes. If serving as a casserole, place in 2 quart dish; top with crumbs and bake at 375° for 30 minutes. Yields: 8-10 servings.

OYSTER AND WILD RICE CASSEROLE

1 quart oysters, drained
½ cup butter, melted
12 ounces wild rice, cooked according to directions
salt
pepper
hot pepper sauce to taste
10¾ ounces canned cream of mushroom soup
1 cup whipping cream
1½ teaspoons onion powder
¾ teaspoon thyme
1½ tablespoons curry powder, dissolved in 2 tablespoons hot water
½ cup parsley, finely minced

Preheat oven to 325°. Add butter to rice; place ½ the mixture in bottom of a 3 quart casserole. Cover rice with oysters which have been seasoned with salt, pepper and pepper sauce. Top with remaining rice. Heat soup; add cream, onion powder, thyme and curry powder. Pour over rice and oysters in baking dish. Bake 45 minutes. Garnish with parsley. Yields: 8-10 servings.

A bushel of oysters serves 10 people.

Roast oysters on a barbecue grill — cover with a wet towel to steam.

SALMON CUSTARD PIE

"Excellent for a luncheon."

1 pound canned red salmon (save liquid)
2 tablespoons butter
2 tablespoons green onions, finely chopped
3 tablespoons fresh dill, snipped
¼ teaspoon black pepper, freshly ground
¼ cup salmon liquid
1 cup whipping cream, scalded
4 eggs, lightly beaten
9 inch pie shell, partially baked

Preheat oven to 375°. Melt butter. Sauté onion until tender. Place salmon, dill, pepper and salmon liquid in a bowl; mash with a fork. Add onion. Pour hot cream over the eggs while beating. Combine egg mixture with salmon mixture and pour into the pie shell. Bake for 30 minutes, or until set in the middle. Yields: 6 servings.

COCKLE SHELL SCALLOPS

2 pounds scallops
1 cup white wine
6 tablespoons butter
¼ cup onion, finely chopped
6 tablespoons self-rising flour
2-3 cups milk
dash salt
dash pepper
4 ounces sliced mushrooms, drained
2 tablespoons sherry
1 cup dry bread crumbs
1 cup Parmesan cheese, grated
paprika

Bring white wine to a boil. Add scallops, bring back to boil; simmer until tender, about 5 minutes. Drain liquid. Sauté onions in butter until tender. Stir in flour, allow to cook 2 minutes. Add milk gradually, stirring constantly. Cook over low heat until smooth and thick. Remove from heat; add salt, pepper, mushrooms, sherry and scallops (cut in bite-size pieces, if desired). Return to heat just until heated thoroughly. In small mixing bowl, combine crumbs and cheese. Divide scallops among shells or individual baking dishes, sprinkle with cheese-crumb mixture. Sprinkle with paprika. Place on cookie sheet and heat under broiler until crumbs are browned. Yields: 6-8 servings.

"Shrimp may also be used."

COQUILLES ST. JACQUES

"May be used as a filling for crepes or served in traditional shells."

½ pound scallops, cut into small pieces
⅓ cup dry white wine
2 tablespoons green onions, chopped
1 cup fresh mushrooms, sliced
3 tablespoons butter
3 tablespoons plain flour
½ teaspoon salt
1½ cups half and half
2 tablespoons parsley, chopped
8 cooked crepes (see Index for recipe)
1 cup Swiss cheese, grated

Preheat oven to 350°. In saucepan, combine wine, onion, scallops and mushrooms. Cover and simmer 5 minutes. Meanwhile, melt butter in skillet. Stir in flour and salt. Pour in half and half; cook, stirring constantly, until thickened. Add parsley, then scallop-mushroom mixture. Fill cooked crepes and fold over in shallow baking dish. If crepes are not used, individual shells may be filled with mixture. Sprinkle with cheese. Heat for 10-15 minutes or until cheese melts. Yields: 8 crepes.

To determine cooking time for fish, lay on counter & measure at thickest point (bottom to top). Cook 10 min. per inch — double time if fish is frozen.

SHRIMP AND CRAB MEAT MORNAY

2 pounds shrimp, cleaned, cooked and coarsely chopped
13 ounces canned crab meat
6 tablespoons butter
6 tablespoons plain flour
2 cups milk, heated
8 ounces chicken broth, heated
1 pound Velveeta cheese, grated
Hollandaise Sauce, see Index for recipe
Parmesan cheese, grated

Preheat broiler in oven. In saucepan, melt butter and add flour. Cook until bubbly. Gradually add milk and chicken broth, stirring constantly until thick. Add Velveeta cheese and stir until well blended. Combine shrimp and crab meat with the sauce; divide among 8 individual baking dishes. Top with 1 tablespoon Hollandaise sauce. Run baking dishes under broiler to lightly brown. Sprinkle with Parmesan cheese and serve. Yields: 8 servings.

"Any single seafood or combination of seafood may be used in this delicious recipe."

SHRIMP ROCKEFELLER

1½ pounds shrimp, cooked and cleaned
10 ounces chopped spinach
1 cup sour cream
1 teaspoon horseradish
½ cup catsup
½ teaspoon onion powder
1 teaspoon fresh parsley, minced
1 teaspoon lemon juice
salt and freshly ground pepper to taste
1 cup buttered bread crumbs

Preheat oven to 450°. Cook spinach according to directions and drain well. Combine shrimp, spinach, sour cream, horseradish, catsup, onion powder, parsley, lemon juice, salt and pepper. Blend thoroughly and turn into a buttered 1½ quart casserole. Sprinkle top with bread crumbs. Bake approximately 15 minutes. Yields: 4 servings.
"For an added special touch, add crumbled bacon."

To eliminate odors when cooking fish, simmer ½ c vinegar in a pan on stove or in oven.

CREOLE SHRIMP CASSEROLE

"Easy to prepare ahead, freeze and have on hand when company drops in. Delicious!"

1½-2 pounds shrimp, cooked and cleaned
1½ cups raw rice, cooked according to directions
1 medium green pepper, chopped
1 medium onion, chopped
½ pound mushrooms, sliced
2 tablespoons butter
10¾ ounces canned tomato soup
15 ounces spaghetti sauce
⅓ cup sherry
1 teaspoon salt
¼ teaspoon pepper
1 teaspoon garlic salt (or to taste)
2 teaspoons Worcestershire sauce
dash of cayenne pepper
dash of paprika
dash of ground oregano
½ cup slivered almonds, toasted and divided
6 ounces sharp Cheddar cheese, grated

Preheat oven to 350°. Sauté green pepper, onion, and mushrooms in butter. Drain off liquid. Combine all ingredients together, with the exception of ¼ cup almonds and grated cheese. Put into a greased 2 quart casserole. Sprinkle remaining almonds and grated cheese on top. Bake for 20-30 minutes. Yields: 8-10 servings.

SHRIMP CREOLE

2-3 cups shrimp, cleaned
5 slices bacon
½ cup celery, sliced
½ cup onion, chopped
⅓ green pepper, chopped
2 tablespoons parsley, chopped
3 tablespoons plain flour
32 ounces tomatoes, chopped
1 teaspoon salt
¼ teaspoon pepper
2 tablespoons Worcestershire sauce
1 garlic clove, minced
⅓ teaspoon paprika
1 teaspoon celery seed
1 tablespoon lemon juice
2 bay leaves
hot cooked rice

Fry bacon in large frying pan until crisp. Remove and drain. Reserve drippings. In bacon drippings, brown celery, onion and green pepper. Blend in parsley and flour; stir until lightly browned. Add tomatoes, seasonings and shrimp. Simmer over low heat 15-30 minutes. Five minutes before serving, remove bay leaves and add cooked bacon which has been crumbled. Serve over a bed of hot cooked rice. Yields: 4-5 servings.

GARLIC BUTTERED SHRIMP

1 pound fresh shrimp (large preferable)
2 tablespoons butter
3 spring onions, minced
1 or 2 cloves garlic, according to taste
2 teaspoons lemon juice
1 teaspoon fresh parsley, minced
1 teaspoon chives
¼ teaspoon thyme
¼ teaspoon tarragon
¼ teaspoon oregano
½ teaspoon paprika

Cook shrimp in salted water for 3 minutes. Drain, remove body shell, but leave the tail shell. Cut each shrimp in half through the back, but keep it attached to the tail. Devein the shrimp. Melt butter and sauté spring onions and garlic until soft. Add shrimp, lemon juice, herbs and paprika, mixing thoroughly and making sure shrimp are well coated. Continue to sauté in pan for approximately 3 minutes. Yields: 4 servings.

SHRIMP ORLEANS

1½ pounds shrimp, cooked and cleaned
1 tablespoon butter
1 medium onion, chopped
1 clove garlic, minced
10¾ ounces canned cream of mushroom soup
1 cup sour cream
⅓ cup catsup
4 ounces mushrooms
4 drops Tabasco
¼ cup dry white wine
4 cups hot cooked rice
chives

Heat electric skillet to 325° (or on medium heat on stove). Sauté onion and garlic in butter. Stir in soup, sour cream, catsup, mushrooms, Tabasco, wine and shrimp. Simmer 5 minutes. Serve with hot rice ring. Garnish with chives. Yields: 4-6 servings.

"To make a rice ring, butter a 9 inch mold generously, pack with hot cooked rice and invert onto serving platter; garnish with fresh parsley."

SWEET AND PUNGENT SHRIMP

"So very, very good!"

2 pounds shrimp, cooked and cleaned
20 ounces pineapple chunks, reserve juice
1 cup brown sugar
1 cup vinegar
¼ cup soy sauce
3 tablespoons catsup
½ teaspoon curry powder
2½ cups water, divided
6 tablespoons cornstarch
2 medium green peppers, cut in strips
2 onions, cut in rings
4 cups hot cooked rice
½ cup slivered almonds, toasted

Drain syrup from pineapple into a skillet or wok. Add brown sugar, vinegar, soy sauce, catsup, curry powder and 2 cups water. Bring to a boil. Combine cornstarch and remaining ½ cup water. Add to skillet. Cook, stirring constantly, until thickened. Add green pepper, onion and pineapple. Cook 3 minutes. Add shrimp and heat through. Serve immediately with rice. Sprinkle almonds on top. Yields: 8 servings.

SEAFOOD CASSEROLE

1 pound crab meat
1 pound shrimp, cooked and cleaned
1 green pepper, chopped
1 medium onion, finely chopped
4 tablespoons butter, melted
5 ounces Durkee's dressing
1 cup mayonnaise
dash of Worcestershire sauce
dash of Tabasco
dash of salt
bread crumbs
butter

Preheat oven to 400°. Cook pepper and onion slowly in butter until tender, not brown. Mix with all other ingredients; place in buttered 2 quart casserole. Top with bread crumbs and dot with butter. Bake for 20-30 minutes. Yields: 6-8 servings.

SEAFOOD CASSEROLE SUPREME

3 cups shrimp, cooked and cleaned
1 pound crab meat
8 ounces fresh mushrooms, sliced
2 cups celery, finely diced
1 large onion, finely diced
1 green pepper, finely diced
4 tablespoons butter, divided
2 ounces pimento, drained and chopped
2 10¾-ounce cans cream of mushroom soup
6 ounces Uncle Ben's long grain and wild rice, cooked
½ cup milk
1 cup slivered almonds

Preheat oven to 325°. Sauté mushrooms, celery, onions and green pepper in 2 tablespoons butter until soft but not brown. Add pimento and soup. Mix well. Add shrimp, crab meat and cooked rice; stir in milk. Heap into a 2 quart casserole. Bake for 45 minutes. Garnish with almonds that have been tossed in remaining butter. Yields: 10-12 servings.

TUNA AND BROCCOLI SOUFFLÉ

4 tablespoons butter
3 tablespoons onion, minced
3 tablespoons plain flour
1 cup half and half
1 cup Swiss cheese, grated
⅛ teaspoon cayenne pepper
4 eggs, separated
6½ ounces canned tuna, drained and flaked
1 teaspoon lemon juice
¼ teaspoon dill weed
½ teaspoon parsley, chopped
10 ounces frozen broccoli, cooked, drained and puréed
¼ teaspoon nutmeg
½ teaspoon salt
½ teaspoon cream of tartar
½ cup Parmesan cheese, grated and divided

Preheat oven to 400°. Melt butter in 8 inch skillet. Add onion and sauté until translucent. Stir in flour, blend well and cook over moderate heat 1 minute. Remove from heat; add half and half, stirring constantly. Return to heat; stir until mixture thickens and simmer 1 minute. Add Swiss cheese and cayenne pepper; blend. Beat egg yolks slightly; add to mixture and stir well. Set aside. In a 2 quart bowl combine tuna, lemon juice, dill weed and parsley. In another 2 quart bowl combine puréed broccoli and nutmeg. Divide basic sauce between tuna mixture and broccoli mixture. Beat egg whites with salt and cream of tartar until stiff but not dry. Fold half of beaten egg whites into tuna mixture and half into broccoli mixture. Butter a 1½ quart soufflé dish and dust with 2 tablespoons of Parmesan cheese. Using foil, make a "collar" about 3 inches wide and long enough to wrap around dish. Butter foil and sprinkle with cheese. Wrap around dish and secure with a paper clip. Gently spoon half of broccoli mixture into dish. Gently spoon tuna mixture over and top with remaining broccoli mixture.

Spread with a spatula so that tuna mixture is thoroughly covered. Sprinkle with remaining Parmesan cheese. Place soufflé in lower third of oven, reduce oven temperature to 375°. Bake 25-35 minutes. Serve immediately. Yields: 6 servings.

SEAFOOD CREPES

1 cup crab meat
1 cup shrimp, cooked and cleaned
1 cup lobster or scallops, cooked and diced
2 tablespoons butter
½ cup fresh mushrooms, chopped
2 tablespoons onion, minced
2 tablespoons plain flour
½ teaspoon salt
¼ teaspoon white pepper
¾ cup milk, scalded
⅛-¼ teaspoon ground cloves (optional)
¼ teaspoon Worcestershire sauce
2 tablespoons Parmesan cheese, grated
3 tablespoons sherry or dry white wine
2 teaspoons fresh parsley, chopped
2 teaspoons chives
12-14 crepes (see Index for recipe)
Cheese Sauce
½ cup Parmesan cheese, grated

Preheat oven to 350°. Melt butter, add mushrooms and onion. Sauté until onion is transparent. Blend in flour, salt and pepper. Heat until well blended. Remove from heat, add scalded milk gradually, stirring constantly. Mix in ground cloves, Worcestershire sauce and 2 tablespoons Parmesan cheese. Return to heat and rapidly bring to boiling. Cook 1-2 minutes, stirring constantly. Remove from heat, mix in crab, shrimp, lobster or scallops. Add sherry or wine, parsley and chives. Chill. Prepare crepes and Cheese Sauce.

Cheese Sauce:
3 tablespoons butter
3 tablespoons plain flour
½ teaspoon salt
¼ teaspoon white pepper
1½-2 cups milk
3 tablespoons sherry
1 cup Cheddar cheese, grated
½ cup Parmesan cheese, grated

Melt butter, blend in flour, salt and pepper. Gradually add half and half, stirring constantly over medium heat until thickened. Cook 1-2 minutes. Add sherry and cheeses. Cook and stir until cheese melts. (Double recipe if you prefer crepes in heavy sauce.)

To assemble, spoon 2-3 tablespoons of the seafood filling into the center of each crepe. Fold one edge of the crepe over filling and roll. Lightly grease a flat 3 quart casserole. Spread with a thin layer of cheese sauce. Place filled crepes in casserole with folded side down. Spoon remaining Cheese Sauce over crepes. Cover and bake 20 minutes. Remove cover. Sprinkle with Parmesan cheese and place under broiler 3-4 minutes, or until lightly browned. Yields: 12-14 crepes.

COLLECTION OF FAMOUS TAR HEELS

Frances Bavier — actress "Aunt Bea" on Andy Griffith Show
David Brinkley — TV commentator
Howard Cosell — sports commentator
Davy Crockett — frontiersman (Tennessee then part of N.C.)
Elliot Daingerfield — artist
Josephus Daniels — Secretary of Navy; journalist; publisher
James B. Duke — founder of American Tobacco Co.; Duke University named for him
Sam Ervin — former U.S. Senator; chairman of Watergate committee
William C. Fields — artist
Raymond Floyd — professional golfer
Ava Gardner — actress
Richard Gatling — invented Gatling gun
Billy Graham — evangelist
Paul Green — playwright: *Lost Colony; Common Glory*
Andy Griffith — actor
Luther Hodges — former governor; founder of Research Triangle; former Secretary of Commerce
Catfish Hunter — professional baseball player
Andrew Jackson — 7th President of U.S.
Sonny Jerguson — professional football player
Andrew Johnson — 17th President of U.S.
Charlie "Choo Choo" Justice — football player
William Rufus King — Vice President of U.S. 1853-1857
Juanita Kreps — Secretary of Commerce, Carter Administration
Charles Kuralt — commentator
Meadowlark Lemon — Globetrotters
Dolly Madison — wife of 4th President of U.S.
Kathy McMillian — olympic track star
Elizabeth MacRae — actress
John M. Morehead — governor and railroad builder; Morehead Planetarium and scholarships named for him
O'Henry (William S. Porter) — short story writer
Richard Petty — professional race car driver
James K. Polk — 11th President of U.S.
Carl Sandburg — poet; novelist; biographer of Lincoln
Terry Sanford — President Duke University; former governor
Susie M. Sharp — Chief Justice State Supreme Court
Arthur Smith — entertainer
Ruth Carter Stapleton — evangelist
Bob Timberlake — artist
David "Carbine" Williams — invented Carbine Rifle

oups

and

sandwiches

THE CAROLINA COLLECTOR'S CONCOCTIONS

. . . Add nutmeg to chicken or mushroom soup; curry powder to chicken with rice soup; chili powder to bean soup; thyme to clam chowder; oregano or bay leaf to tomato soup.

. . . Add curry powder to New England clam chowder for unusual treat.

. . . In blender, blend 2 avocados, 2 c light cream, 1 can clam chowder & heat with 2 c chicken consommé; add ¼ c sherry last.

. . . Make a basic chicken soup adding 4 whole cloves & ½ t crushed rosemary.

. . . Add sautéed onion & curry powder to canned tomato soup & garnish with egg yolks.

. . . Easy chilled borsch is made with diced beets, canned bouillon, minced onion & lemon juice to taste. Garnish with sour cream.

. . . Cool avocado soup calls for 1 chopped avocado, 1 can chicken broth, 1 soup can water, 1 c light cream, dash hot sauce. Chill.

. . . Combine tomato soup & 1 c shredded cheese; heat until cheese melts. Add water until desired consistency.

. . . Spread deviled ham on toast, top with asparagus spears & cheese sauce. Serve hot.

. . . Toast English Muffins & spread with cream cheese; top with deviled ham.

. . . Sauté 2 onions, ½ c catsup, 1 T mustard & 1 T Worcestershire. Add 16 oz. roast beef with gravy for an easy barbecue.

. . . Combine 1 can corn beef, ¼ c pickle relish, horseradish & chopped onion with mayonnaise.

. . . A delightful spread is made from ½ c peanut butter, 1 c shredded cheese & ⅓ c milk.

. . . Add Chinese vegetables to frankfurters on hamburger buns.

. . . Sauté green pepper rings; arrange on toast & cover with a cheese sauce. Garnish with bacon.

. . . Spread a mixture of tuna, cheese, onion, green pepper & mayonnaise on buns; broil until golden.

. . . Serve thinly sliced frankfurters in a barbecue sauce over hamburger rolls.

. . . Layer a hamburger patty, dry onion soup mixed with water, slice of cheese & another patty. Press edges together, top with onion sauce, wrap in foil & cook 20 min. over hot coals. Serve on buns.

. . . A pizza sandwich made on English muffins with mozzarella cheese, tomato sauce, Parmesan cheese, oregano & any other topping is delicious.

LIL'S BRUNSWICK STEW

"The longer it cooks, the better it tastes – and leftovers are even better."

4 chicken breast halves, skinned
4 cups water
1½ teaspoons salt
10¾ ounces canned tomato soup
16 ounces canned tomatoes
1 onion, chopped
3 potatoes, diced
1½ cups lima beans
1½ cups white corn
3 tablespoons sugar
⅛ teaspoon pepper
salt to taste

Simmer chicken in salted water until tender, about 1½ hours. Remove chicken breasts; cool. Cut meat into small pieces; return to broth. Add remaining ingredients, bring to boil. Simmer for several hours. Thicken with 1 to 2 tablespoons flour if necessary. Yields: 6-8 servings.

Appetizer soups are thin; main course soups are creamy & heartier.

BRUNSWICK STEW Á LA GEORGIA

"A different stew using 3 meats."

1 pound beef chuck, cubed
1 pound pork shoulder, cubed
½ pound lamb shouder, cubed
16 ounces canned tomatoes
3 cups potatoes, diced
16 ounces canned lima beans
1 cup onions, diced
16 ounces whole kernel corn
1 tablespoon sugar
2 teaspoons salt
½ teaspoon basil, crushed
¼ teaspoon thyme, crushed
1 bay leaf, crushed
¼ teaspoon pepper
2 slices white bread

Place meat in 6 quart pot; add water, cover. Simmer 1 hour or until meat is tender. Remove meat, measure broth and add enough water to make 4 cups. Return broth to boiling; add vegetables. Cook, covered, 15 minutes or until tender. Add cubed meat and seasonings; cook, covered, 3 minutes more. Season to taste with salt and pepper. Break bread into pieces. Add to stew, stirring constantly. If desired, chill overnight to let flavors blend, then reheat before serving. Yields: 8-10 servings.

CANADIAN CHEESE SOUP

½ cup butter
½ cup onion, minced
1 cup carrots, diced
1½ cups celery, finely chopped
2 cups chicken broth (or bouillon)
½ cup plain flour
6 cups milk
4 cups (1 pound) Cheddar cheese, grated
parsley, minced for garnish

Melt butter in large heavy pan. Add onion. Sauté until tender. Add carrots, celery and chicken broth. Cover; simmer about 15 minutes or until vegetables are tender. Make a paste with flour and 1 cup of milk; add to vegetable mixture. Add remaining milk. Cook, stirring constantly, until slightly thickened. Add cheese; stir over low heat until melted. Serve in warm soup bowls; sprinkle with minced parsley. Yields: 10-12 servings.

CORN CHOWDER

"Great for lunch."

6 slices bacon
16 ounces cream style corn
1 cup milk
1 medium onion, diced
1 small green pepper, diced
3 medium potatoes, diced
salt to taste
pepper to taste

Cook bacon until crisp; drain well. To bacon grease, add corn, milk, onion, green pepper and potatoes; cook until vegetables are tender. Add salt and pepper to taste; serve with bacon crumbled on top. Yields: 4 servings.

SHE-CRAB SOUP

13 ounces white crab meat
10¾ ounces canned celery soup
10¾ ounces canned tomato soup
6 ounces cream cheese, softened
2 cups milk
10½ ounces canned Harris She-Crab soup
1 cup sherry
dash of salt and pepper
dash of Worcestershire sauce

Combine all ingredients except sherry. Cook on top of stove until cream cheese is melted. Add sherry. Stir constantly to prevent sticking. Serve hot. Yields: 10 servings.

Hint: This recipe makes a large quantity and does freeze well. It is excellent served with ham biscuits and congealed salad.

CRAB BISQUE

"Serve in small cups with a salad and sandwich for a summer luncheon."

10½ ounces canned beef bouillon
10¾ ounces canned tomato soup
11¼ ozs. can green pea soup
1 soup can of milk
8½ ounces white crab meat
½ cup dry sherry

Mix and heat all ingredients in a saucepan. Yields: 4-6 servings.

MANHATTAN CLAM CHOWDER

6 slices bacon
1 onion, chopped
2 potatoes, diced
1 teaspoon salt
8 ounces clam juice
15 ounces minced clams, drained
32 ounces canned tomatoes, drained
½ teaspoon thyme

Sauté bacon until crisp; crumble. Stir onions into drippings; sauté until soft. Add potatoes, salt and clam juice. Cover; simmer until potatoes are done — about 15 minutes. Stir in clams, tomatoes, thyme and bacon. Simmer 15 minutes longer. Add a little water if necessary. Yields: 6-8 servings.

GAZPACHO

"A special treat on a hot summer day."

3 tablespoons olive oil
5 tablespoons wine vinegar
4 peppercorns (or ¾ teaspoon pepper)
3 garlic cloves
1 teaspoon salt
1 medium onion, chopped
1 cucumber, peeled, seeded and chopped
5-6 red juicy fresh tomatoes, chopped
1 green pepper, chopped
additional chopped vegetables for garnish
bread cubes for garnish

In a blender, combine olive oil, vinegar, peppercorns, garlic and salt. Add onion, cucumber, green pepper and tomatoes. Blend. Pour mixture into a large bowl. Mixture should be of fairly smooth consistency. Put in a few ice cubes for cooling and thinning. Cover and chill thoroughly. Serve with chopped vegetables and bread cubes, allowing each person to garnish his own soup. Yields: 6 servings.

OLD-FASHIONED NAVY BEAN SOUP

16 ounces small navy beans
4 tablespoons butter or margarine
1 cup onion, chopped
1 cup celery, chopped
1 quart water
2 pound meaty ham bone
1 teaspoon salt
¼ teaspoon pepper
1 large bay leaf
1 tablespoon parsley, minced
¼ teaspoon thyme
⅛ teaspoon garlic powder

Wash beans thoroughly; soak overnight. Drain. Sauté onion and celery in butter in large Dutch oven. Add water, ham bone and remaining ingredients. Bring to a boil; reduce heat, cover and simmer 2½ to 3 hours or until beans are well done and liquid is creamy. Yields: 8-10 servings.
Note: Check occasionally, stir and add more water if necessary.

RICH OYSTER STEW

4 tablespoons butter
2 onions, sliced
1 clove garlic, slivered
1 carrot, sliced
1 stalk celery, sliced
few sprigs parsley
pinch thyme
1½ cups milk
1½ cups whipping cream
24 oysters with their liquor
1 teaspoon salt and pepper to taste
¼ teaspoon Worcestershire sauce
¼ teaspoon Tabasco

Melt butter in a large, heavy saucepan. Add onions, garlic, carrot, celery, parsley, and thyme. Cover; cook over moderate heat about 10 minutes. Add milk, cream, and oyster liquor. Heat to boiling point but *do not* boil. Strain into another saucepan. Add oysters and heat until oysters curl at the edges. Season with salt, pepper, Worcestershire and Tabasco. Ladle into hot soup bowls. Yields: 4 servings.

WRIGHTSVILLE SEAFOOD CHOWDER

1 tablespoon margarine
1 onion, thinly sliced
1 pound fish fillet (cod, haddock, king, flounder or mackerel may be used)
3½ cups boiling water
2 ribs celery, minced
4 cups potatoes, diced
¼ cup cold water
1 tablespoon plain flour
13 ounces evaporated milk
salt
white pepper
paprika for garnish
parsley, minced for garnish

In a nonstick saucepan, heat margarine and onions until onions are soft but not brown. Cut fish into bite-sized pieces; add to saucepan, along with boiling water, celery and potatoes. Cover; simmer over very low heat until potatoes are just tender, about 10 minutes. Combine cold water and flour to make a paste; stir into saucepan over low heat until mixture is thick. Stir in milk and heat gently, until chowder is thick and bubbly. Season to taste. Pour into bowls and sprinkle with paprika and parsley. Yields: 6 servings.
Hint: The chowder is best served right away – the flavor is not enhanced by long simmering.

VICHYSOISSE

1 pound leeks
½ cup onion, chopped
4 tablespoons margarine
1 pound potatoes (2 cups), cubed
½ teaspoon salt
dash white pepper
2 13¾ ounce cans chicken broth
2 cups milk
1 cup half and half, chilled
chives for garnish

Sauté leeks and onions in margarine but do not brown. Add potatoes, salt, pepper and chicken broth. Cook until done. Heat milk and add to potato mixture. Put in blender; blend until smooth. Chill thoroughly. Before serving, gradually add half and half; mix well. Garnish with chives. Yields: 6 servings.

Substitution for chicken or beef stock: 2 c canned beef bouillon or chicken broth, 3 T each sliced onions, carrots & celery, ½ c vermouth, 2 sprigs parsley, ⅓ bay leaf & pinch thyme. Simmer 30 min. & strain.

ZUCCHINI SOUP
"Very, very good!"

1 pound zucchini, sliced
¼ cup onion, chopped
10¾ ounces canned cream of chicken soup
1⅓ cups water
salt to taste
pepper to taste
¼-½ cup white wine

Combine all ingredients except wine. Cook over medium heat 10-12 minutes or until squash is tender. Cool. Pour into container of electric blender; blend until smooth. Stir in wine. Chill thoroughly. Yields: 4-6 servings.

BACON ROLL-UPS

"Excellent served with a cold soup for lunch."

4 tablespoons butter or margarine
½ cup water
1½ cups herb-seasoned stuffing mix
1 egg, beaten
¼ pound hot or mild sausage
½-⅔ pound bacon

Preheat oven to 375°. Melt butter or margarine in water in saucepan. Add stuffing mix, egg and sausage. Mix thoroughly; cool. Roll into oblongs about ½x3 long. Cut bacon strips into thirds; wrap around each sausage stick. Secure with a toothpick. Place on a rack in shallow pan. Bake 35 minutes, turning halfway during cooking time. Drain on paper towels. Serve hot. Yields: 20-24 servings.

Hint: These may be prepared the day before baking. They also freeze well.

CHEESE RAREBIT

11 ounces canned Cheddar cheese soup
½ cup mayonnaise
¼ cup dry white wine
½ clove garlic, crushed
8 slices ham
8 slices tomato
8 slices toast

Mix first 4 ingredients in a saucepan. Cook over low heat about 5 minutes or until heated. Place ham and tomato slices on toast. Top with cheese mixture. Yields: 4 servings.

HOT CORNED BEEF AND SLAW SANDWICHES

2 tablespoons butter or margarine
1 small onion, thinly sliced
3 cups green cabbage, finely shredded
1 teaspoon caraway seed
2 teaspoons Dijon mustard
¼ teaspoon garlic salt
½-¾ pound corned beef, thinly sliced and heated
4-6 slices rye bread (or dark whole wheat bread)
butter
6 slices Swiss cheese, thinly sliced
4-6 tablespoons Russian dressing

Melt butter in pan; sauté onion. Stir in cabbage; cook until hot. Add caraway seed, mustard and garlic salt; stir well to blend. Cover and keep warm. Cabbage should be limp. Toast and butter bread. Arrange cheese on toast. Top with corned beef and hot slaw. Spoon 1 tablespoon Russian dressing over each. Serve with knife and fork. Yields: 4-6 sandwiches.

CROQUE-MONSIEUR

"May be served as an appetizer or as a main course."

½ cup butter
8 slices firm bread
4 slices baked ham, thinly sliced
4 slices roasted chicken or turkey, thinly sliced
4 slices mozzarella cheese
pepper to taste, freshly ground
pinch allspice

Lightly butter one side of each slice of bread. Place one slice of ham, chicken or turkey and cheese on the buttered side of 4 slices of bread. Season with pepper and allspice. Top each with another slice of bread, buttered side down. Heat enough of remaining butter to cover bottom of a heavy skillet. Sauté sandwiches slowly, browning each side until cheese has melted. Cut into quarters or leave whole. Yields: 16 appetizers or 4 whole sandwiches.

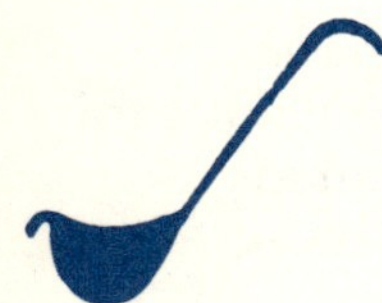

To freeze sandwiches, always spread bread with butter instead of mayonnaise. This prevents fillings from soaking in bread.

CRUNCHY CHICKEN SANDWICHES

"Great for lunch served with broccoli and a congealed salad."

1½ cups cooked chicken, chopped
10¾ ounces canned cream of mushroom soup
10½ ounces canned chicken gravy
2 tablespoons pimento, chopped
2 tablespoons onion, chopped
8 ounces water chestnuts, drained and thinly sliced
20 slices white bread
4 eggs, beaten
2 tablespoons milk
potato chips, crushed

Preheat oven to 300°. Mix first 6 ingredients. Trim crust from bread; spread with chicken mixture. Cover with a second slice of bread. Wrap individually in waxed paper; freeze. Dip frozen sandwiches in mixture of eggs and milk to coat. Cover with crushed chips. Place on buttered cookie sheet. Bake 50-60 minutes or until brown and bubbly. Yields: 10 servings.
Hint: These sandwiches are nice to keep in freezer for a special lunch.

GOLDEN DELIGHT SANDWICHES

12 slices white bread
soft margarine
3 cups Cheddar cheese, shredded
1 cup cooked shrimp, chopped
¾ cup mayonnaise
1 tablespoon lemon juice
1 teaspoon Worcestershire sauce
⅛ teaspoon curry powder
paprika

Trim crust from bread. Cut 6 slices in half diagonally; spread slices with margarine. Combine remaining ingredients, except paprika. Spread mixture on each slice of bread. Sprinkle with paprika. Broil until cheese bubbles. Arrange 1 whole and 2 half slices of bread on plate, open face to form a diamond. Serve hot. Yields: 6 servings.

Variation: The shrimp mixture can also be mounded on English muffins or halves of sandwich rolls. Crab meat may be substituted for shrimp.

HAM DELIGHT

1 pound boiled ham
1 medium onion
½ pound Swiss cheese
1 tablespoon Worcestershire sauce
3 tablespoons poppy seed
3 tablespoons prepared mustard
2-3 tablespoons mayonnaise
3 packages party rolls (or sandwich rolls)

Preheat oven to 350°. Grind ham, onion and cheese together. Add Worcestershire sauce, poppy seeds and mustard. Mix well. Add mayonnaise if it is needed to make mixture a good spreading consistency. Using a long knife, slice the tops off entire pan of party rolls at one time, leaving bottom of rolls in original container. Spread mixture on rolls. Replace top half. Bake, covered with foil, 30 minutes. Yields: 72 party rolls or 8 sandwich rolls.

Note: These may be wrapped and frozen until needed. Leftover ham may be substituted for boiled ham.

CHEESEBURGER IN A BUN

1 pound lean ground beef
1 tablespoon onion, chopped
½ teaspoon salt
¼ teaspoon pepper
2 tablespoons catsup
cheese topping
4 hamburger buns, split and lightly buttered

Preheat oven to 350°. Combine first 5 ingredients. Mix well and shape into 4 patties. Fry until done. Prepare cheese topping.

Cheese Topping:

1 cup sharp Cheddar cheese, shredded
2 tablespoons butter or margarine, softened
1½ teaspoons catsup
½ teaspoon prepared mustard
1 tablespoon onion, finely chopped

Combine all ingredients; mix well. Place each patty on a bun half; top with about ¼ of cheese topping. Place remaining bun on top. Wrap each burger individually in aluminum foil. Heat in oven until warm and cheese has melted. Yields: 4 sandwiches.

PIZZABURGERS

"Great for lunch, light suppers or late night snacks."

1 pound ground beef
1 onion, diced
2 tablespoons oil
1 teaspoon garlic salt
salt to taste
pepper to taste
15½ ounces canned pizza sauce
8 ounces Cheddar cheese, grated
4 ounces canned mushroom pieces, drained
1 teaspoon oregano
8-10 English muffins, halved

Brown beef and onion in oil. Drain. Add garlic salt, salt and pepper; cook until onion is done. Add sauce, cheese, mushrooms and oregano. Spread on English muffins. Toast under broiler until cheese is melted. Yields: 8 servings.

"Mixture may be prepared ahead of time. It also freezes well. Sprinkle Parmesan cheese on top for an extra cheesy flavor."

PUFFY HAM SANDWICHES

2 egg whites
¾ cup mayonnaise
1 tablespoon lemon juice
6 slices bread
6 slices ham
6 slices cheese
6 slices tomato

Preheat oven to 300°. Beat egg whites until stiff; fold in mayonnaise and lemon juice. Make an open face sandwich using remaining ingredients. Pour egg mixture over sandwich. Bake 5-10 minutes, then broil until golden brown. Yields: 6 servings.

COLLECTION OF N.C. LEGENDS AND GHOST STORIES

Devil's Tramping Ground:

Speaking of the Devil, there is a widely accepted legend that the Devil has his very own tramping ground in the piedmont near the geographical center of the state, not too far from the town of Siler City. In the midst of a wooded area there is a perfect circle, forty feet in diameter which is without vegetation. Curiosity seekers have tossed sticks and other objects into the circle and returned the next day to find them gone. Legend has it that the Devil tramps around the circle thinking up evil and plotting against the good.

Joe Baldwin:

Among other legends common to N.C. is the mystery of the Maco light. Near this small community southwest of Wilmington there frequently appears an unexplained light moving alongside the railroad track. Tradition has it that the light is from a lantern being carried by Joe Baldwin still searching for his head. Baldwin, railroad brakeman, was decapitated at this spot in 1867 while trying to prevent a railroad accident. Curiosity seekers frequently go to Maco on quiet summer evenings in hopes of catching a glimpse of old Joe Baldwin's lantern.

Brown Mountain Lights:

Perhaps North Carolina's most spectacular spook story is that of the Brown Mountain Lights. The following is reprinted from National Geographic Magazine. "From three points near Linville there may be witnessed a curious and some North Carolinians insist, a yet unexplained phenomenon, known as the Brown Mountain Lights. These appear with fairly dependable regularity and at all seasons, especially on dark nights. They have been variously described as "globular, glowing red, like toy fire balloons, or a pale, white light with a faint halo around it." Although frequently seen, the lights have never been satisfactorily explained.

Magic Horse Tracks:

A few miles from the town of Bath are a series of shallow holes in the ground which measure about the size of a hoof print. The holes have been there, empty and bare, for some 150 years. The story is that a Bath citizen who liked to race his horse on Sunday, one Sabbath shouted to his horse, "Take me in a winner or take me to hell." With that the horse dug its hoofs into the dirt and threw the rider against a tree, killing him instantly. When filled up with dirt, the holes are again empty on the following day. Many suggestions have been offered for this strange occurrence but Beaufort County folks insist that they are merely the marks of a horse who complied with his master's wish.

vegetables

THE CAROLINA COLLECTOR'S CONCOCTIONS

. . . Top baked potatoes with sour cream mixed with finely chopped pimento-stuffed green olives.

. . . Hot French dressing seasons okra or green beans with a flair.

. . . Add a little chopped pimento to the melted butter added to cauliflower at serving time.

. . . Top a vegetable casserole with buttered bread crumbs to which a little grated lemon peel has been added.

. . . Add celery for crunch to packaged macaroni and cheese for something different.

. . . Stir a little dry sherry into frozen macaroni & cheese; sprinkle with almonds.

. . . Sprinkle chopped mint over cooked carrots, peas or green beans.

. . . Broil peach halves with marmalade or mincemeat in center.

. . . Add rum to baked carrots.

. . . Spread applesauce mixed with butter over partially cooked winter squash halves. Sprinkle with apple pie spice & bake until tender.

. . . Bake tomato halves with butter at 350° for 10 min. Sprinkle with Parmesan cheese.

. . . Stir sesame seeds in buttered squash.

. . . Mix dry onion soup mix with butter; drizzle over asparagus & sprinkle with mozzarella & Parmesan cheeses. Bake 10 min.

. . . Simmer cabbage wedges in crushed pineapple and tomato sauce for 8 min. until tender crisp.

. . . Add maple syrup to lima beans, tomatoes, onion & green pepper creole.

. . . Heat 2 cans baked beans in 1 jar chunky applesauce & ½ t ginger.

. . . Mix ½ c sour cream in 1 package dry blue cheese dressing mix & mix with thawed spinach. Heat through.

. . . Fry patties of sliced okra, diced peppers, green tomatoes, onion & ½ c cornmeal.

. . . Glaze vegetables in 1 can whole berry cranberry sauce, 1 bottle chili sauce & 1 T Worcestershire. Heat.

. . . Layer apricot halves, brown sugar, ritz crackers crumbled & top with butter. Bake 1 hr. at 350°.

. . . To make curry sauce for vegetables, mix 1 can mushroom soup, 3 T water & 1 t curry powder.

ARTICHOKES AND MUSHROOMS IN CHEESE SAUCE

28 ounces canned artichoke hearts
1 pound mushrooms, sliced, drained and sautéed
4 spring onions, chopped
4 tablespoons butter
2 tablespoons olive oil
2 tablespoons wine vinegar
¼ teaspoon garlic salt
1 tablespoon fresh parsley, snipped
½ teaspoon paprika
¼ teaspoon seasoned salt
⅛ teaspoon cayenne pepper
2 cups cheese sauce

Cheese Sauce:
4 tablespoons butter
¼ cup plain flour
1½ cups chicken broth
½ cup whipping cream
1 teaspoon lemon juice
salt to taste
pepper to taste
1½ cups sharp Cheddar cheese, grated
1 cup buttered bread crumbs

Preheat oven to 350°. Drain and slice artichoke hearts; add to mushrooms which have been sautéed with spring onions in butter and drained. Combine olive oil, wine vinegar, garlic salt, parsley, paprika, seasoned salt, and cayenne pepper. Mix thoroughly with artichokes, mushrooms and onions. To make Cheese Sauce, melt butter; blend in flour. Add chicken broth; stir until thickened. Add cream and lemon juice gradually with salt, pepper and cheese, stirring until smooth. Pour sauce over artichoke mixture, stirring gently. Turn into a 2 quart casserole. Cover with bread crumbs. Bake 30 minutes. Yields: 8 servings.

ARTICHOKE-MUSHROOM VELVET

18 ounces frozen artichoke hearts, cooked, drained and sliced
6 ounces sliced mushrooms, drained
1 envelope chicken gravy mix
dash crushed thyme
dash crushed marjoram
4 ounces Swiss cheese, grated
3 tablespoons dry white wine
1 cup soft bread crumbs, buttered

Preheat oven to 350°. Combine artichokes and mushrooms; divide among 4 or 5 ramekins or place in 1 quart casserole. In small saucepan, prepare chicken gravy mix according to package directions. Remove from heat; add thyme, marjoram and cheese. Stir just until cheese melts. Add wine; pour over vegetables. Top with buttered crumbs. Bake, uncovered, 24 minutes for ramekins or 30 minutes for casserole. Yields: 4-5 servings.

ARTICHOKE AND SPINACH CASSEROLE

"This is truly delicious!"

6 ounces artichoke hearts, drained and chopped
20 ounces frozen chopped spinach, cooked and drained
½ cup onion, chopped
4 tablespoons butter or margarine
2 eggs, beaten
½ cup sour cream
¼ teaspoon garlic salt
2 tablespoons lemon juice
¾ cup Parmesan cheese
1 cup bread crumbs, buttered

Preheat oven to 350°. While spinach is cooking in a small amount of salted water, sauté onions in butter. Beat eggs; add sour cream, garlic salt, lemon juice and most of the Parmesan cheese. (Reserve some cheese for top.) Combine onions, drained spinach and artichokes. Add to sour cream mixture. Pour into a greased 2 quart casserole. Sprinkle crumbs and remaining cheese on top. Bake 25-30 minutes. Yields: 6 servings.

ASPARAGUS CASSEROLE SUPREME

"Easy and always draws raves."

20 saltine crackers
32 ounces canned asparagus, drained and juice reserved
4 hard-cooked eggs, chopped
10 ounces sharp Cheddar cheese, grated
8 ounces fresh mushrooms, sautéed and chopped
2½ ounces almonds, toasted
2 10¾-ounce cans cream of mushroom soup
pepper to taste
butter
1 cup milk

Preheat oven to 350°. Crumble 5 saltine crackers in bottom of a 2 quart casserole. Layer ⅓ asparagus spears, cut up, ⅓ chopped eggs, ⅓ grated cheese and ⅓ of mushrooms and almonds in casserole. Dot with ⅓ mushroom soup, dot with butter and sprinkle with pepper. Repeat layering 2 more times, ending with 5 crumbled saltine crackers. Mix milk with 2-3 tablespoons asparagus juice. Pour evenly over casserole. Bake 30-40 minutes, or until bubbly. Yields: 6-8 servings.

MARINATED ASPARAGUS

10 ounces asparagus spears, drain and reserve liquid
juice of ½ lemon
½ cup vinegar
½ cup sugar
1 teaspoon salt
1 teaspoon pepper
pimento strips, for garnish
hard cooked eggs, grated, for garnish (optional)

Combine all ingredients except asparagus; mix well. Place asparagus in flat container; pour marinade over, adding asparagus liquid if needed to cover. Cover container and refrigerate overnight. May garnish with strips of pimento and grated hard cooked eggs, if desired. Yields: 4 servings.

BEAN POT

"Perfect to take for a potluck dinner."

6 slices bacon
1 garlic bud, finely chopped (optional)
3 medium onions, sliced into rings
16 ounces pork and beans, undrained
16 ounces red kidney beans, drained
16 ounces lima beans, drained
½ cup brown sugar, firmly packed
2 tablespoons vinegar
½ cup catsup
1 teaspoon mustard
1 teaspoon Worcestershire sauce
salt to taste
pepper to taste
1 cup sharp Cheddar cheese, grated (optional)

Preheat oven to 350°. Fry bacon until crisp. Sauté onions and garlic in bacon fat until soft. Combine all ingredients (including cheese, if used); mix well. Put in 2 quart casserole. Bake, uncovered, approximately 1 hour, stirring twice. Yields: 8 servings.

"This recipe is excellent for plain, quick and easy baked beans by omitting the kidney and lima beans."

GREEN BEAN CASSEROLE

"Perfect accompaniment for ham."

¾ pound fresh mushrooms
1 large onion, sliced in rings
½ cup butter
¼ cup plain flour
1 cup milk
1 cup half and half
12 ounces sharp Cheddar cheese, grated
⅛ teaspoon Tabasco (or to taste)
3 teaspoons soy sauce
1 teaspoon salt
½ teaspoon pepper
30 ounces frozen French-style green beans, cooked and drained
16 ounces bean sprouts, drained
5 ounces water chestnuts, drained and sliced
½ cup slivered almonds

Preheat oven to 350°. Sauté mushrooms and onions in butter until soft. Add flour; stir until smooth. Add milk and half and half slowly, stirring over low heat until mixture thickens. Add cheese, Tabasco, soy sauce, salt and pepper. Mix until cheese melts. Add green beans, bean sprouts and water chestnuts to sauce. Pour into a 3 quart, flat casserole. Sprinkle almonds on top. Bake 20-25 minutes. Yields: 10-12 servings.

GREEN BEANS WITH HORSERADISH

32 ounces canned or fresh whole green beans
1 large onion, sliced
country ham bits, bacon pieces or salt pork
1 cup mayonnaise
2 hard-cooked eggs, chopped
1 heaping tablespoon horseradish
1 teaspoon Worcestershire sauce
½ teaspoon mustard
2 teaspoons onion, grated
2 teaspoons lemon juice
1½ teaspoons parsley, minced
salt to taste
pepper to taste
garlic salt to taste
celery salt to taste

Cook beans and onion in lightly salted water, with choice of seasoning meat, 30 minutes. Blend mayonnaise with remaining ingredients; set aside at room temperature. When beans are ready to serve, drain and spoon mayonnaise mixture over. Yields: 8 servings.

GREEN BEANS AND ONION SAUCE

"So very, very good!"

20 ounces frozen French style green beans
8½ ounces small pearl onions, drained
½ cup butter
½ cup almonds, slivered
¼ cup dry white wine
2 tablespoons brown sugar
1 teaspoon garlic clove, minced
½ teaspoon salt
¼ teaspoon pepper

Cook beans according to directions; drain. Melt butter in saucepan and stir in remaining ingredients. Simmer on low heat 20 minutes, coating onions well. Pour over beans, which have been kept hot, and serve. Yields: 6 servings.

CREAMED MASHED BEETS

"These beets are so good, this recipe will quickly become a favorite."

3 cups cooked beets, mashed
1 tablespoon lemon juice
½ teaspoon salt
½ cup whipping cream or sour cream
½ cup crumbs
1 tablespoon butter

Drain beets and add lemon juice and salt. Fold in sour cream or stiffly beaten heavy cream. Top with crumbs and dot with butter. Slip under broiler to brown lightly and serve hot. Yields: 4 servings.

DIFFERENT SAUCES WITH FRESH BROCCOLI

Curry Sauce:

1 cup mayonnaise
1½ teaspoons lemon juice
1 teaspoon curry powder

Blend all ingredients together in top of double boiler; slowly warm. Be careful not to let curdle. This may be doubled or altered as to amounts of lemon juice and curry used, depending upon one's taste.

Deviled Cream Sauce:

2 tablespoons butter
2 tablespoons plain flour
1½ teaspoons dry mustard
1 teaspoon brown sugar
½ teaspoon lemon juice
1 tablespoon sherry (or to taste)
½ teaspoon Worcestershire sauce
¼ teaspoon salt
dash pepper
1 cup milk
½ cup sour cream

Melt butter in saucepan. Blend in flour and rest of ingredients, except milk and sour cream. Add milk all at once; cook and stir until bubbly. Stir small amount of hot mixture into sour cream. Return all to hot mixture. Heat, do not boil. Pour over broccoli and top with toasted almonds, if desired.

Sour Cream Sauce:

1 cup sour cream
¼ cup prepared mustard
1 teaspoon salt
¼ teaspoon white pepper

Preheat oven to 350°. Combine ingredients. Spoon over broccoli. Bake 8-10 minutes or until sauce sets.

BROCCOLI-RICE CASSEROLE

20 ounces chopped broccoli, cooked and drained
2 cups cooked rice
½ cup onion, chopped
½ cup celery, chopped
4 tablespoons butter, melted
10¾ ounces canned cream of celery soup
⅔ cup milk
8 ounces Cheese Whiz
salt to taste
pepper to taste
garlic salt to taste
½ cup bread crumbs, buttered
½ cup almonds (optional)
¼-½ teaspoon paprika

Preheat oven to 350°. Cook broccoli and rice, separately, as directed. Drain broccoli; set aside broccoli and rice. Sauté onion and celery in butter. Stir in celery soup, milk, cheese and seasonings. Mix well; combine with broccoli and rice. Place in a 2 quart casserole, top with bread crumbs and almonds; sprinkle with paprika. Bake 30 minutes. Yields: 8-10 servings.

BROCCOLI AND SHRIMP CASSEROLE

"A delightful combination."

½ cup butter or margarine
8 ounces Cheese Whiz
3 ounces cream cheese
10¾ ounces canned cream of shrimp soup
2 tablespoons sherry (optional)
½ teaspoon Worcestershire sauce (optional)
½-1 pound shrimp, cleaned and cooked
30 ounces frozen broccoli, cooked and well drained
almonds, toasted
cracker crumbs, buttered

Preheat oven to 350°. Melt butter and cheese in top of double boiler. Blend until cheeses are thoroughly dissolved. Stir in soup. Add sherry and Worcestershire sauce, if desired. Add shrimp; pour over broccoli in a 2 quart rectangular casserole. Top with toasted almonds and cracker crumbs. Bake 20-25 minutes or until bubbly. Yields: 8-10 servings.

Note: Use minimum amount of salt while cooking broccoli as sauce is salty due to soup.

CREAMY BROCCOLI AND ZUCCHINI

2 cups fresh broccoli, chopped
2 cups zucchini, unpared and chopped
½ cup onion, chopped
1 clove garlic, minced
2 tablespoons butter or margarine
3 tablespoons plain flour
2 tablespoons parsley, snipped
½ teaspoon salt
½ teaspoon dried oregano, crushed
¾ cup milk
1½ cups ricotta cheese (or cream-style cottage cheese)
8 ounces thin egg noodles, cooked, drained and buttered
Parmesan cheese, grated

In medium saucepan, cook broccoli and zucchini together, covered, in small amount of boiling salted water. Cook until tender, about 8-10 minutes. In large saucepan, cook onion and garlic in butter or margarine until onion is tender but not brown. Blend in flour, parsley, salt and oregano. Add milk all at once. Cook and stir until thick and bubbly. Add ricotta cheese; cook and stir until cheese is nearly melted. Stir in cooked and well drained vegetables. Heat through. Serve over hot noodles. Pass Parmesan cheese. Yields: 4-6 servings.

Variation: Green noodles may be used instead of egg noodles.

KENTUCKY CABBAGE CASSEROLE

"Even those who don't like cabbage will like this."

1 small head cabbage
1 cup celery, thinly sliced
1 cup boiling water
¼ teaspoon salt
10¾ ounces canned cream of celery soup
⅓ cup milk
4 teaspoons soy sauce
1 tablespoon onion, minced
generous dash Tabasco
2 tablespoons butter
½ cup round crackers, finely crushed

Preheat oven to 350°. Shred cabbage coarsely with knife, making approximately 5 cups. Put cabbage, celery, water and salt into a large saucepan; cover, boil 5 minutes. Drain well. In a 1½ quart casserole, mix soup, milk, soy sauce, onion and Tabasco. Add drained cabbage and celery; mix well. Melt butter in small pan, add crumbs; mix well. Sprinkle over cabbage mixture. Bake 40 minutes, or until bubbly and top is browned. Yields: 4-6 servings.

A few drops of vinegar added to cabbage cooking water keeps odor away.

Add a few drops of lemon juice to canned or frozen vegetables to make them taste fresh.

CABBAGE GOURMET

"Such a distinctive flavor."

1 small head cabbage
½ cup Chablis or other white dinner wine
½ cup chicken broth or bouillon
1 tablespoon wine vinegar
2 tablespoons butter or margarine
1 tablespoon instant minced onion
¼ teaspoon dried dill
½ teaspoon salt
dash of pepper

Wash cabbage, shred or cut coarsely in strips. There should be about 6 cups. Add remaining ingredients. Cover; simmer 12-15 minutes. Serve with pan liquid which may be thickened, if desired. Yields: 4-6 servings.

CARROT DELIGHT

2 pounds carrots, cooked and mashed
4 tablespoons butter
1 medium onion, finely chopped
⅓ cup green pepper, finely chopped
8 ounces sharp Cheddar cheese, grated
½ teaspoon salt
⅛ teaspoon pepper
bread crumbs, buttered
parsley (optional)

Preheat oven to 350°. Pare, slice and boil carrots in lightly salted water until tender. Meanwhile, sauté onion and green pepper in butter. Mash carrots well when cooked; add onion and green pepper mixture, cheese, salt and pepper. Place in buttered 1 quart casserole, top with buttered crumbs. Bake 30 minutes or until bubbling. Garnish with parsley, if desired. Yields: 4-6 servings.

CURRIED CAULIFLOWER

"This is a delicious party dish – quick and easy."

1 large head cauliflower
½ teaspoon salt
10½ ounces canned cream of chicken soup
1 cup Cheddar cheese, grated
⅓ cup mayonnaise
1 teaspoon curry powder
½ cup bread crumbs
3 tablespoons butter, melted

Preheat oven to 350°. Break cauliflower into florets. Cook 15 minutes in boiling salted water; drain. Mix together soup, cheese, mayonnaise and curry powder in a 2 quart casserole. Add cauliflower; mix well. Toss bread crumbs in melted butter; sprinkle on top. Bake 25 minutes or until hot and bubbly. Yields: 8 servings.
"This freezes well."

SWISS CAULIFLOWER CASSEROLE

"This is a most attractive-looking and delicious-tasting dish."

1 medium cauliflower
6 medium tomatoes
1 mediun onion, chopped
4 tablespoons butter or margarine, divided
2 hard cooked eggs, chopped
1 tablespoon parsley, minced
¾ cup Swiss cheese, grated
salt to taste
pepper to taste

Preheat oven to 375°. Cook the cauliflower whole in boiling, salted water 5 minutes; drain. Wash tomatoes, remove cores and prick skins with a fork. Sauté onion in 2 tablespoons butter until soft. Arrange onion in bottom of a deep casserole. Place cauliflower in center with tomatoes around it. Dot with remaining butter. Bake 30 minutes. Remove from oven; sprinkle with chopped eggs, parsley, Swiss cheese, salt and pepper. Bake 5 minutes longer. Yields: 6 servings.

SWISS CORN SOUFFLÉ

"This can be a year-round treat."

6 ears fresh corn (or 9 ounces frozen)
6 slices bacon
¼ cup plain flour
¼ teaspoon salt
dash pepper
1 cup milk
4 egg yolks
4 ounces Swiss cheese, shredded
4 egg whites

Preheat oven to 350°. Cut kernels from cob; cook, covered, in small amount of boiling salted water 6-8 minutes or until done. Drain; set aside. In skillet, cook bacon until crisp. Drain, reserving ¼ cup drippings. Crumble bacon; set aside. In saucepan, blend flour, salt and pepper into reserved drippings; add milk. Cook and stir until thick and bubbly; remove from heat. Beat egg yolks until very thick and lemon-colored. Blend a moderate amount of hot mixture into egg yolks; return to saucepan. Cook, stirring rapidly, until blended. Stir in cheese until melted. Stir in corn and bacon. Remove from heat. Beat egg whites until stiff peaks form. Fold hot mixture into egg whites. Turn into ungreased 1½ quart soufflé dish. Bake 45 minutes or until knife, inserted off-center, comes out clean. Yields: 4-6 servings.

CUCUMBERS AU GRATIN

4 medium cucumbers
2 tablespoons scallions, minced
6 tablespoons butter, divided
3 tablespoons plain flour
1¼ cups half and half
1 beef bouillon cube
¼ teaspoon salt
dash Tabasco
dash pepper
⅛ teaspoon allspice
2 tablespoons parsley, minced
¼ teaspoon onion juice
1 cup sharp cheese, grated
⅓ cup fine bread crumbs, buttered

Preheat oven to 350°. Melt 3 tablespoons butter in saucepan. Add cucumbers, which have been pared, cut lengthwise into strips, and seeds removed, with minced scallions. Cook over low heat, stirring frequently, 5-7 minutes or until cucumbers are tenderly crisp but not browned. Melt remaining 3 tablespoons butter; blend in flour. Add half and half gradually, stirring until thickened. Stir in remaining ingredients, except bread crumbs; blend until cheese melts. Place cucumbers and scallions in a shallow 2 quart dish. Pour sauce over. Put buttered crumbs on top. Bake 20-25 minutes, uncovered. Yields: 4-6 servings.

EGGPLANT CASSEROLE

2 eggplants
salt
½ cup flour
1 cup vegetable oil
½ cup onion, chopped or sliced in rings
¼ cup butter
3 cups tomato sauce
1 bay leaf
Salt and pepper to taste
parsley, oregano and basil to taste
1 tablespoon sugar
2 cups Parmesan cheese, freshly grated
12 ounces mozzarella cheese, sliced

Preheat oven to 400°. Slice eggplant into ¼ inch slices. Salt slices and let sit 30 minutes. Wipe off salt and water; flour eggplant and brown slowly in oil. Remove to a paper towel and drain. Sauté onion in butter until golden. Add tomato sauce and seasonings; simmer 15 minutes. Pour 1 cup tomato sauce on bottom of 3 quart casserole; sprinkle with ½ cup Parmesan cheese. Cover with slices of eggplant. Top with slices of mozzarella, ½ cup Parmesan and 1 cup tomato sauce. Repeat again, ending with last of mozzarella and Parmesan cheeses. Bake uncovered 20 minutes. Serve hot. Yields: 8-10 servings.

FRIED EGGPLANT ITALIANA

2 medium eggplants, peeled and cut in ¼ inch rounds
2 tablespoons salt
2 eggs, beaten
4 tablespoons milk
1 cup plain flour
1 teaspoon salt
1 cup Italian-flavored bread crumbs
¼ cup Parmesan cheese, grated

Prepare eggplants. Place slices in deep container with cold water to cover and 2 tablespoons salt. Let soak 20 minutes. In shallow dish combine eggs and milk; mix to blend. In another dish combine flour, salt, bread crumbs and cheese. Drain eggplant slices. Dip each in egg mixture and then into crumb mixture; coat well. Fry until golden brown in hot oil in deep fat fryer. Drain well on paper towels. Yields: 6-8 servings.

MEATLESS MOUSSAKA

1 eggplant (approximately 1¼ pounds)
2 eggs, beaten
1 cup cooked rice
15 ounces cottage cheese
½ cup instant non-fat dry milk
¼ cup onion, finely chopped
¼ teaspoon salt
¼ teaspoon sage
15 ounces canned meatless spaghetti sauce
6 ounces mozzarella cheese, sliced

Preheat oven to 375°. Peel eggplant; cut into slices ¼ inch thick. Drop into rapidly boiling, salted water. Cover; boil 4 minutes. Drain on paper towels. Beat eggs; add rice, cottage cheese, milk powder, onion, salt and sage. Blend thoroughly. Spread ½ cup spaghetti sauce in 11x7x2 dish. Layer half of eggplant, half of egg mixture and half of remaining sauce. Repeat, ending with sauce. Top with mozzarella strips in lattice pattern. Bake 30-40 minutes until bubbly. Yields: 5 servings.

COMPANY GRITS

1½ cups quick cooking grits
4 cups water
1 teaspoon salt
½ cup butter or margarine
6 ounces garlic cheese spread
4 ounces Swiss cheese, grated
½ cup milk
1 cup sour cream
3 eggs, slightly beaten
salt and pepper to taste
⅓ cup Parmesan cheese, grated
paprika

Preheat oven to 325°. Cook grits in salted water according to package directions. While hot, add butter, garlic and Swiss cheese; blend well. Cool slightly. Combine milk, sour cream, beaten eggs, salt and pepper to taste. Blend with grits. Pour into a greased 3 quart casserole. Sprinkle with Parmesan cheese and paprika. Bake approximately 50 minutes. Yields: 8 servings.

GRITS SUPREME

"Such a unique flavor!"

¾ cup quick grits
1 cup boiling water
1½ teaspoons salt, divided
¼ teaspoon white pepper
4 tablespoons butter, divided
2 cups milk, scalded and divided
1 egg, beaten
⅓ cup sour cream
1 tablespoon horseradish

Preheat oven to 350°. In top of double boiler, mix boiling water with 1 teaspoon salt, gradually stir in grits. Add 2 tablespoons butter; boil about 5 minutes, until water is absorbed. Add 1 cup scalded milk; blend thoroughly, cook 15 minutes. Remove from heat. Add remaining 2 tablespoons butter. In a bowl, blend egg, sour cream, horseradish, ½ teaspoon salt and ¼ teaspoon white pepper with second cup of scalded milk which has cooled. Add grits; beat 1 minute with electric mixer. Butter a 2 quart casserole. Turn grits into casserole. Bake 30-35 minutes, until lightly browned. Yields: 6-8 servings.

Note: Topped with small link sausages, this is great for a brunch.

MUSHROOM-CHEESE BAKE

½ cup celery, chopped
¼ cup onion, chopped
3 tablespoons butter
¾ pound fresh mushrooms, chopped
4 cups day old whole-wheat bread, cubed
2 cups Cheddar cheese, shredded
2 eggs
2 cups milk
2 teaspoons dry mustard
1 teaspoon salt
½ teaspoon pepper

Preheat oven to 325°. Sauté celery and onion in butter until crisp-tender, stir in mushrooms; continue to cook until tender. Drain. In a buttered 1½ quart casserole, layer ½ the bread, ½ the mushroom mixture, and ½ the cheese. Repeat the layers. Beat together eggs, milk, and seasonings. Pour evenly over bread mixture. Bake approximately 45 minutes. Let stand 5 minutes before serving. Yields: 6 servings.

MUSHROOMS FLORENTINE

"Outstanding and simple to prepare."

2 tablespoons butter
1 pound fresh mushrooms, sliced
20 ounces frozen chopped spinach
1 teaspoon salt
¼ cup onion, finely chopped
4 tablespoons butter, melted
1 cup Cheddar cheese, grated

Preheat oven to 350°. Melt 2 tablespoons butter; sauté mushrooms until done. Cook spinach according to package directions; drain well. Put spinach in bottom of greased shallow 1½ quart casserole. Sprinkle with salt, onion, and butter. Layer ½ cup of cheese over spinach mixture. Add drained mushrooms. Top with remaining cheese. Bake 20 minutes. Yields: 6 servings.

STUFFED MUSHROOMS

"This may be used as a main dish or as an appetizer."

1 pound large fresh mushrooms
2 tablespoons butter
¼ cup onion, finely chopped
¼ pound ground veal (or ground beef)
¼ teaspoon garlic salt
¼ teaspoon celery salt
¼ teaspoon pepper, freshly ground
1 tablespoon parsley, minced

Preheat oven to 375°. Wash mushrooms, remove stems and chop. Melt butter in a heavy skillet. Add chopped stems, onion and veal. Brown lightly. Stir in seasonings, mixing well. Fill mushroom caps. Place in greased shallow casserole. Bake 20-25 minutes. Spoon the following sauce over the mushrooms and serve as a main dish. Yields: 4-6 servings.
Note: Omit sauce if served as an appetizer.

Sauce:
2 tablespoons butter
¼ cup onion, finely chopped
1½ tablespoons plain flour
¼ teaspoon dry mustard
½ teaspoon marjoram, crushed
½ teaspoon celery salt
1 teaspoon Worcestershire sauce
1 tablespoon lemon juice
½ cup sauterne (or other white wine)
½ cup sour cream

Melt butter, add onion and brown lightly. Blend in flour, seasonings, lemon juice and wine. Cook over low heat, stirring until thickened. Add sour cream just before serving. To serve on toast, add ½ cup milk to sauce to make it thinner.

Eggplant should be soaked in salted water for 20 minutes prior to cooking to remove bitter taste.

NOODLES DELUXE

"Superb flavor – great with hamburgers or steak."

8 ounces medium egg noodles
1 medium onion, chopped
½ pound fresh mushrooms, cleaned and chopped
3 tablespoons butter
1 cup sour cream
8 ounces cottage cheese
½-¾ cup milk
1 tablespoon Worcestershire sauce
½ teaspoon salt
¼ teaspoon pepper
½ teaspoon garlic salt
1 teaspoon parsley
½ cup Parmesan cheese, grated
chopped chives (optional)

Preheat oven to 350°. Cook noodles in boiling water; drain. Sauté onion and mushrooms in butter; drain. Mix sour cream and cottage cheese; add enough milk to make it soupy. Add Worcestershire sauce, salt, pepper, garlic salt, parsley and Parmesan cheese. Combine this mixture with noodles, onion and mushrooms. Add chives, if desired. Place in 2 quart casserole. Bake 30 minutes. Yields: 4-6 servings.
Note: Additional Parmesan cheese may be sprinkled on top before baking.

NOODLE BROCCOLI CASSEROLE

8 ounces uncooked lasagne noodles
20 ounces frozen broccoli, cooked, drained and ¼ cup liquid reserved
1 cup Cheddar cheese, grated
1 cup medium white sauce

Preheat oven to 350°. Cook noodles in 2½ quarts water with 1 teaspoon salt 10 minutes. Cook broccoli according to package directions. Drain, reserving ¼ cup liquid. Place alternate layers of noodles, broccoli and cheese in a 1½ quart casserole. Pour white sauce over the layers. Bake 30 minutes. Yields: 6-8 servings.

White Sauce:
2 tablespoons butter
1 tablespoon plain flour
¼ cup broccoli liquid
¾ cup cream
½ teaspoon salt
1 teaspoon Worcestershire sauce

Melt butter, add flour; cook until golden. Add liquid slowly, stirring constantly. Add salt and Worcestershire sauce. Blend well and continue stirring until slightly thickened.

ALMOND POPPY SEED NOODLES

1 cup butter
1½ cups almonds, sliced
½ cup poppy seeds
1 teaspoon salt
16 ounces dry egg noodles

Melt butter, add almonds and poppy seeds; sauté until almonds are slightly browned. Cook noodles according to package directions. Drain; turn into serving dish. Pour warm butter mixture over. Toss to coat. Yields: 6 servings.

STEWED OKRA

2 strips bacon
⅔ cup onion, chopped
1 clove garlic, minced
4 cups okra, sliced
10 ounces canned tomato sauce
2 tablespoons catsup
2 teaspoons Worcestershire sauce
¼ teaspoon hot pepper sauce
½ teaspoon pepper
1 teaspoon salt
1-2 teaspoons chili powder, according to taste

Cut bacon in small pieces and partially fry. Sauté onions with bacon and garlic. Add remaining ingredients. Cover tightly; cook 30 minutes over low heat. Yields: 4-5 servings.

TAR HEEL OKRA AND TOMATO GUMBO

4 or 5 slices bacon (or ham chunks)
3 small onions, chopped
1 green pepper, chopped
16 ounces canned tomatoes, drained and cut up
8 ounces cocktail vegetable juice
16 ounces okra, cut up
1 teaspoon parsley
salt, pepper, garlic salt, seasoned salt, rosemary, thyme, and chives; any, or all, according to taste
cooked rice

Cut bacon into small pieces. Sauté slowly over low heat until soft but not crisp. Add onion and green pepper, continuing to sauté until soft. Add tomatoes; mix well. Add cocktail vegetable juice; cook slowly 5-10 minutes. Add okra; continue cooking slowly until okra is done. Season according to taste. Cook over very low heat 20-30 minutes. Serve on rice. Yields: 4 servings.

Note: Naturally, this is much better when fresh vegetables are used.

To get a bit of onion juice, sprinkle a cut onion with salt & then scrape with a spoon to obtain the juice.

To prevent onion centers from popping out while cooking, poke a hole through the center of each onion.

FRIED ONION RINGS

1½ cups plain flour
1½ cups beer
3 large yellow onions
3-4 cups shortening

Combine flour and beer in a large bowl; blend thoroughly with a whisk. Cover; let sit at room temperature at least 3 hours. Twenty minutes before batter is ready, heat oven to 200°. Peel and slice onions in ¼ inch slices; separate into rings. Heat oil in electric skillet or deep fat fryer to 375°. Dip rings in batter; fry until batter is lightly browned. Drain on biscuit pans covered with brown grocery bags. Put in oven to keep warm until all are fried. Yields: 6 servings.

Note: To freeze, put onion rings, on biscuit pans, in freezer until frozen. When frozen, place in plastic bags. To serve, bake 4-6 minutes at 400°.

SPANISH ONION CUSTARD

2 Spanish onions (1 quart) sliced thin
4 tablespoons butter, melted
2 eggs, beaten
1½ cups milk
3 shakes hot sauce
½ teaspoon salt
¼ teaspoon Worcestershire sauce
sharp Cheddar cheese, grated

Preheat oven to 325°. Cook onions in butter in covered pan over low heat until onions are transparent. Place in shallow 1½ quart casserole. Combine eggs, milk, hot sauce, salt and Worcestershire sauce. Pour over onions. Sprinkle grated cheese on top. Bake 30 minutes or until a knife comes out clean. Yields: 4-6 servings.

PEAS BONNE FEMME

8 scallions, sliced
2 tablespoons butter, melted
1 cup consommé (canned or made with a cube)
20 ounces frozen green peas
1 head lettuce, cut in 1 inch cubes
1 teaspoon salt
⅛ teaspoon white pepper
dash cayenne
⅛ teaspoon thyme
⅛ teaspoon marjoram
4 slices crisp bacon, crumbled

Cook scallions in melted butter until tender. Add consommé; bring to a boil. Cook peas in this until tender (about 4 minutes after liquid comes to a boil again). Add lettuce. Cover pan; cook about 5 minutes or until lettuce is tender. Add seasonings. Serve very hot topped with crumbled bacon. Yields: 8 servings.

Wrap baked sweet potatoes in a towel for 20 min. after removing from oven. This crystallizes the sugar & keeps in flavor.

DELICIOUS PEAS

"Excellent flavor."

4 cups freshly shelled garden peas
½ cup butter
½ teaspoon salt
1 tablespoon parsley, freshly chopped
½ teaspoon thyme
¼ teaspoon marjoram
⅛ teaspoon garlic salt
⅛ teaspoon white pepper
½ pound fresh mushrooms, sliced and sautéed

Gently boil peas in lightly salted water 15-20 minutes. Meanwhile, melt butter; add the next 6 ingredients. Drain all water from cooked peas, add butter sauce and mushrooms, which have been sautéed and drained. Mix gently and heat thoroughly. Yields: 6-8 servings.

Variation: Canned, sliced artichoke hearts are an excellent substitution for mushrooms.

GREEN PEA CASSEROLE

"Terrific casserole for a covered dish dinner!"

17 ounces canned small green peas (reserve liquid)
1 cup celery, diced
1 cup onion, chopped
½ cup green pepper, chopped
4 tablespoons butter, melted
½ cup liquid from peas
10¾ ounces canned cream of mushroom soup
2 tablespoons Worcestershire sauce
1 teaspoon Tabasco sauce
salt to taste
pepper to taste
4 tablespoons butter, melted
¾ cup Ritz cracker crumbs
½ cup sharp Cheddar cheese, grated

Preheat oven to 300°. Combine first 6 ingredients; cook over medium heat 20 minutes. Add next 5 ingredients. Place mixture in a 1½ quart casserole. Mix 4 tablespoons butter with crumbs; sprinkle on top of casserole. Sprinkle with cheese. Bake 30 minutes or until bubbly. Yields: 6 servings.

GOURMET POTATOES

"Marvelous recipe; perfect with steak."

3 pounds (about 7 cups) potatoes, thinly sliced
1 teaspoon salt
¾ teaspoon white pepper
⅛ teaspoon nutmeg, grated
2 cups Beaufort or Swiss cheese, grated
6 tablespoons butter
1¼ cups chicken stock

Preheat oven to 425°. Place potatoes in cold water. Butter heavily a deep 3 quart casserole. Mix salt, white pepper and nutmeg together. Drain potatoes. Place ⅓ in bottom of casserole. Sprinkle with ⅓ of the seasonings, ⅓ of the cheese and ⅓ of the butter. Repeat same procedure 2 more times. Add chicken stock. Place casserole on cookie sheet. Bake 70 minutes. By this time, all liquid, except butter, should be evaporated and top nicely browned. Let stand 10 minutes before serving. Yields: 8 servings.

Note: Placing dish on cookie sheet allows for good transfer of heat during cooking. A variation using sliced onions between the layers is also very good.

COTTAGE POTATOES

5 large potatoes, cooked and diced
1 cup Cheddar cheese, grated
1 medium onion, finely chopped
¼ cup parsley, chopped
½ cup fresh bread crumbs, very fine
1 teaspoon salt
¼ teaspoon pepper
½ cup butter, melted
½ cup milk
½ cup corn flakes, crumbled

Preheat oven to 400°. Grease 2 quart casserole. In bowl, combine potatoes, cheese, onion, parsley and bread crumbs; mix well. Put into casserole. Blend salt, pepper, butter and milk; pour over potato mixture. Sprinkle with corn flakes. Bake 30 minutes. Yields: 6 servings.

POTATOES SUPREME

1 cup sour cream
2 cups cottage cheese
2 teaspoons salt
2 tablespoons onion, grated
1 small clove garlic, minced
6 medium potatoes, cooked and diced
1 cup Cheddar cheese, shredded
paprika

Preheat oven to 350°. In mixing bowl, combine sour cream, cottage cheese, salt, onion and garlic. Gently fold in cooked, diced potatoes; put in buttered 1½ quart baking dish. Top with cheese. Sprinkle lightly with paprika. Bake 40-45 minutes or until lightly browned on top. Yields: 6 servings.

"HOT" RICE

1 cup raw rice
4 ounces green chili peppers; chopped, seeded, and with liquid
10¾ ounces canned cream of celery soup
½ pint sour cream
¾ cup sharp Cheddar cheese, grated

Preheat oven to 350°. Cook rice according to package directions. Place in flat 1½ quart casserole. Add green chili peppers, soup and sour cream, blending the mixture together. Top with cheese. Cover; bake approximately 30 minutes. Yields: 4-6 servings.

PARSLIED RICE

"Especially attractive; an excellent buffet dish."

1 medium green pepper, chopped
1 onion, chopped
3 tablespoons butter, melted
1½ cups raw rice
1 cup fresh parsley, minced
4 ounces mushrooms, sliced and drained
2 eggs, well beaten
2 cups Cheddar cheese, grated
2 cups milk
1½ teaspoons salt
pepper to taste

Preheat oven to 350°. Sauté green pepper and onion in melted butter until soft. Prepare rice according to package directions. Add parsley, mushrooms, green pepper and onion to cooked rice. Add milk, eggs, cheese, salt and pepper. Blend well. Place in 2½ quart casserole. Bake 1 hour. Yields: 8 servings.

Cook rice in orange juice — it is good with curry.

For foolproof rice — cook 1 c rice, 2 c water, 1 T butter, 1 t salt. Cover & boil 10 min., turn off & let stand 20 min. without peeking.

CURRIED RICE AND MUSHROOMS

¾ pound fresh mushrooms
4 medium fresh tomatoes
1 clove garlic
7 tablespoons butter, melted and divided
¾ tablespoon curry powder
¼ cup onion, finely chopped
dash nutmeg
salt and pepper to taste
2½ cups rice, cooked
2 tablespoons butter
1 cup soft bread crumbs
1 cup Cheddar cheese, grated

Preheat oven to 350°. Wash and slice mushrooms. Peel and slice tomatoes. Peel garlic clove; heat with 4 tablespoons butter. Discard garlic; add mushrooms. Cook over medium heat until nearly tender, stirring often. Add 3 tablespoons butter, curry powder, onion, nutmeg, salt and pepper to cooked rice. Mix with cooked mushrooms. Lay tomato slices in flat 2 quart casserole. Cover evenly with rice-mushroom mixture. Dot with 2 tablespoons butter. Cover with bread crumbs and cheese. Bake 40 minutes. Cover if top browns too quickly. Yields: 6 servings.

Note: An excellent addition to this recipe is ⅓ cup toasted almonds.

SPINACH SOUFFLÉ ROLL

"Delicious and well worth the effort."

4 tablespoons butter or margarine
½ cup plain flour
½ teaspoon salt
⅛ teaspoon white pepper
2 cups milk
5 egg yolks
5 egg whites
Spinach Chicken Filling

Preheat oven to 400°. Grease a 15½x10½x2 baking pan, line with waxed paper, grease again and dust with flour. In saucepan, melt butter or margarine; blend in flour, salt and pepper. Add milk all at once; cook and stir until thick and bubbly. Remove from heat. Beat egg yolks until very thick and lemon-colored. Gradually add white sauce to beaten eggs, stirring constantly. Cool slightly. Beat egg whites to soft peaks; fold into cooled sauce. Spread evenly in prepared pan. Bake 20-25 minutes or until puffed and brown. Turn out immediately onto a clean towel. Spread with Spinach Chicken Filling.

Spinach Chicken Filling:
2 tablespoons butter or margarine
1 tablespoon shallots, finely chopped
½ cup mushrooms, chopped
10 ounces frozen chopped spinach, cooked and well drained
1 cup cooked chicken, finely chopped
1 tablespoon Dijon mustard
¼ teaspoon ground nutmeg
6 ounces cream cheese, softened

Melt butter in skillet; cook shallots in butter until tender. Add mushrooms; cook 3 minutes. Add spinach, chicken, mustard and nutmeg; heat through, stirring occasionally. Stir in cream cheese. Season to taste with additional salt and pepper. Spread base with filling; roll up jelly roll style, beginning with long edge, by lifting edge of towel. Transfer to serving plate, seam side down. Yields: 8 servings.

"This is attractive garnished with paprika and fresh parsley sprigs."

To give carrots a shiny coating, cook them in a little meat stock to which sugar has been added.

Add 1 t vinegar to water when boiling potatoes for extra white results.

SAVORY SPINACH

10 ounces frozen chopped spinach
3 ounces cream cheese, softened
4 slices bacon
½ cup sour cream
2 tablespoons green onion, minced
1 tablespoon horseradish
salt to taste
½ cup Parmesan cheese, grated

Preheat oven to 350°. Cook spinach according to package directions. Drain thoroughly. Add cream cheese; stir until blended. Cook bacon until crisp; drain and crumble. In a greased 1 quart casserole, combine spinach mixture with bacon and remaining ingredients. Sprinkle with Parmesan cheese. Bake 20-30 minutes. Yields: 4 servings.

HERB SPINACH BAKE

10 ounces chopped frozen spinach
1 cup cooked rice
1 cup Cheddar cheese, grated
2 eggs, slightly beaten
2 tablespoons butter, softened
⅓ cup milk
2 tablespoons onion, chopped
½ teaspoon Worcestershire sauce
⅛ teaspoon rosemary
⅛ teaspoon thyme
⅛ teaspoon marjoram

Preheat oven to 350°. Cook and drain spinach; mix with cooked rice. Combine remaining ingredients; mix with spinach and rice. Turn into 1½ quart casserole. Bake 25 minutes or until knife comes out clean. Yields: 4-6 servings.

GREEN AND GOLD SQUASH

5 strips bacon
1 large onion, chopped
1 pound zucchini, shredded
1 pound yellow squash, shredded
2 tablespoons parsley, minced
1 teaspoon salt
¼ teaspoon pepper
½ teaspoon ground oregano
2 teaspoons sesame seeds, toasted (optional)
3 eggs, slightly beaten
½ cup milk
1 cup Cheddar cheese, grated
1 cup bread crumbs

Preheat oven to 325°. Fry bacon until crisp; remove and crumble. Pour off all but 3 tablespoons grease. Sauté onion until tender; add to zucchini and squash along with crumbled bacon. Mix with all remaining ingredients except cheese and bread crumbs. Butter a 1½ quart casserole. Layer ½ squash mixture, ½ cheese and ½ bread crumbs. Repeat. Bake 35-45 minutes. Yields: 6 servings.

SUMMER SQUASH CASSEROLE

6 ounces herb-seasoned stuffing mix
4 tablespoons butter, melted
2 pounds yellow squash, sliced
1 medium onion, chopped
1 cup carrots, shredded
6 tablespoons butter, melted
2 tablespoons bacon fat
2 tablespoons pimento, chopped
10¾ ounces canned cream of chicken soup
1 cup sour cream
¼ cup water chestnuts (optional)

Preheat oven to 350°. Mix together stuffing mix and 4 tablespoons melted butter. Set aside. Sauté yellow squash, onion, and carrots in 6 tablespoons melted butter and bacon grease. Mix together the pimento, soup, sour cream and water chestnuts; blend with squash mixture. Place half of stuffing mix on bottom of a 2 quart rectangular casserole. Put squash mixture on top. Top with remaining stuffing. Bake 25-30 minutes. Yields: 6 servings.

Asparagus Casserole Variation:
20 ounces canned asparagus and 16 ounces canned cream of shrimp soup may be used in place of squash and chicken soup. Combine other ingredients; drain the asparagus and fold into cream mixture. Asparagus does not need to be sautéed.

SWEET POTATO CASSEROLE

2½ pounds sweet potatoes, cooked and mashed
6 tablespoons butter, melted
3 eggs, slightly beaten
½ cup brown sugar
½ cup pecans, chopped
½ cup coconut, flaked
½ cup orange juice
1 tablespoon orange rind, grated
½ teaspoon salt
1 teaspoon vanilla extract
10 orange slices
10 large marshmallows

Preheat oven to 350°. Add all ingredients, except orange slices and marshmallows, to mashed potatoes. Blend thoroughly. Place in a 1½ quart casserole. Bake 30 minutes. Top with orange slices. Place a marshmallow on each slice. Return to oven until marshmallows are golden brown —about 5 minutes. Yields: 6-8 servings.

Variations: Mandarin oranges are a good substitute for orange slices; also ⅔ cup drained, crushed pineapple may be added to body of recipe.

NORTH CAROLINA YAM CUSTARD

"A Christmas and Thanksgiving favorite!"

1⅔ cups half and half
1 tablespoon butter
3 cups yams, cooked and mashed
2 eggs, slightly beaten
¾ cup sugar
½ teaspoon salt
½ teaspoon cinnamon
½ teaspoon ginger
½ teaspoon nutmeg
1 teaspoon vanilla extract

Topping:
½ cup brown sugar
3 tablespoons plain flour
3 tablespoons butter, melted
½ cup pecans, chopped
½ cup coconut, flaked

Preheat oven to 400°. Heat 1 cup half and half with butter. Combine the warm cream and yams in blender. Add remaining half and half, eggs, sugar, salt, spices and vanilla. Blend until smooth. Pour into a 2 quart casserole. Cover with topping. Bake in hot water bath 50 minutes or until knife inserted comes out clean. Yields: 6-8 servings.

Note: 1. This may be used as a dessert with whipped cream.
2. Substitute brandy or bourbon for some of the cream for an extra special flavor.

SWEET POTATOES AND APPLE CASSEROLE

6 medium sweet potatoes, cooked and sliced
6 medium cooking apples, peeled and sliced
1 tablespoon lemon juice
6 tablespoons butter, melted
⅔ cup brown sugar, firmly packed
½ cup red wine
3 tablespoons maple syrup
¾ teaspoon cinnamon
½ teaspoon ginger
¼ teaspoon nutmeg
⅔ cup golden raisins (optional)
½ cup pecans, chopped

Preheat oven to 325°. Arrange sweet potatoes and apple slices in a buttered 2 quart casserole. Cover tightly to prevent discoloration. Combine lemon juice, butter, brown sugar, wine, maple syrup and spices. Bring to a boil; boil slowly 10 minutes, stirring constantly. Pour sauce over sweet potatoes and apples. Add raisins, if desired. Sprinkle with pecans. Bake 25-30 minutes, basting occasionally. Yields: 6-8 servings.

Variation: Apricots may be substituted for apples.

TOMATOES STUFFED WITH MUSHROOMS

8 firm ripe tomatoes
1 pound mushrooms, sliced
6 tablespoons butter, melted
8 ounces sour cream
4 teaspoons plain flour
3 ounces Roquefort cheese
¼ teaspoon ground oregano
1 teaspoon parsley
3 tablespoons dry sherry
salt to taste
pepper to taste
Parmesan cheese
paprika

Preheat oven to 375°. Cut a slice from top of each tomato. Scoop out pulp, leaving shells in tact. Invert tomatoes; drain. Sauté mushrooms in butter until tender. Drain. Combine sour cream, flour, Roquefort cheese, oregano, parsley and sherry. Cook over low heat until smooth and thickened, stirring constantly. Add mushrooms, salt and pepper. Stir well. Spoon mixture into tomato shells. Place in shallow baking pan. Sprinkle with Parmesan cheese and a dash of paprika. Bake 15 minutes. Yields: 8 servings.

Cauliflower and potatoes will remain white if a piece of lemon or 1 T white vinegar is added to the cooking water.

A pinch or 2 of sugar in vegetables gives them a fresher taste, never makes them sweet.

SPINACH STUFFED TOMATOES

10 medium firm tomatoes
20 ounces frozen chopped spinach, thawed and squeezed dry
6 tablespoons butter, softened
1½ tablespoons green onion, minced
1 garlic clove, minced or ⅛ teaspoon garlic powder
1½ tablespoons parsley, minced
¼ teaspoon salt
freshly ground pepper
½ cup Parmesan cheese, grated
¼ cup bread crumbs

Preheat oven to 350°. Wash tomatoes and slice off ⅛ inch of top. Remove center core and some seeds, leaving most of pulp. Sprinkle cavities with salt and fill with spinach. Thoroughly mix together softened butter, green onion, garlic, parsley, salt and pepper. Spread approximately a tablespoon of this mixture on each tomato. Combine Parmesan cheese and bread crumbs and top each tomato with this. Bake 15-20 minutes or until soft. Place briefly under broiler to brown. Yields: 10 servings.

BAKED TOMATOES AND ZUCCHINI

2 cups onions, chopped
1 green pepper, chopped
½ cup celery, chopped
2 garlic cloves, minced
3 tablespoons butter, melted
4 cups tomatoes, peeled and chopped
1 bay leaf
1 teaspoon dried basil
¼ cup fresh parsley, minced
salt to taste
freshly ground black pepper to taste
4 zucchini, sliced
½ cup plain flour
¾ cup olive oil
¾ cup fresh soft bread crumbs
¼ cup Parmesan cheese, grated
2 tablespoons butter

Preheat oven to 450°. In a medium size saucepan, cook onions, pepper, celery and garlic in melted butter until onions are translucent. Add tomatoes, bay leaf, basil, parsley, salt and pepper to taste. Simmer 30 minutes. Scrub zucchini and trim; cut into thick slices. Dredge the slices in flour, shake to remove excess flour. Quickly brown in olive oil. Transfer to paper towels to drain. Add zucchini to tomato mixture and continue to cook 10 minutes or until zucchini is tender. Do not let the vegetables become mushy. Pour mixture into 2 quart casserole. Sprinkle with a mixture of the bread crumbs and Parmesan cheese; dot with butter. Bake until bubbling. The top should be golden brown. Yields: 6-8 servings.

ZUCCHINI CASSEROLE

"The flavor of this end result is superb."

6-8 zucchini
½ cup butter
¾ cup Cheddar cheese, grated
½ cup Monterey Jack or Gruyére cheese, grated
1 cup sour cream
½ teaspoon salt
¼ cup chives
½ teaspoon paprika
1 cup fine bread crumbs, buttered
butter
Parmesan cheese, grated

Preheat oven to 350°. Thoroughly scrub zucchini and trim off ends. Cut into ½ inch slices. Cook 3-4 minutes in lightly salted boiling water; drain thoroughly. Make a sauce from butter, Cheddar cheese, Monterey Jack or Gruyére cheese, sour cream, salt, chives and paprika. Put zucchini in a 3 quart casserole; pour the sauce over. Sprinkle crumbs on top, dot with butter and finish with Parmesan cheese. Bake 15-25 minutes. Yields: 6-8 servings.

CHEESE-STUFFED ZUCCHINI

"Company will love this one."

6 large zucchini (about 8 inches long)
1 cup onion, minced
4 tablespoons butter
Béchamel Sauce
¼ cup bread crumbs, toasted
2 tablespoons Parmesan cheese, grated
salt to taste
pepper to taste
additional Parmesan cheese
additional butter, melted

In a saucepan, sauté onion in melted butter until soft. Stir in flour and cook roux over low heat, stirring constantly, for 3 minutes. Remove pan from heat; add scalded milk and cream in a stream, stirring until mixture is thick and smooth. Add salt and pepper to taste; simmer over low heat 15 minutes. Strain sauce through a fine sieve. Yields: 1¼ cups.

Béchamel Sauce:
½ tablespoon onion, minced
1½ tablespoons butter, melted
2 tablespoons flour
1¼ cups milk, scalded
¼ cup whipping cream
salt to taste
white pepper to taste

Preheat oven to 450°. Scrub zucchini and trim stem ends. Slice off top third of each zucchini, lengthwise. In a saucepan blanch top and bottom sections in boiling water 10 minutes. Refresh zucchini under running cold water. Scoop out pulp from the top and bottom sections with a small spoon, being careful not to tear bottom shells. Invert bottom shells on paper towels to drain. Discard tops. Mince pulp; squeeze out as much moisture as possible. In a large skillet, sauté onion in melted butter until soft and golden. Add minced zucchini; simmer 5 minutes. Remove skillet from heat; add Béchamel Sauce, bread crumbs, Parmesan cheese, salt and pepper. Dry inside of shells with paper towels. Spoon mixture into shells. Sprinkle tops with Parmesan cheese and butter. Place zucchini in a lightly buttered gratin dish. Bake 10-15 minutes. Yields: 6 servings.

ZUCCHINI AND SPINACH CASSEROLE

6 slices bacon
1 large onion, chopped
2 pounds zucchini, shredded
10 ounces frozen chopped spinach, cooked and drained
1 cup seasoned bread crumbs
¾ cup evaporated milk
2 eggs, slightly beaten
salt to taste
pepper to taste
1 cup Cheddar cheese, grated
1 cup Swiss cheese, grated

Preheat oven to 350°. Fry bacon until crisp; drain on paper towel. Sauté onion in 2 tablespoons bacon fat until soft; remove from heat. Crumble bacon; mix with onion in frying pan. Add remaining ingredients except the cheeses; mix well. Place half of the mixture in a buttered 2 quart casserole. Sprinkle with half of each of the cheeses, add remaining zucchini-spinach mixture. Top with remaining cheeses. Bake 50-60 minutes. Yields: 6-8 servings.

VEGETABLES SUPREME

10 ounces frozen chopped spinach or broccoli
3 medium carrots, sliced
½ cup celery, chopped
½ cup onion, chopped
14 ounces artichoke hearts, drained and quartered
10¾ ounces canned cream of mushroom soup
½ cup mayonnaise
2 eggs, slightly beaten
1 teaspoon lemon juice
1 teaspoon Worcestershire sauce
1 cup Cheddar cheese, grated
buttered bread crumbs

Preheat oven to 350°. Cook spinach or broccoli in a small amount of lightly salted boiling water. Drain; set aside. Repeat for the carrots, celery and onions, boiling until just tender. Place artichokes in bottom of a buttered 1½ quart rectangular casserole. Layer spinach or broccoli over artichokes. Combine soup, mayonnaise, eggs, lemon juice and Worcestershire sauce, mixing well. Mix soup mixture with the carrots, celery and onions. Pour over vegetables. Sprinkle with cheese and buttered crumbs. Bake 25 minutes. Yields: 4-6 servings.

SUMMER VEGETABLE CASSEROLE

3 cups chicken broth
1 teaspoon salt
½ teaspoon basil
½ teaspoon thyme
1 cup brown rice, uncooked
2 tablespoons salad oil
1½ cups (about ½ pound) eggplant, diced
½ cup onion, chopped
1 clove garlic, crushed
1 cup (about ¼ pound) zucchini, sliced
½ cup green pepper, chopped
1 large tomato, peeled and cubed
2 cups Swiss cheese, grated

Preheat oven to 350°. In medium saucepan, heat chicken broth to boiling point. Add salt, basil, thyme and rice. Reduce heat to low. Cook, covered, until liquid is absorbed, about 30-40 minutes. In medium skillet heat oil. Add eggplant, onions and garlic. Sauté 5 minutes or until tender. Mix all vegetables, onion and garlic with rice. Spoon half the rice-vegetable mixture into a greased 2 quart casserole. Sprinkle 1½ cups grated Swiss cheese on top. Top with remaining vegetable mixture; sprinkle rest of cheese on top. Bake until thoroughly heated. Yields: 6-8 servings.

HOT FRUIT CASSEROLE

"Expensive, but a special treat."

17 ounces apricot halves, drained
17 ounces peaches, reserve ¼ cup of juice
17 ounces pears, reserve ¼ cup of juice
20 ounces pineapple chunks, reserve ¼ cup of juice
11 ounces mandarin oranges, drained
6 ounces maraschino cherries, drained and sliced
2 bananas, sliced
fresh strawberries (optional)
5½ tablespoons butter, melted
2 tablespoons plain flour
¾ cup brown sugar, firmly packed
½ teaspoon cinnamon
1 teaspoon curry powder or to taste
⅓ cup dry sherry

Preheat oven to 325°. Drain all fruit; arrange in shallow 2 quart rectangular casserole. Melt butter, add flour and reserved juices. Cook over low heat until thickened. Add brown sugar, cinnamon, curry powder and sherry; blend thoroughly. Pour over fruit. Bake 40-45 minutes. Yields: 8-10 servings.

Note: Apricot or peach brandy may be substituted for the sherry.

PINEAPPLE CASSEROLE

"An excellent accompaniment for ham or pork."

3 eggs
½ cup sugar
2 teaspoons plain flour
20 ounces crushed pineapple, undrained
2 cups soft bread crumbs
½ cup butter

Preheat oven to 400°. In a 2 quart casserole, beat eggs. Add sugar, flour and pineapple; mix well. Cover with soft bread crumbs. Dot with butter. Bake, uncovered, 50-60 minutes or, covered, 45 minutes. Yields: 6 servings.

BAKED SHERRIED FRUIT

"Delicious served with turkey, chicken, or ham."

29 ounces peach halves, drained and sliced, reserve juice
29 ounces pear halves, drained and sliced, reserve juice
16 ounces Queen Anne cherries, drained, reserve juice
2 cups boiling water
½ cup raisins
1½ oranges, peeled and thinly sliced
1 cup sugar
3 tablespoons plain flour
¼ teaspoon salt
4 tablespoons butter
½ cup medium-dry sherry

Place peaches, pears and cherries in a buttered 2 quart casserole. Pour boiling water over raisins and orange slices. Cover; let simmer in saucepan 20 minutes; discard water. Sift sugar, flour and salt into saucepan; add 1½ cups of reserved fruit juices and butter. Cook over medium heat until thick; cool and add sherry. Add oranges and raisins to fruit in casserole. Pour sherry sauce over. Cover. Refrigerate overnight. Bake at 350° 1 hour. Yields: 10-12 servings.

CAROLINA BAKED APPLES

"This is also delicious as a dessert – very, very rich."

4 cups water
3 tablespoons lemon juice
8 large baking apples
½ cup pecans, chopped
½ cup seedless raisins
½ cup brown sugar, firmly packed
2 cups apple juice
1 cup butter, softened
2 cups brown sugar, firmly packed
½ teaspoon cinnamon
¼ teaspoon nutmeg

Preheat oven to 350°. Combine water and lemon juice; set aside. Peel ¼ inch of skin from tops of apples. Remove core and seeds, being careful that bottoms remain intact. As each apple is peeled, dip in lemon juice and water. Combine nuts, raisins and ½ cup brown sugar. Stuff into centers of apples. Place in deep baking dish. Add apple juice. Cover. Bake 50-60 minutes, until apples are soft, not mushy. While apples are baking, prepare sauce. Whip butter with 2 cups brown sugar, cinnamon and nutmeg. Place in top of double boiler. Cook over low heat about 20 minutes; keep warm. When apples are done, pour sauce over. Cover. Bake 5 minutes. Yields: 8 servings.

CRANBERRY-APPLE BAKE

"Perfect for brunch."

5-6 large apples, peeled and sliced
16 ounces whole cranberry sauce

Preheat oven to 350°. Place apples in 2 quart casserole. Spread cranberry sauce over apples.

Topping:
1 cup regular oatmeal
½ cup margarine, softened
⅔ cup dark brown sugar

Mix thoroughly; sprinkle over apples. Bake, covered, 1 hour, uncover and bake ½ hour to brown. Yields: 8 servings.

COLLECTION OF FAVORITE NORTH CAROLINA RESTAURANTS

GROVE PARK INN, Asheville — Robert A. Guth, Manager, Farokh Nanavaty, Food & Beverage Manager

JARED'S, Asheville — Bob and Jared,Satz, Proprietors

HOUND EARS CLUB, Blowing Rock — Mrs. Mildred Bunting, Asst. Club Manager; Tony Wilson, Chef; Jeff Hutchins, Bartender

NUWRAY INN, Burnsville — Rush T. Wray, Manager

HIGH HAMPTON INN, Cashiers — Miss Agnes Crisp Reservations Manager

PEKING PALACE, Charlotte — K. P. Lau, President

OLD BRICK CHURCH, Concord — Mrs. Mary Frances Ridenhour Owner

BIRD CAGE, Capitol Department Store, Fayetteville — Ruth M. Poe, Pat L. Exum, Proprietors

LEONARDO'S RESTAURANT, Fayetteville — Ralph Potter, Steve Paris, Owners

CANDLEWICK INN, Greenville — Bob Sauter, Chef

LEE'S INN, Highlands — Dick Lee, Innkeeper

SANITARY FISH MARKET AND RESTAURANT, Morehead City — Tony Seaman, Owner

BLUE STOVE CAFE, Pinehurst — Henry M. Schliff, Chef

RESTAURANT LA RESIDENCE, Pittsboro — Bill Neal, Chef

FRENCH COUNTRY INN, LTD., Selma — Phillip Forman Chef and Owner

We are deeply indebted for the interest and participation of these restaurants and their staff who chose to contribute their favorite recipes to *The Carolina Collection.*

Recipes are presented as submitted and have not been tested by the Cookbook Committee.

CONNOISSEUR'S
CORNER

STRAWBERRY PEACH TRIFLE
Grove Park Inn, Asheville, North Carolina

1 11½ ounce pound cake
2 cups vanilla pudding
1 pint fresh strawberries, halved
1 pint fresh peaches, cubed
sweetened whipped cream

Cut pound cake into ½ inch slices. Reserve five slices. Arrange remaining slices in bottom of 2½ quart glass bowl. Spoon pudding over cake. Cover with fruit. Stand remaining five slices in star shape on top of fruit. Fill spaces between cake with whipped cream and garnish with more fruit.

FLAMING SALAD
Grove Park Inn, Asheville, North Carolina

1½ pounds fresh spinach
½ pound diced bacon
½ cup wine vinegar
2 tablespoons Worcestershire sauce
juice of 1 lemon
½ cup sugar
¼ cup Triple Sec

Wash spinach, pat dry. Poach bacon for 10 minutes, dry and sauté. Add vinegar, Worcestershire sauce, lemon juice and sugar. When sauce boils; pour over spinach. Add Triple Sec to pan, flame and pour flaming over the salad.

QUICHE SPECIALITÉ
Jared's, Asheville, North Carolina

9 inch pie crust
1½ pounds fresh spinach
10 ounces fresh mushroom buttons
3 whole eggs
13 ounces sour cream
2 pounds grated Swiss cheese

Prebake pie shell 10 minutes at 400°. Wash spinach and mushrooms twice. Cook mushrooms in a skillet with butter, salt, pepper and garlic. Drain well. Cook spinach in boiling salted water. Drain and cool. Extract all water. In a large bowl combine spinach, mushrooms, and sour cream. Recheck seasoning. Mix well together. Pour into pie shell. Sprinkle cheese on top making a full covering. Bake at 350°-400° for 30 minutes. Cool before serving so the mixture will set better. Can be kept in refrigerator for several days. Will not freeze.

Note: As the Quiche Lorraine is now popular everywhere, we at Jared's have created a tasty and unusual quiche, made of fresh spinach and mushrooms, blended in sour cream and egg, and crowned by a very good imported Swiss cheese.

LE GATEAU ST. CHARLES

Jared's, Asheville, North Carolina

"A delicious dessert – light and rich. The perfect way to crown an unusual event."

2 pounds graham cracker crumbs
½ cup sugar
1 cup melted butter
1 pound non dairy topping
6 egg yolks
3 whole eggs
12 ounces sugar
5 ounces (or more to taste) French brandy
1½ cups water
3 tablespoons unflavored gelatin

Combine graham cracker crumbs, sugar and butter and line 9 inch springform pan. Bake for a few minutes at 350°. Cool completely in refrigerator and leave there until needed. In a large bowl, combine egg yolks, whole eggs and sugar; mix well. Dissolve the gelatin in cold water. Boil and watch closely. Add gelatin to egg mixture and mix well. The sugar should dissolve. Cool down to body temperature. In the meantime, whip the topping til hard. Add eggs and gelatin mixture slowly to the cream topping. Blend well and then add brandy. Pour into shell. Set in refrigerator overnight. When the cake starts to set, top with full layer of Chocolate Mousse. Serves 12.

Chocolate Mousse:

1 quart heavy cream
7 ounces sugar
4 ounces semi-sweet chocolate
2 egg whites

In a mixing bowl, whip 1 quart of heavy cream; add while mixing 7 ounces sugar. Melt the chocolate over low heat. Cool to body temperature. Add to cream and fold in. Whip into meringue the 2 egg whites and add 2 ounces sugar. Fold in chocolate and cream. With a piping bag, decorate the cake.

HOUND EARS HOT BUTTERED RUM

Hound Ears Club, Blowing Rock, North Carolina

Preheat 6 ounce mug using hot water. Pour in 1 jigger rum (or a mixture of rum and brandy, or rum and whiskey may be used), add ½ to one teaspoon of batter (according to taste) and stir until dissolved. Fill with hot apple cider. Float pat of butter on top and garnish with a cinnamon stick.

Batter:

1 pound brown sugar
¼ pound soft butter
¼-½ teaspoon ground nutmeg
¼-½ teaspoon ground cinnamon
¼-½ teaspoon ground cloves
pinch of salt

Beat sugar and butter together until thoroughly creamed and fluffy; beat in nutmeg, cinnamon, cloves, and salt.

SMOTHERED LETTUCE

(Mountain Spring Salad)

Nu Wray Inn, Burnsville, North Carolina

Select fresh spring lettuce before it heads. Chop enough lettuce to fill bowl. Add 3 young onion heads and onion tops chopped fine. Add teaspoon of sugar, and salt to taste. Pour over 2 tablespoons of vinegar. Fry five slices of cured country bacon crisply, and place strips upon lettuce. Pour hot bacon grease over all. Serve immediately.

WILL'S SUNDAY CAKE

Nu Wray Inn, Burnsville, North Carolina

2 cups sifted cake flour
2 teaspoons baking powder
¼ teaspoon salt
½ teaspoon soda
½ cup butter or other shortening
2 eggs, unbeaten
3 squares unsweetened chocolate, melted
1 cup buttermilk
1 teaspoon vanilla
1½ cups sugar

Sift flour once, measure, add baking powder, and salt and sift together three times. Cream butter thoroughly, add sugar gradually, and cream together until light and fluffy. Add eggs, one at a time, beating thoroughly after each. Add chocolate and blend. Add flour, alternately with milk, in which soda has been dissolved, beating after each addition. Add vanilla. Bake in two greased 9 inch layer pans about 30 minutes at 350°. Put together with custard filling, and cover sides and top of cake with chocolate frosting.

OLD-FASHIONED CUSTARD FILLING

Combine ½ cup sugar, 3 tablespoons flour, and ¼ teaspoon salt in top of double boiler. Add 1½ cups milk gradually, and stir until mixed. Put over boiling water and cook 10 minutes, stirring constantly. Take small amount of cooked mixture and pour over 2 slightly beaten egg yolks, stirring well; return to boiler and cook about 2 minutes longer, stirring constantly. Add 1 teaspoon vanilla and cool. If deeper yellow is wanted, add a few drops of coloring. Spread bountifully between layers of cake, then cover with frosting.

FROSTING

Cream 4 tablespoons butter, add ¾ cup sifted confectioners' sugar and blend. Add 1 teaspoon vanilla, 3 squares of bitter chocolate, melted and ¼ teaspoon salt. Beat two egg whites until stiff, but not dry. Add ¾ cup sifted confectioner's sugar, 2 tablespoons at a time, beating until mixture is stiff. Fold this mixture into chocolate part, only enough to blend, spread on sides and top of cake.

SUNNY SILVER PIE

High Hampton Inn, Cashiers, North Carolina

⅓ cup cold water
grated rind of 1 lemon
½ tablespoon gelatin
1 cup sugar
4 eggs
few grains salt
3 tablespoons lemon juice
1 cup whipping cream

Set gelatin to soak in ⅓ cup cold water. Place the 4 egg yolks, lemon juice, lemon rind, and half cup of sugar in a rounded bottom enamel bowl. Set bowl in larger pan of boiling water. Keep boiling. Whip the egg mixture until it becomes quite firm and creamy. When it reaches this stage, turn the heat down and fold in the gelatin. Turn off stove. Beat the egg whites very stiff and combine with remaining ½ cup sugar. Then fold this into yolk mixture. Pour the filling into a baked pie shell and set in refrigerator for 2 hours. Whip cream stiff and spread over top of pie just before serving.

DOUBLE FRIED PORK

Peking Palace, Charlotte, North Carolina

½ pound pork loin
green pepper, cut into 1 inch squares
1½ tablespoons chopped fresh garlic
1 cup cabbage
2 tablespoons dry sherry
½ teaspoon sugar
1 cup dried bean curd (optional)
1 teaspoon salt
1-2 tablespoons Chinese chili paste with garlic
1 cup peanut oil
1 tablespoon soy sauce
1 cup chopped green onion
1 teaspoon chopped ginger

Boil pork in water with ginger 3 minutes. Slice pork in thin slices against the grain after it has cooled and been dried. Heat oil (high heat) and add garlic. Cook 30 seconds then add sliced pork and stir fry til pork is cooked. Add cabbage and green pepper and 1 cup of broth. Stir for 2 minutes. Add optional bean curd. Add salt, sugar, sherry, soy sauce and chili paste; stir til blended. Serve with green onion sprinkled on top.

GINGER SHRIMP

Peking Palace, Charlotte, North Carolina

2 pounds fresh shrimp
1 teaspoon salt
½ teaspoon sugar
2 tablespoons diced scallions
1 tablespoon soy sauce
1 tablespoon finely diced fresh ginger
4 tablespoons catsup
2 tablespoons wine
1 tablespoon cornstarch
1 cup oil

Shell the shrimp, clean and drain. Mix salt, sugar, soy sauce, catsup, wine and cornstarch in a bowl. Heat oil in a skillet (or wok) til very hot. Add shrimp and stir vigorously for 5 minutes or til shrimp turn red. Add ½ the liquid mixture and stir til half dried. Add other half with ginger and scallions. Stir and serve when sauce is thick.

CHEESE STRAWS

The Old Brick Church, Concord, North Carolina

1½ sticks butter
1 pound New York state cheese
2-2½ cups sifted plain flour
salt and pepper to taste
paprika to taste

Blend together butter and cheese with mixer. Gradually add flour, salt, pepper and paprika to taste. Squeeze out in "S" shapes. Bake 10-12 minutes at 350°.

VEAL MARSALA

Leonardo's Restaurant, Fayetteville, North Carolina

2-2½ pounds veal cut from the top round of the leg
all purpose flour
6 tablespoons sweet butter
2 tablespoons olive oil
4 slices Prosciutto, diced
1 garlic clove, mashed
1 teaspoon crumbled, dry rosemary
⅓ teaspoon salt
⅓ teaspoon fresh, ground black pepper
6 tablespoons Marsala or sherry wine
2 cups tiny French peas
8 fresh parsley sprigs, leaves only, chopped fine

Slice veal into cutlets. Pound them thin and sprinkle with flour on both sides. Shake off any excess flour. Place butter and olive oil in a large skillet and heat. Add the veal slices and the ham. Sauté for 3 minutes in the skillet, then turn and add garlic, rosemary, salt and pepper. Cook for 2 minutes. Add the wine, cover and sauté for 3 minutes. Discard bits of garlic. Warm the peas but do not boil, and drain well just before adding to the skillet. Uncover the skillet, add peas and the parsley. Cook slowly for 6 minutes longer. Taste for salt and cooking. Serve with a green salad. Serves 4.

CHUTNEY RICE

Bird Cage, Fayetteville, North Carolina

1 cup chopped onion
1 cup sliced celery
4 tablespoons butter
3 cups cooked rice (approximately ¾ cup raw rice)
½ cup flaked coconut
¼ cup chopped mango chutney
½ teaspoon ground ginger
1 teaspoon curry powder

Sauté the onions and celery in butter until barely tender in a skillet, then add everything else. Toss lightly together making sure it is hot clear through. Serves 6.

CORNISH HENS WITH CRANBERRY STUFFING

Bird Cage, Fayetteville, North Carolina

1 cup chopped cranberries
3 tablespoons sugar
2 cups dry raisin bread cubes
1 teaspoon grated orange peel
½ teaspoon salt
⅛ teaspoon ground cinnamon
2 tablespoons melted margarine
2 tablespoons orange juice
4 1-pound cornish game hens

In mixing bowl, combine cranberries and sugar. Add bread cubes, orange peel, salt, and cinnamon; toss with a little margarine and orange juice until well mixed. Salt cavity of birds. Stuff each with cranberry mixture; push drumsticks under band of skin at tail. Place birds on rack in shallow baking pan. Cover loosely with foil and roast for 30 minutes. Uncover and roast 60 minutes more brushing occasionally with Orange Glace. Makes 4 servings.

Orange Glace:
Combine ¼ cup orange juice and 3 tablespoons melted butter.

BEEF STROGANOFF

Bird Cage, Fayetteville, North Carolina

2 pounds sirloin steak
flour
⅓ cup butter
3 medium onions, chopped
½ pound mushrooms
salt and pepper
⅔ cup tomato juice
½ cup sherry
1½ cups water
⅔ cup sour cream

Cut meat into strips, dredge in flour and brown in skillet with half the butter. Remove meat and add remaining butter, onions and mushrooms. Sprinkle with salt and pepper and cook 5 minutes. Add tomato juice, sherry and water, return to boiling. Cover and simmer until tender, approximately 2 hours. Add sour cream just before serving. Serve over rice or noodles.

STEAK AU POIRVE

Candlewick Inn, Greenville, North Carolina

6-8 ounce steak of choice
cracked whole peppercorns
brandy
Dijon mustard
brown sauce
heavy cream

Season both sides of steak with cracked peppercorns to taste. Cook in skillet to proper degree of doneness. Flambé with ¾ ounce brandy. Remove steak and hold on warmer. Add ½ teaspoon of Dijon mustard, 1-1½ ounces brown sauce, and 1 ounce heavy cream to skillet and blend over low heat. Garnish steak with sauce and serve. Serves 1.

CRAB STUFFED MUSHROOMS

Candlewick Inn, Greenville, North Carolina

4-5 large fresh mushrooms
4-5 ounces back fin lump crabmeat
2 ounces Imperial Sauce

Clean and stem mushrooms. Fill with 1 ounce crab meat each. Top each filled mushroom with ½ ounce of Imperial Sauce. Bake 375° for 5 minutes or until sauce browns.

Imperial Sauce:
4 egg yolks
1 cup heavy mayonnaise
1 finely diced pimento
½ finely diced green pepper
1 ounce cream sherry

SOUTHERN PORK CHOPS

Lee's Inn, Highlands, North Carolina

6 center-cut loin pork chops, cut 1½ inches thick
3 cups cooked dry rice
6 large slices onion, cut ¼ inch thick
6 large green pepper slices, cut 1 inch thick
6 large slices tomato, cut ¼ inch thick
salt

On a grill or frying pan, brown pork chops on both sides for 10 minutes on high heat. Place chops in a 3 inch deep baking pan. Cover each with onion slice, then a tomato slice; sprinkle well with salt. Put cleaned pepper ring around onion and tomato slices. Stuff pepper ring with cooked rice. Pour 2 cups water into pan, cover with aluminum foil. Bake in 300° oven for 3½ hours. Baste every 1½ hours with pan drippings, covering rice well. Serves: 6.

TOASTED ALMOND CREAM PIE

Lee's Inn, Highlands, North Carolina

⅔ cup sugar
½ teaspoon salt
2½ tablespoons cornstarch
1 tablespoon flour
2½ cups milk
3 egg yolks, slightly beaten
1 tablespoon butter
½ teaspoon almond extract
½ cup finely chopped toasted almonds
whipped cream
finely chopped almonds

Mix sugar, salt, and cornstarch and flour in saucepan. Gradually stir in milk. Cook over moderate heat, stirring constantly until mixture thickens. Boil 1 minute. Stir small amount of hot mixture into egg yolks. Add to hot mixture and cook 1 minute stirring constantly. Remove from heat and blend in butter, almond extract and ½ cup almonds. Cool and put in baked pie shell. Top with whipped cream and finely chopped almonds.

BOGUE SOUND CLAM CHOWDER

Tony's Sanitary Fish Market & Restaurant, Morehead City, North Carolina

1 quart clams
1⅓ cups onion, chopped
⅓ cup salt pork or bacon fat
3 cups potatoes, diced
salt and white pepper, to taste

Clean and chop clams to desired size. Add onions to clams. Cover with water (or clam juice), add fat drippings or cubed pork and cook 30 minutes or until tender. Then add potatoes; let come to boil. Cook until potatoes are creamy. Season to taste. Serves 6.

SWEDISH APPLE CAKE

Blue Stove Cafe, Pinehurst, North Carolina

2 medium apples, peeled, cored and diced
½ cup white sugar
½ cup brown sugar, firmly packed
enough hazelnuts, toasted and skins rubbed off, to make ½ cup chopped
⅓ cup melted butter

Combine above ingredients. Beat one egg with one teaspoon vanilla and add to apple mix. In a separate bowl sift 1 cup flour, 1 teaspoon each baking soda and cinnamon, ½ teaspoon each nutmeg and ground cardamon, and ¼ teaspoon salt. Stir into apple mix. Bake in 8 inch cake pan at 350° for 50 minutes or until cake tester comes out clean. Cool in pan on wire rack. Remove from pan and wrap tightly in plastic wrap and foil and let stand at room temperature for at least one day. Serves 6-8.

FRENCH CHOCOLATE CAKE

Blue Stove Cafe, Pinehurst, North Carolina

½ cup butter, at room temperature
1 cup almonds (slivers or slices)
4 ounces semisweet chocolate
⅔ cup sugar
3 eggs
grated rind of one orange
¼ cup fine dry bread crumbs

Butter and line one 8 inch round cake pan. In a blender grind the almonds fine. Spread on ungreased cookie sheet and lightly toast in moderate oven. Melt chocolate in double boiler and remove from heat. Beat butter with electric mixer until very soft and light. Beat in sugar, then eggs one at a time, beating well after each addition. Stir in chocolate, almonds, bread crumbs and orange rind. Bake at 375° for 30 minutes. Remove from oven. (Don't worry if the cake appears to be slightly underdone. It is supposed to be very moist.) Cool in the pan for 30 minutes. Turn out on rack. Glaze when cool.

Glaze:

Combine 2 ounces unsweetened chocolate, 2 ounces semisweet chocolate, ¼ cup softened butter, and 2 teaspoons honey in double boiler. Melt and remove from heat. Beat over bowl of ice until cool but still pourable. Pour glaze over top of cake and spread around sides. (If the chocolate should harden too much for spreading, simply reheat in double boiler.) Refrigerate. Serve with whipped cream and orange segments.

TOURNEDOS HENRI IV
Blue Stove Cafe, Pinehurst, North Carolina

In a saucepan, sauté four frozen or canned artichoke hearts or bottoms. Remove from heat and sprinkle with salt, pepper, and lemon juice. Panfry four 6 ounce filet mignons. After turning, salt the tops. When blood appears on tops and steaks are medium rare, remove steaks from pan and pour out grease from pan. Then deglaze pan over heat by pouring a small amount of Madeira wine and stirring. Pour liquid over steaks, which are placed on toasted and buttered fruit bread rounds. Place sautéed artichokes on steaks and top with Bearnaise Sauce and parsley sprig. Serves 4.

BLENDER BEARNAISE SAUCE
Blue Stove Cafe, Pinehurst, North Carolina

¼ cup wine vinegar
¼ cup dry white wine
1 tablespoon minced scallions or shallots
½ teaspoon dried tarragon
¼ teaspoon salt
⅛ teaspoon pepper

Combine above ingredients in saucepan. Boil until liquid has reduced to about 2 tablespoons. In blender, place 3 egg yolks and whiz several seconds at high speed. By driblets pour vinegar mixture into blender while still whizzing. (You may wish to use a funnel.) By driblets add 6 ounces (1½ sticks) butter which has been heated to bubbling (about 170°). Blend until mixture is thick. Makes 1 cup.

VEAL KIDNEYS ROASTED WITH MUSTARD
Restaurant La Residence, Pittsboro, North Carolina

1 fresh veal kidney per person
1 cup chopped celery, carrots, onions
butter
Dijon mustard

Peel the membrane off the kidney and cut out the center core of fat. Place the chopped vegetables in a small roasting pan with about ⅓ cup melted butter. Place the kidney on top, coat well with Dijon mustard, sprinkle with salt and pepper. Roast in a hot oven for about 15-20 minutes. Remove, slice thinly and strain the butter over the kidney. Brush all the slices lightly with Dijon mustard and serve immediately.

Note: This makes the most excellent sort of small roast which can be easily and quickly done for a few people. The kidneys must be fresh.

QUICHE WITH CRAB

Restaurant La Residence, Pittsboro, North Carolina

½ pound backfin only crab
1 cup grated Gruyere cheese
8 whole eggs
1¼ cups half and half
pie crust, preferably made of all butter (should weigh about 20 ounces)

Roll out pie crust to fit 9 inch cake pan. Prick with fork, line with wax paper, fill with dried beans. Bake at 375° until half done, remove beans, return to oven til no longer damp feeling. Brush bottom well with Dijon mustard to prevent leakage. Sprinkle cheese in, add crab. Meanwhile, beat eggs with half and half, season with salt, white pepper, cayenne, and nutmeg. Pour over crab, bake at 350° for about 35-45 minutes. It should be solid but do not let puff. Yields: 6 luncheon servings.

Note: Use a cake pan with high sides so the quiche will be thick and luscious throughout.

AIOLI

(Garlic Mayonnaise)

The French County Inn, Ltd., Selma, North Carolina

6 cloves garlic, peeled and chopped
2 egg yolks
1 cup olive oil
juice of 1 lemon
1 teaspoon cold water

Place the chopped garlic in an electric blender along with the egg yolks, lemon juice and a little salt. Cover and blend at low speed for 5 seconds. Add the oil a teaspoonful at a time until the sauce thickens. Then add the remaining oil and water. Blend well. Makes 1-1½ cups.

Note: *This is a sauce used on vegetables, fish, meat and eggs in Provence. It is delicious.*

SOUPE A L'OIGNON

The French Country Inn, Ltd., Selma, North Carolina

6 large onions (5 cups) thinly sliced
2 tablespoons butter
7 cups rich beef broth
salt
pepper, freshly ground
1 tablespoon flour

Melt butter in large saucepan. Add onions and sauté until golden brown. Add flour and mix well. Gradually stir in beef broth. Add salt and pepper to taste. Cover pan and simmer gently for 30 minutes. Pour serving of soup over a slice of toast, in serving dish, which has been sprinkled with Parmesan or Gruyere grated cheese. If the serving is to be part of a light meal, it may be heavily sprinkled with more cheese and placed under a broiler to melt and brown. Yields: 6 servings.

Index

Index

D

Q

R

S

Re-Order Additional Copies

The Carolina Collection
The Junior League of Fayetteville, Inc.
Post Office Box 53232
Fayetteville, North Carolina 28305

Please send me______copies of *The Carolina Collection*. I am enclosing $9.95 for each book ordered, plus $1.50 shipping per book, plus 4% sales tax for N.C. residents.

Name____

Address______________________________________

City____________________State__________Zip__________

The Carolina Collection
The Junior League of Fayetteville, Inc.
Post Office Box 53232
Fayetteville, North Carolina 28305

Please send me______copies of *The Carolina Collection*. I am enclosing $9.95 for each book ordered, plus $1.50 shipping per book, plus 4% sales tax for N.C. residents.

Name____

Address______________________________________

City____________________State__________Zip__________

The Carolina Collection
The Junior League of Fayetteville, Inc.
Post Office Box 53232
Fayetteville, North Carolina 28305

Please send me______copies of *The Carolina Collection*. I am enclosing $9.95 for each book ordered, plus $1.50 shipping per book, plus 4% sales tax for N.C. residents.

Name____

Address______________________________________

City____________________State__________Zip__________